DETACHED

AMERICA

□ □ □ □ □

MIDCENTURY: ARCHITECTURE, LANDSCAPE, URBANISM, AND DESIGN
Richard Longstreth, Editor

25 September 2015

Detached America

□ □ □ □ □   *Building Houses in Postwar Suburbia*

JAMES A. JACOBS

UNIVERSITY OF VIRGINIA PRESS

Charlottesville and London

CAROL —
Thanks for
everything over the years.
Your friendship &
knowledge were
a great support
w/ this project!

love to Jim

for Phillip

UNIVERSITY OF VIRGINIA PRESS
© 2015 by the Rector and Visitors of the University of Virginia
All rights reserved
Printed in the United States of America on acid-free paper

First published 2015

9 8 7 6 5 4 3 2 1

LIBRARY OF CONGRESS CATALOGING-IN-PUBLICATION DATA

Jacobs, James A., 1974–
   Detached America : building houses in postwar suburbia / James A. Jacobs.
      pages   cm — (Midcentury : Architecture, Landscape, Urbanism, and Design)
   Includes bibliographical references and index.
   ISBN 978-0-8139-3761-8 (cloth : alk. paper) — ISBN 978-0-8139-3762-5 (ebook)
      1. Home ownership—Social aspects—United States—History—20th century.
2. Suburban homes—Social aspects—United States—History—20th century.
3. Suburban life—United States—History—20th century. 4. Construction
industry—Social aspects—United States—History—20th century. I. Title.
   HD7287.82.U6J33 2015
   333.33'80973—dc23   2014050145

COVER ART: *Children Coming Home from School*, photograph by Clyde Hare, 1951.
   (© Clyde Hare)

Contents

Acknowledgments

NO BOOK COMES TO FRUITION without the insight, knowledge, and, most of all, sustained encouragement of many individuals. This project has, in some ways, been decades in the making. Its roots extend back to a set of house-plan catalogs that my parents, Albert and Barbara, gave to me for my eighth birthday and to an unknown number of trips with them to see newly completed model houses. They and my siblings were my earliest intellectual mentors.

I am extremely grateful to Chad Heap, Phyllis Palmer, Isabelle Gournay, John Vlach, Pamela Simpson, and—especially—Richard Longstreth for their guidance and critique as the project took shape and matured. Anna Andrze-jewski, Amy Niedzalkoski Brown, Justine Christianson, Lisa Pfueller Davidson, Michael Harrison, Catherine Lavoie, and Alexandra Lord were indispensable as readers and co-conspirators as I reworked and refined my ideas and arguments. I thank Paul Davidson, as the creator of many of the images in this book, for setting a high standard for the graphics, and Ina Gravitz for her expertise in formulating the index. I also commend Glenn Hennessey and Cameron Logan for both suggesting *detached* as I wrestled with the title. Finally, I am highly appreciative of Boyd Zenner, Mark Mones, and the University of Virginia Press staff for their hard work and steadfast support throughout this project.

A number of individuals were generous with their time and professional expertise: Martin Aurand, architecture librarian and archivist in the Carnegie Mellon University Architecture Archives; Bill Davis, reference librarian for the National Association of Home Builders; Megan Moholt, archivist at Weyer-haeuser; Stephen E. Patrick, former director of museums, and Pamela Wil-liams, present manager of historic properties and museums, for the City of Bowie, Maryland; C. Ford Peatross, director of the Center for Architecture,

Design, and Engineering, and the staff of the Prints and Photographs Division, Library of Congress; and Jobi Zink, senior collections manager at the Jewish Museum of Maryland.

For access to houses to photograph, for images and other materials shared from family albums/collections, and for waived or reduced fees for permissions, I am indebted to Martin Aurand; Grace H. Crane; Paul Dolinsky; Roland L. Freeman; Jeffrey Herr; Tim B. Lavoie; Warren K. Leffler; Charles and Helen Lodge; Alexandra Lord and Benjamin Apt; Paul Lusignan; Paul Markow; Megan Moholt; Judi Siani O'Connell; John and Dorothy Petrancosta; Roger G. Reed; Shirley Robick; Geoff Siemering; Albert, Dolores, and Pamela Sybo; Marion S. Trikosko; Ellis Yochelson; and GE (General Electric), the Mortgage Bankers Association, Poists Studio, and Simmons-Boardman Publishing.

A very special thanks goes out to over forty residents of fieldwork sites in Glenshaw, Pennsylvania, and in metropolitan Washington, DC, who returned one or more survey forms, granted me personal or telephone interviews, and/ or shared primary documents related to their houses. Laura Trieschmann and Kate Reggev deserve thanks for accompanying me on various trips into the Washington-area suburbs. Ongoing dialogues about my research with Emily Cooperman, Andrew Dolkart, Laura Feller, Chris Madrid French, Margaret Grubiak, Dianne Harris, Kim Hoagland, Kenneth Horrigan, Karen Kingsley, Barbara Miller Lane, Linda McClelland, Chad Randl, Kate Solomonson, and Abby Van Slyck proved extremely helpful over the course of the project.

My sincere gratitude goes out to my friends and colleagues in the Historic American Buildings Survey/Historic American Engineering Record/Historic American Landscapes Survey Division and the National Historic Landmarks Program, in particular Caridad de la Vega, Dan DeSousa, Patty Henry, Dana Lockett, Paul Loether, Kristin O'Connell, Rich O'Connor, Gigi Price, Erika Martin Seibert, and others mentioned elsewhere. A special thanks to Robbie Caldwell, technology guru, and Bill Blatt, cheerleader. Love and admiration, always, go to my exceptional husband, Phillip Anderson. Willingly or not, he, too, has also come to intimately know the residential landscape of postwar America.

DETACHED AMERICA

❑ ❑ ❑ ❑ ❑

Introduction

DURING THE QUARTER CENTURY between 1945 and 1970, Americans crafted a new manner of living that shaped and reshaped the design of millions of detached, single-family suburban houses designed, built, and marketed by residential builders. These dwellings were the basic building blocks and the single most important components of the explosive suburban growth during the postwar period, luring families to the metropolitan periphery from both crowded urban centers and the rural hinterlands. Favorable government policies, and sympathetic and widely available print media such as trade journals, popular shelter magazines, and newspapers, emboldened the residential building industry while informing the public of these new possibilities. They permitted builders to establish, for the first time, a strong national presence and to make a more standardized product available to prospective buyers everywhere. A vast and long-lived collaboration involving government and business, fueled by millions of homeowners, established the financial mechanisms, consumer framework, domestic ideologies, and architectural precedents that permanently altered the geographic and demographic landscape of the nation. This book explores the design and marketing of houses during the postwar period as an immensely understudied dimension of this deeply transformative period of domestic expansion in the United States.

A generation of academic scholarship has sharpened knowledge of mid-twentieth-century suburbanization in the United States. Professionals ranging from sociologists, economists, and popular commentators to social, architectural, and urban historians have produced critical appraisals and more objective studies about the various catalysts, mechanisms, and consequences of this geographic revolution.[1] All of this energy and insight has both affirmed and overturned popular narratives and widely held beliefs, yet virtually nothing is known about the details of the extraordinary growth and spatial evolution of the houses themselves.

If they are mentioned at all in histories of the period, houses are usually folded into the broader discussion of suburbanization, a process that is often portrayed as immediate, monolithic, and static. In these histories, massive residential subdivisions spring up like weeds on former farmland, newly linked to existing urban centers by high-speed freeways. Their curvilinear streets are more often than not lined with one of the iconic house forms—Cape Cods, ranch houses, or split-levels—that are used as interchangeable backdrops for various types of historical narrative rather than as individual, tangible records of past cultural change. This book places the postwar suburban house and the contexts most directly influencing its design and physical evolution at the center of the story, rather than at its margins.

This book is loosely divided into two parts. The first articulates the sustained process of mutual education and interaction whereby builders became master marketers and buyers became savvy consumers within a buoyant consumer economy.[2] Chapter 1 defines the diverse industry that created the houses and how the federal government devised a solid foundation on which builders could reinvent themselves in the years following World War II. In particular, it chronicles the way the industry reorganized and expanded as a key part of the period's energetic consumer culture.[3] Chapter 2 articulates the manner in which postwar builders designed and marketed their models with a specific type of buyer in mind: a nuclear family that was middle class, upwardly mobile, and white. The characteristics of this generic buyer are presented here in aggregate, but these characteristics did not all have equal sway over the design of houses.

The racial components of suburbanization have been well documented, and in restricting access, builders were fully implicated in the sharply defined racial segregation of the postwar suburbs. Access to the suburbs and the complex way in which various types of postwar media represented the house and suburban life include dominant racial components in their narratives.[4] Few people would attempt to argue that the postwar suburban landscape was not highly racialized and restricted, or that houses were not consciously and unconsciously imbued with meanings of confidence and superiority—whether related to race, class, or their intersection. The evolution in domestic design in the suburbs, however, is best approached as material remnants of class aspirations and patterns of family life. Race here is not discounted as a focal point of postwar suburbanization: chapter 2 goes on to discuss the increased numbers of black Americans moving to existing suburbs during this period, as well as the way consumer desire for domestic space and certain house forms was not limited by race, even while race severely curtailed the freedom to purchase a new house. Nonetheless, race is not one of the primary and conscious forces at work in the design of postwar single-family houses.

Builders formulated their business outlook on the belief that nonhomeowners would become owners and many home-owning households would be willing to "trade up" to something new and better for either practical or aspirational reasons or both. The evolution of rooms, plans, and house forms during the postwar period presents an underutilized body of evidence that documents middle-class expansion and adaptation, as well as changing expectations and configurations of ideal home life in the middle decades of the twentieth century.[5] In the process of training an inexperienced generation of prospective buyers to become formidable and discerning house consumers, the building industry, tastemakers, and housing journalists also pitched an entirely new and casual lifestyle to the middle class. Even while economic division and homogeneity heightened as buyers sorted themselves into specific areas, neighborhoods, and subdivisions, casual living—through its stresses on easy sociability and material comfort—forged a common link between the various strata of middle-income households. Its eventual acceptance and full adoption by suburban households helped to facilitate the rapid rise of a considerably more immense middle class. Critics and pundits frequently ponder why so many Americans across the income spectrum identify as "middle class." The universal establishment of casual living in the postwar suburbs and the design of houses to accommodate it are part of the explanation for this tendency.[6]

Class identity and the adoption of a new style of living and its bearing on house design were directly related to widespread opinions about optimal family structure. Most postwar suburban households were nuclear family units in which the male head left daily for paid work, and the female head remained at home engaged in unpaid domestic work. It is well established that this type of gendered household organization was a sign of middle-class affluence and privilege and that women's daily lives were circumscribed by the manage-ment of their homes through housework, childcare, and consumer activities.[7] Extremely limiting though they were, these conditions and expectations did mean that women had considerable direct and indirect effects on the design of houses. The *Washington Post* reported in 1961: "Surveys show that while the man of the house concerns himself with the 'major' problems of life such as determining who will win the national elections and how to pay for Christmas in December, it is the woman of the house who generally makes the 'minor' decisions, including what home to buy in the spring."[8] Although articles that touched on gender roles within the family usually contained less hyperbole, and those promoting the ease of a house purchase generally did not even joke about this purchase being "minor," most shared the same sentiment: men earned the money, and women spent it.

Builders adhered to this formula in their business methods. Literature about marketing inevitably observed that couples approached a possible new house from different directions. It presented men as being concerned with such things as the quality of construction and mechanical systems that affected the overall long-term investment while women seemed to be sold on an attractive and well-equipped kitchen alone. These gender-based sales and marketing conclusions about the concerns of men and women were likely overstated and overgeneral-ized; however, gender-based roles within the nuclear family unit did have spe-cific spatial outcomes. For example, lacking the servants of the past, middle-class women spent considerable parts of their days in the kitchen. Their interest in larger kitchens was not tied just to easing the preparation and cleanup of meals but also to lessening women's solitude by providing space for friends to visit or for family members to be present while engaged in their own activities. At the same time, men's desire to avoid having to battle for time in the bathroom as they got ready for work encouraged the trend for attaching a small, private en suite bathroom to the master bedroom. Certain rooms and components of the house were influenced to greater and lesser degrees by men and women, but all houses were designed to accommodate heterosexual couples and their children within predominant notions of ideal environments for happy and healthy family life.

It is hard to know definitively whether men and women had equal input when choosing a house, and like all aspects of a marriage, this process was surely based on variable compromise. Still, articles and advertisements in the postwar period repeatedly and especially stressed the importance of impressing women with the features of a house. A 1967 study of buyer motivations took this idea even further, articulating: "The female is the prime motivational force in the family's decision to buy a house. . . . She provides the impetus within the family. She is the one who most readily becomes discontent with the family's present home . . . [and] the female desire to move seems to hold true at all age and income levels."[9]

The agency accorded to women concerning when to buy a house and which house to buy did not necessarily extend to the actual purchase. In most cases lacking their own incomes, women needed final approval from their husbands when buying a house. On the other side of the table, men continued to make up most or all of the sales staff for building companies large enough to have such a staff, even while women began to move into the residential real estate profession in greater numbers. Women's activities within building businesses were largely restricted to the decoration of model houses, sometimes through the services of a hired professional from a department or furniture store and other times with the input of the builder's wife. Larger building companies at times also employed "a housewifely looking woman in the [model] house as hostess or to demonstrate kitchen facilities," a function distinct from that of salesmen.[10] In contrast to the sales environment, in which women played a limited role, the actual design and construction of houses in the postwar period were almost wholly limited to men.

With the principal players affecting house design and their roles identified in the first two chapters, the second part of the book turns to the detached, single-family house itself and its expansion, reconsideration, and successive reinventions during the postwar period. This part unfolds in a loosely chronological progression, with each chapter thematically organized around the dominant factor or group of factors most influencing design during a specific time period. These themes delineate three distinct phases of architectural development for the postwar house.

Chapter 3 discusses the degree to which households found "livability" in the small rooms and uncomplicated plans of the modest yet fully up-to-date "minimum houses" constructed in the years immediately following the war. Whether members of the rising middle-income working class or the established middle class, homeowners and prospective buyers initially believed that minimum houses were livable based mostly on the fact that they were new and suburban, and they featured a full range of up-to-date systems and modern household equipment.

This contentment, generated to a degree under the duress of a lack of housing options, faded very quickly as growing households pursued daily life within the spatial limitations of the minimum house. For members of the existing middle class, who were more likely to have lived in houses that were larger, as well as organized into a distinct hierarchy of spaces mirroring social conditions and class-oriented functions, the size and simplicity of the minimum house undoubtedly frustrated many occupants from the start.

Members of the rising middle-income working class—whether coming from urban or rural areas—were more likely to move from crowded or substandard dwellings of various shapes and sizes that were also less consistently modernized with utility systems, fixtures, and equipment. Additionally, daily life within their households historically tended to be less formal relative to the middle class and included greater functional overlap. For these reasons, the minimum house would not have seemed so "minimum" to a significant part of this cohort and in all likelihood proved livable to these households for a longer period. Still, as time passed and families grew; as the novelty of complete and modern bathrooms, kitchens, and systems wore off; as incomes and equity increased; and as a casual lifestyle took hold in the suburbs, even families for whom minimum houses were initially welcome often entertained the thought of a larger house, through either purchasing another house or adding to their own. Significantly, a majority of houses built in the late 1940s and early 1950s were classifiable as "minimum" as compared to those that would become widely available in subsequent decades. Their relative inadequacies became evident to many households, independent of origin and background, a shared experience that contributed to the expansion and redefinition of the middle class in the postwar suburbs.

The response to these shortcomings is investigated in chapter 4, as builders expanded and devised novel house forms that distinguish the second phase of development, forms such as the split-level, the split-foyer, and the bi-level. In these newer houses, builders enlarged existing rooms and increased their number, but, far more significantly, they also both met and fostered changed expectations for livability in new houses by integrating new types of space for casual living, most notably the family room. Builders joined popular tastemakers and receptive suburbanites in the integral positioning of this new type of living within the emergent, consumption-based, suburban lifestyle that very quickly came to define the middle class and its phenomenal growth.

The first forms of house designed for casual living were inventive—at times even experimental—highly marketable, and broadly popular. However, their nascent and limited accommodation of casual living fell short of what growing and aging suburban families found most useful in their day-to-day lives, which were still largely based on activities at home. In the final stage of development, covered in chapter 5, new designs fully integrated casual living into the house as one of two distinct zones intended for daytime use: active and casual and quiet and formal. The zoned house was spatially efficient yet sophisticated in its overall planning and function. Its success set a new standard for livability that strongly guided domestic design for the remainder of the century. The astonishing and largely unpredicted architectural and cultural transformation of the postwar house from pinched minimum models to spacious zoned ones is one of the great milestones in the history of domestic architecture in the United States.

It should be noted that the low-density suburban expansion of the period was not limited to the United States. In North America, cities in Canada experienced a similar type of expansion, and Australia and New Zealand also became even more highly suburbanized on the backs of their own phenomenal growth.[11] Timing was important; all of these countries were wholly or largely spared the physical destruction of World War II, which devastated the economies of Europe and parts of Asia. More peculiarly American than the low-density pattern of development is that development's underlying contexts. In particular, government intervention in the workings of the private housing industry distinguished the process in the United States, as did the period's feverish consumerism, which extended to the design, marketing, and purchase of houses.

The staggering scale of the postwar housing boom in the United States also sets it apart. At the end of the war, the United States had an approximate population of 140,000,000, as contrasted with Canada (12,100,000) and Australia (7,400,000), both having massive land areas, and New Zealand (1,700,000).

During the next twenty-five years, private builders and building companies constructed about 35,500,000 housing units in the United States, with an average of 1,420,000 units per annum.[12] The overwhelming majority of these units were the detached, single-family houses that define suburbia.[13] The total number of houses constructed in a country having one of the largest land areas in the world and strong regional building traditions might have deterred an attempt to place the new construction in a national context or continuum. In fact there is, conceivably, a counterexample for every conclusion drawn. Still, viewing the residential building industry—its practices, products, and target audience of prospective purchasers—through a national lens is not only possible but essential. This outlook recognizes the degree to which the United States became even more connected through mechanisms such as direct dialing, interstate highways, and movies and television shows. It also acknowledges the extent of the period's veneer of national unity and purpose that, while actively and legitimately questioned, still broadly colors popular opinion about postwar America.

THE FEDERAL HOUSING ADMINISTRATION AND THE BEGINNING OF THE POSTWAR PERIOD: 1945

The "postwar period," as defined by its houses and their closely associated contexts, refers to the quarter century following World War II. The starting year of 1945 is straightforward enough. Nonetheless, the fundamental role of the Federal Housing Administration (FHA), in the continued overhaul of the building industry and residential financing, in the design of houses, and in the widening of the pool of potential buyers, also suggests the alternate possibility of a longer period, beginning with the FHA's establishment in 1934.

One of a number of Depression-era programs concerned with housing, the FHA ultimately became the most broadly influential even while its reputation was tarnished by inbuilt racial and socioeconomic discrimination. The Depression-era collapse of the residential construction industry brought about, for the first time, a far-reaching dialogue about the appropriate role of the federal government in the production of housing to its highest levels. A major source of contention was whether the government should engage in the construction of a majority of new housing directly or provide such things as loan guarantees to private companies in order to stimulate residential construction. Builders, real estate professionals, and lending institutions not surprisingly preferred the latter, and their energetic lobbying paid off with the passage of the National Housing Act of 1934, which created the FHA. The racial, social, and economic exclusion built into the policies of the FHA and their execution are well known. These unsavory aspects of the agency stand in counterpoint to its economic successes, which have also been well documented, as it reinvigorated the building industry through a process of reduced economic risk for builders and lenders.[14]

Importantly, the influence of the FHA spread well beyond the confines of its program. Its policies normalized the long-term, amortizing home loan, which was first introduced and tested on a large scale with the Home Owners Loan Corporation, a government program established in 1933 to refinance mortgages for homeowners under threat of default or foreclosure. This type of loan was central to the operations of the FHA, and its success demonstrated its viability to lenders who at first doubted its efficacy. Homeowners seeking conventional mortgages outside the FHA benefited not only from the regularized terms of the mortgage but also from the increased availability of mortgage funds. This increase in large part resulted from the creation of the secondary mortgage market, an outcome of the same legislation that founded the FHA. This kind of market required a uniform, tradable product—the mortgage—whose value was clearly discernible through the character of the loan itself, as well as the physical traits of the real property, the latter of which was underpinned by minimum standards for design and construction. The widespread publicity about the FHA and the characteristics of the housing it required meant that few builders after World War II constructed houses that did not meet its standards, even those built using conventional financing, if for no other reason than the fact that prospective buyers came to expect a certain level of quality regardless of the loan type.[15]

The direct and indirect architectural outcomes of the FHA have not been broadly engaged, nor has the degree to which the FHA helped to position the suburban house as a primary indicator of middle-class attainment. The exclusionary nature of FHA policy aided the building industry in limiting its outlook to a target demographic—white, middle-income families—that builders kept in mind as they designed and marketed houses independent of a specific client. The FHA also had a strong effect on the products of the building industry in the form of minimum standards for design and construction required for FHA loan guarantees. These standards immediately raised the base quality for new residential construction to a similar level everywhere in the country; however, the outcomes of their bearing on the design process in the late 1930s and early 1940s were quite marked when compared with the late 1940s and early 1950s.

The FHA codified minimum standards through the production of technical bulletins, in particular *Technical Bulletin No. 4: Principles of Planning Small Houses,* first issued in 1936 and periodically revised and updated. This government publication was a tangible outcome of the Central Housing Committee, an advisory body to President Franklin Roosevelt, established in 1935. The committee was made up of officials from various New Deal programs concerned with housing, having backgrounds in such areas as architecture, construction, development, and finance and banking. *Principles of Planning Small Houses* addressed such things as square footage, mechanical systems, and the number of closets and other amenities considered essential for the modern house. Although clearly valuing modern systems and technologies over space, the minimum standards were not conceived to be literally interpreted into three dimensions. This unplanned postwar occurrence sets the houses of that era apart from the ones built at the outset of the FHA.

The various mechanisms of the FHA made possible the late-1930s resurgence of residential construction in the United States, resulting in houses unlike those seen a decade later. The uptick in the construction of single-family houses in the late 1930s and early 1940s mostly met the needs of households that were already solidly in the middle class and coming out of the Great Depression with the resources to purchase a newly constructed house. Generally speaking, these houses contained rooms and features comfortably above the minimum ones required by the FHA. In contrast, during the second half of the 1940s, the immense demand for new houses at a time when the material and labor costs of building a house were rising meant that typical houses were far more likely to be more exact representations of the FHA's minimum standards. This simplification was also an outcome of the favorable lending terms available through the FHA and the Veterans Administration (VA). These benefits, often augmented by builders who reduced or waived down payments for veterans, allowed many members of the rising middle-income working class to consider the purchase of a suburban house for the first time, yet their comparatively lower incomes necessitated less expensive ones.

This is not to say that all houses built in the 1940s were architecturally reduced; many looked indistinguishable from what had appeared at the end of the 1930s. Rather, the overwhelming majority of houses were discernibly more modest in size and planning features, and a much larger percentage were considerably simplified to capture a less affluent and previously excluded segment of the market. Within a decade after the war, the FHA's minimum standards had returned to their intended role as a solid base for the design of larger houses with greater amenities, and the program saw, as related in one period retrospective of the FHA, "a shift of emphasis from volume housing alone to quality housing."[16] The temporary architectural outcomes of this transition period are the reason for the start date of 1945, rather than 1934, for a history of the postwar house.

BUSINESS MODEL DISINTEGRATION AND THE END OF THE POSTWAR PERIOD: 1970

There is no clear event or milestone ending the postwar period as it related to the design of houses, yet the choice of 1970 is not merely an arbitrary bookend closing off a tidy quarter-century timespan. For two decades, the building industry had prospered by maintaining laser-sharp focus on the design and marketing of a single product—the detached, single-family house—to a specific demographic—nuclear families who were middle class, upwardly mobile, and white. Profound cultural transformations in the 1960s, with particular regard to race, and a range of economic troubles culminating in the decade following rendered this narrow business model increasingly obsolete and unworkable by 1970.

The postwar civil rights movement and the Civil Rights Acts of the

1960s—especially the 1968 legislation that included Title VIII, better known as the Fair Housing Act—laid bare how housing inequality based on race had significantly intensified during the postwar period. More and more, the American public became aware that they might not be able to afford the costs, both economic and social, of creating such homogenized and stratified suburban worlds. These developments began the slow change of opening up the suburbs to Americans of all races, and the beginning of meaningful suburban housing integration was one of the major achievements of the civil rights era.

The building industry of the 1960s also saw its leaders advocating more and more for different types of housing. Literature of the period increasingly discussed new groups with distinct needs, such as low-income families; couples whose children had left home; retirees; people not wanting the work and responsibility associated with owning a detached, single-family house; and the single men and women and "young marrieds" of the baby boom, then coming of age. A splintering consumer market and the deepening concern of the government, if not wholeheartedly of the building industry, to sponsor and promote affordable housing for low-income Americans led to significant diversity in housing offerings by the decade's end.[17] Increasingly, apartments, townhouses, and condominiums, often arranged in fully planned communities with built-in density variations, flooded the trade presses and were translated into physical forms throughout the country.[18] The high cultural value placed on the detached, single-family house did not seriously diminish, but it was no longer the lone motivation for the building industry and the only reasonable option for new housing available to consumers.

The final component marking the end of the postwar period was inflation and its cooling effect on design innovation. Land, labor, and material costs for housing had risen steadily throughout the postwar period but began to turn more sharply upward in the 1960s before running rampant in the 1970s and early 1980s. Rising interest rates and a tightening of the credit market made mortgages and development loans harder to obtain and more expensive to service. The rapid pace of change in domestic design, discernible almost yearly over the course of the postwar period, decelerated as builders made decisions to continue selling existing models with few or no improvements. This strategy limited the adverse effects of inflation on consumers while keeping builders in business. The slowdown in design that began in the late 1960s and lasted into the early 1980s likely seemed more dramatic and even retrograde when weighed against the frenetic pace of earlier development.

SPACE OVER STYLE

From the street, houses constructed simultaneously in two subdivisions located outside Washington, DC, have little in common (fig. 1 and fig. 2). The traditional houses in famed Levitt and Sons' Belair at Bowie, Maryland (hereafter Belair), and the modern ones in Robert C. Davenport (developer) and Charles M. Goodman's (architect) Hollin Hills, in Alexandria, Virginia, are actually far more analogous when one peeks behind their façades at their similarity in terms of rooms and spaces and their functions. This type of approach moves away from the all-too-frequent preoccupation with architectural style, which usually occurs at the expense of architectural space and the contexts that shaped it.

Using domestic space as evidence of social and cultural change has been upheld as a valid and fruitful scholarly method for a generation.[19] Although primarily having focused on different types of housing in the Colonial, Victorian, and Progressive eras, this body of scholarship presents workable models for how the types, functions, and interrelationships of rooms in houses document postwar social change. This approach is also essential for creating a common baseline that bridges the outward distinctions between houses, which is especially important when weighing the relative significance of stylistic differences versus functional similarities in postwar houses.

Advances in construction techniques, new types of materials and building components, and changed aesthetic sensibilities made the correlation between a house's floor plan and exterior elevations more tenuous than in the past. Floor plans could be translated into three dimensions with unlimited expressive (stylistic) possibilities for exteriors, and builders frequently offered façade variations for a given model. This flexibility, divorcing the elevation from the plan, at times even separated the design of the street façade from the other

FIGURE 1. Two-story Colonial model in Belair at Bowie, Maryland, built ca. 1960-61 by Levitt and Sons. (Library of Congress, Prints and Photographs Division, HABS/HAER/HALS Collection; photograph by James Rosenthal)

exterior walls, resulting in a designated "style" that is only evident at the front of the house. Further muddying the waters for understanding postwar houses is the present-day conflation of form and style in surveys of postwar suburban neighborhoods; common references to the "split-level style" house are just one example.

The choice to value space over style in this book is based not just in the development of a methodological framework but also in postwar consumer desire with regard to housing. For prospective buyers, the amount and type of space in a house, and its cost, outpaced specific concerns about style. In April 1954, the Housing and Home Finance Agency (HHFA) concluded a study carried out by its Division of Housing Research and two contracted university research centers.[20] *U.S. News & World Report* digested the results of the HHFA study later that year, conveying that participants indicated a preference for one-story houses having no "special style of architecture" and concluding: "The typical family seems to be more practical than artistic."[21] The following year the HHFA released the full survey as a publication titled *What People Want When They*

FIGURE 2. One-story model built in 1963 in Hollin Hills, a ground-breaking Modern tract development. (Photograph by the author)

Buy a House. Author Edward T. Paxton, a housing economist for the agency, further elaborated, explaining that a prospective purchaser "would rather buy a house in the location of his choice, with the number and size and arrangement of rooms best adapted to his family's needs, even though he does not like, or perhaps even dislikes, the style of its architecture."[22]

Field surveys conducted in the Lyndhurst Estates, Pictwood, and New Glen Manor subdivisions, all developed between roughly 1960 and 1970 in Glen-shaw, a northern suburb of Pittsburgh, Pennsylvania, also demonstrated that space was more important than style. Original purchasers who valued an "open" interior for public spaces tended to be more interested in contemporary designs, and those drawn to the two-story form usually associated it with "Colonial" detailing. When prompted about their reasons for buying a particular house, most respondents and interviewees revealed that they were far more concerned with square footage, room type, and number of stories than with how a house specifically looked.[23] Builders wisely spent the postwar period designing models that wrapped conventional, even humdrum exteriors around interiors containing the most up-to-date rooms and amenities thought to be ideal for a high degree of livability.

A NATIONAL PERSPECTIVE ON POSTWAR HOUSES

Postwar houses physically document the presence of trends in domestic space that were national in extent and record a spatial evolution that can be traced with remarkable similarity throughout the country. A national range for this study was concretely established through a complete review of mid-twentieth-century building journals, shelter magazines, and articles relating to housing in other types of popular periodicals.

The contents of two trade journals—*American Builder* and *House & Home*—are relevant to nearly all topics and themes underpinning changes in the building industry and in house design. Of the two, *American Builder,* whose publishing history extends back into the nineteenth century, afforded greater balance in describing the varied scales of business and products of the building industry as a whole. Created in 1952 as part of Henry Luce's publishing empire, *House & Home* more often highlighted versions of avant-garde trends and, not coincidentally, frequently featured articles about better cooperation between builders and architects, all of which gave preference to large-scale builders and building companies. Both of these journals were key chroniclers of the house-building boom in the United States from the perspective of the industry and furnish foundational information on design and planning trends, construction techniques, materials, and products. Central to the postwar transformation of the building industry, annual marketing issues offer a full range of advice and examples on all aspects of marketing new houses.

American Builder and *House & Home* both closely followed and reported on the activities of the National Association of Home Builders (NAHB), which, in 1942, spun off from the National Association of Real Estate Boards (NAREB), one of the primary groups involved with the creation of the FHA. Headquartered in Washington, DC, the NAHB acted both as a professional organization, in the sense that it provided support and educational materials for its members, and as the building industry's lobbying arm. Its library was also open to the public desiring information about residential construction and design. The library and archives of the NAHB include a full run of its journal for members, the *Correlator* (which became the *Journal of Homebuilding* in 1957), for the entire study period. The *Correlator* covered many of the same topics as *American Builder* and *House & Home* but offered greater detail on the workings of the NAHB and somewhat fewer articles about specific builders. A limited amount of manuscript materials in the NAHB's archive was also invaluable, especially the coverage of its annual marketing bonanzas: National Home Week and the Parade of Homes.

The influence that nationally distributed shelter and news magazines had in shaping popular opinion about houses and contributing to the rise and acceptance of a specific type of casual lifestyle in the suburbs cannot be overstated. Since the mid-nineteenth century, homemaking magazines had held increasing amounts of influence over the development of middle-class culture and identity.[24] The role of such magazines attained unprecedented levels of importance in the postwar period, as magazine circulation exploded, and technical advances in publishing conveyed even more information through increased use of photography and other types of graphic representations. Between 1956 and 1973, for example, *Better Homes & Gardens* jumped from an already considerable monthly distribution of 4.25 million to over 7.75 million.[25]

Joining *Better Homes & Gardens, American Home,* the *Ladies' Home Journal,* the *Women's Home Companion,* and *Good Housekeeping* influenced domestic life with articles aimed at women that covered an array of subjects and themes related to house and home. Henry Luce's *Time, Life,* and *Fortune,* as well as the widely read *Business Week* and *Newsweek,* regularly featured articles on many aspects of new houses and suburban life, their content complemented by niche periodicals like *Parents' Magazine* (targeting, or at least promoting, nuclear family life) and *Popular Mechanics* (directed toward the male tinkerer within a do-it-yourself [DIY] culture).

The usefulness of widely read periodicals to divining the timing and trajectory of consumer desire and national trends in domestic design is not limited to present-day researchers and historians. In 1955, industry marketing experts encouraged builders to "keep your eye on the newsstands" because "each month, more than 50 million U.S. magazine readers learn to like (and want) quality design. . . . You can no longer afford to 'build down' to people—or to 'design down' to them, or to fix your valuations on a house with the idea that 'public taste' is way behind your own. In short . . . you are going to be left by the wayside unless you give your customers what the magazines have taught them to want."[26] Builders could peruse individual articles in monthly issues but also utilize comprehensive quantitative data presented in the results of various types of surveys that marked the drift of consumer desire. They were complemented by surveys appearing in building trade journals that chronicled the prevalence of certain spatial features and architectural elements of houses recently constructed by builders and building companies. Together with periodic government reports on the characteristics of newly built houses, the appearance of which increased in regularity over the course of the period, these surveys were a major source of baseline quantitative data on houses.

Statistics collected through consumer and builder surveys and government reports were qualitatively enhanced by the contents of trade journals, popular periodicals, and other publications like house plan catalogs. These articles, broadly categorized as "prescriptive literature," depicted both the houses and the lifestyles they supported. In contrast to their nineteenth- and early-twentieth-century counterparts, which were not always illustrated with even nonspecific plans and elevations, the gap between "ideal" and "real" in postwar publications was considerably more narrow. For example, instead of featuring a nonspecific plan, a 1964 *Better Homes & Gardens* article about "good" two-story houses included images and a floor plan enhanced with the locations of furniture for a house already constructed by a builder in Fort Wayne, Indiana.[27] Articles with prescriptive functions tended not to be illustrated with a generic suggestion of a form of house or a particular prototype; rather, they advocated these things by promoting them with already constructed, and usually decorated, examples. Readers, both builders and prospective buyers, were not introduced just to ideas but also to how they were practically applied. These specifics were revealed through as-built plans, sometimes with furniture layouts, and photographs that conveyed not only knowledge of the physical house but also a vision of the lifestyle supported and encouraged through its rooms and features.[28]

The broad representation of published primary source material is critical in crafting a national context for domestic design and is particularly crucial at a time when few manuscript collections currently exist that document the activities of individual builders or large building companies. In addition to the aforementioned collection of materials at the NAHB archives, the Ryan Homes Collection in the Architecture Archives at Carnegie Mellon University in Pittsburgh, while modest, contains a great deal of pertinent textual and graphic materials. Edward Ryan founded his Pittsburgh building company in 1948, and in only twenty years, Ryan Homes had become the second-largest residential builder in the country. A majority of the materials in this collection date from after the mid- to late 1950s, revealing the activities of a local building company on its rise to regional and, eventually, national prominence. This collection ultimately contributed to a nuanced understanding of a specific housing market—the suburbs of Pittsburgh, Pennsylvania—and significantly underpinned fieldwork conducted in the same metropolitan area during the course of this study.

With a national survey of literature completed through the use of trade and popular publications, fieldwork was completed in targeted developments, all of which revealed that houses constructed throughout the country shared essential commonalities. Specific case study fieldwork resulting in a detailed grasp of the building activities and houses in the Pittsburgh area and, to a lesser degree, the suburbs of Washington, DC, does not undermine the goal of a national study. Rather, such fieldwork permits a deeper appreciation and command of the complex mechanics of the building industry, its interaction with prospective buyers, and the viewpoints of those buyers at a level not afforded through published sources. It also allows the content offered by trade journals and prescriptive popular literature for a national audience to be tested for the extent to which such advice was taken.

Survey work in the Pittsburgh area targeted three subdivisions—the Pictwood Plan, Lyndhurst Estates, and New Glen Manor—where houses for middle-class consumers were constructed between 1960 and 1970. The land for the contiguous Pictwood Plan and Lyndhurst Estates was legally subdivided under these names, and the individual custom builders constructing houses on these subdivisions' lots initially used the names in marketing; however, they never fell into common use for the neighborhoods. Similarly, New Glen Manor was the legal name lodged for a subdivision of land in the 1960s, within an established neighborhood; however, the name was never used in marketing or afterward. The use of the legal subdivision names in this study is for the sake of convenience in discussion.

The identification of probable original owners still living in the Pittsburgh subdivisions occurred through tax information available online and confirmed through blind surveys mailed to households in 2002. Identification was followed up by interviews, either in person or by telephone; visits to a number of the properties; and, when available, a review of personal papers related to the design and construction of individual houses. Records located at the municipal planning department and the local public library were also examined. The survey forms and interviews in particular were extremely useful in understanding the manner in which consumers approached the selection and purchase of a new house. This applied to both the house currently lived in and in some cases to those owned prior to trading up to something seemingly better.

A second survey form distributed in 2004 more specifically focused on the living and family rooms in these houses as a way of measuring the effect of casual living on house design and its consumer appeal. A similar approach was used in the investigation of Levitt and Sons' Belair in Bowie, Maryland, with interviews and onsite fieldwork conducted in 2000 and again in 2006–7.[29]

The depth of insight provided through targeted fieldwork confirmed the local and regional manifestation of national narratives and expanded conclusions that can be drawn about the building industry and its products, particularly for smaller businesses. For example, fieldwork in Pittsburgh's northern suburbs provided an opportunity to learn about the crucial building activities of specific small-volume and custom builders. These individuals constituted a significant majority of active builders nationwide during this period. Although they were frequently referred to and statistically quantified in national publications, the detailed nature of their businesses was generally overshadowed by coverage of large-volume merchant builders in national publications.

Fieldwork coupled with information from the Ryan Homes Collection was indispensable in reaching the important conclusion that merchant builders and custom builders were, for the most part, constructing houses with the same type of domestic space. The difference in cost was not so much a factor of size or floor plan as it was of the location of houses, the quality of their materials, and the more active role of an actual consumer in the design process of a custom builder. The outcome of this interaction—the house—does not seem to significantly depart from that of consumers purchasing comparable merchant-built housing. The intensive outlook on a specific metropolitan area, Pittsburgh and, to a lesser degree, Washington, DC, crafted insightful avenues of investigation that, although documented and discernible in national literature, can be brought into sharper focus through a significant body of detailed information through fieldwork.

Reviews of newspapers put an added spotlight on the relatively even appearance of design trends across the United States. A twenty-five-year examination of the *Pittsburgh Press* was part of the research and fieldwork in that metropolitan area. Checks of the real estate sections in three other newspapers were also conducted, with reviews of the September issues of the *Los Angeles Times,* the *Chicago Tribune,* and the *Washington Post.* September was chosen because that is the month when "National Home Week" was celebrated in most metropolitan areas, an event that usually generated a special or enlarged real estate section related specifically to an area's new housing.

These sources and approaches support the view presented in this book that the design and marketing of new, single-family houses by the postwar building industry for middle-class families is an underutilized body of evidence in the study of the postwar American suburbs. It addresses the appearance of the most pervasive housing forms and furnishes a clear and succinct analysis of spatial change over time, a comprehensive outlook and detailed presentation that currently is lacking in architectural historical scholarship. The houses, as constructed, and their associated documentary evidence, firmly establish the existence of architectural trends that were national in scope and record a spatial evolution that was remarkably uniform across the country. Localism and regionalism most strongly asserted themselves through house form—the way the component rooms were arranged and related to one another—and through materials and applied architectural decoration. The effects of postwar consumerism on builder-buyer relationships and the influence of idealized notions of family life on how the house was used give structure to the analytical framework and keep the study from becoming only a narrative chronicle of physical change. Such a framework does not just explain when and how detached, single-family houses evolved but demonstrates why such houses changed the way they did over the course of the postwar period.

The Housing Industry Reinvented

IN OCTOBER 1947, *American Builder* confidently proclaimed: "The modern home is as attractive and convenient as any other product being turned out today."[1] This hopeful self-promotion was slightly premature, yet the statement would prove to be uncommonly prescient. Residential builders in the United States at the end of World War II were not in any position to immediately alleviate the critical shortage of housing, let alone revolutionize their products. The industry lacked much of the know-how and the financial resources to engage in large-scale development of affordable houses. By 1950, however, when William Levitt appeared on the cover of *Time* magazine as a stand-in for the success of the entire industry, builders were being trumpeted as linchpins in the creation of the latest version of what was widely held to be a peculiarly "American" way of life.

Postwar Americans cast merchant builders like Levitt and other leading businessmen as the primary shapers of a "new order of the world," with frequent comparisons made between the building and auto industries.[2] The comments made by Milton Brock, the president of the Los Angeles Home Builders Institute, in September 1951 are representative of the views held by many people throughout the country: "Under the force and ingenuity of private enterprise builders, lenders, suppliers and labor form a production team that permits mass building technique[s] at lower costs. It is not unlike what Henry Ford did with automobile production that made it possible for everybody in America to own a car. That's what has made this country successful and prosperous."[3] Brock's linking of car and house production shows how strongly the largest merchant-building companies and their practices had come to represent the industry as a whole, masking the true heterogeneity of its makeup and business methods.

While a convenient tie may be made between the two industries, such comparisons overlook the significant contributions of small- and medium-volume builders to the construction of suburbia. They also downplay to the point of disregard the federal government's involvement in the financial stabilization of the building industry. Without this stability individual builders and building companies would have lacked the confidence and capacity to fully reinvent their industry and its practices. These changes also point to mass consumption rather than mass production as a more broadly applicable shared feature of postwar businesses.

The revolution in the private housing industry had two overlapping and interrelated components—a government-supported one and a consumer-oriented one. The government component, while it underpinned builders for the entire postwar period, was quickly and broadly overshadowed by the consumer component. The policies of the Federal Housing Administration (FHA) and similar ones overseen by the Veterans Administration (VA) lessened financial risk for builders by provisionally backing all future mortgages for qualified buyers of houses meeting the FHA's minimum standards for design and construction. These programs provided enormous public subsidies for a range of private entities with interests in housing—builders, developers, and lenders. Under such favorable conditions, builders expanded their businesses to include millions of Americans who could consider home ownership for the first time, even while these policies also facilitated the rise of a business model within the building industry that enshrined exclusion based on race.

The eventual scale of the outcomes resulting from this public-private venture could not have been predicted, as they more than fulfilled the intentions of policy makers and shot stratospherically beyond all industry expectations. With a seemingly never-ending supply of qualified white buyers assured through government programs, builders vigorously engaged the prevailing consumer atmosphere structured around the regular release of new or enhanced products and their associated and intense marketing. Unlike emphasizing the feats of mass production, a narrative that favors large-volume merchant builders—the "Fords" of the industry—recasting houses primarily as a consumer good takes into account the entire spectrum of residential construction. Whether completing five or five hundred houses per year, all builders had to be vigilant in discerning shifts in needs and wants and periodically, sometimes annually, retooling their products and successfully marketing and selling them. Advances in the technology of house production were, without question, significant, but the most powerful revolution in American residential construction in the decades following World War II was an economic one that altered the way Americans perceived houses. "It is an axiom of our present day economy," mused the industrial designer J. Gordon Lippincott in 1947, "that *one cannot have mass production without mass consumption.*"[4]

EXCLUSION AND INCLUSION IN THE PUBLIC-PRIVATE HOUSING COMPACT

The common wartime aspiration—"after total war comes total living"—suggested that the federal government would continue to be involved in the nation's peacetime activities. Sluggish economic conditions even at the end of the 1930s had given way to World War II, preventing the housing industry from realizing the full potential of New Deal policies. Contrary to the period's optimistic rhetoric, builders nationwide were ill equipped to meet the crushing demand for housing that followed the war. The authors of a 1946 article in the *American Journal of Economics and Sociology* proposed: "A huge potential housing market exists. If the bungling housing industry . . . looking towards the past and swamped in the archaic, cannot meet the challenge, the government will be called upon to do so."[5]

Up until that time, residential construction in the United States had proceeded at a snail's pace for an array of oft-cited reasons. The most affordable land for development was frequently located in areas remote from the main bases of employment and often not connected to municipal utility lines. Variations in local zoning and construction ordinances made profitable trans-metropolitan building operations difficult. The terms of mortgage financing were strict, and mortgages were virtually nonexistent for people of modest means and often unavailable to builders for land-development purposes. Finally, house construction was a slow-going and expensive process. Some large-volume builders had gained experience in mass construction with defense housing during the war, but most possessed neither the experience nor the financial capacity to create and market similarly scaled permanent subdivisions in peacetime.

Government studies found that the country required five million new housing units at the war's end, with a projected twelve million more to follow in the coming decade.[6] As it stood in 1945, the private building industry could not even begin to meet this need. The housing legislation passed in the 1930s had substantiated a two-tier system that favored commercially produced housing for middle-income households (through the FHA) and noncommercial housing for low-income households.[7] Yet the building industry feared the tide might turn, given the acute shortage, and set out to decry public housing as a failure in both theory and practice and to convince politicians that private industry could succeed where the government had failed.

Building-industry leaders promoted their "business solution" as appropriate within a capitalist society. Yet, importantly, they also aimed to convince the public that, as "business statesmen," they favored profit-generating activities that were inherently altruistic and community oriented.[8] They continually reiterated the idea that the ownership of detached, single-family houses would provide the bedrock of a strong domestic economy and favorably contribute to social stability in a manner fitting for a democratic nation. Industry leaders editorialized in 1947: "When home builders construct good houses, they can be justifiably proud of a job well done. They should also take pride in the fact that with each home sold to a family, they further the maintenance of good citizenship and perpetuate the desire of the nation's citizens for good government. Destruction of the opportunity for home ownership could well mean destruction of the system which has enabled this nation to become the wealthiest on earth."[9] Thanks to skillful and sustained lobbying by the building industry, the federal government ultimately legitimized this self-proclaimed mandate.

Before the war ended, industry leaders aimed to garner congressional support for their cause and become the sole solution for the problem of housing middle-income Americans. Early in 1944, Frank W. Cortright, the executive vice president of the National Association of Home Builders (NAHB), the residential building industry's professional organization and lobbying entity, spoke before the House Committee on Public Buildings and Grounds. In his remarks, Cortright read a letter from President Franklin D. Roosevelt to the NAHB, which praised the industry's cooperation in constructing defense housing quickly and economically. Roosevelt concluded: "Housing will be one of the most important parts of this nation's postwar program as everyone knows. Upon you will devolve a great responsibility and I am sure you will meet it."[10]

With a virtual charge from the president himself, Cortright moved on to claim that the relatively young "public housing experiment [in the United States] has failed" and outlined how the building industry would succeed. Perhaps most important, he concluded with a thinly veiled request: "I am confident that you, and the entire Congress, are in accord with our philosophy and basic approach . . . by which we can meet the total demands made upon the home building industry of this country."[11] Despite this sort of lobbying, however, the experiences of the Great Depression still haunted the nation, and the government did not immediately turn to private business for a solution to the pressing issue of housing.

In November 1946, Republicans won a majority of seats in both houses of Congress for the first time since 1928. Earlier that year, the Democratic-controlled body had passed the latest version of the National Housing Act, which "extend[ed] to private enterprise the challenge and the opportunity" to meet the housing needs of middle-income families.[12] This legislation had the support of banking institutions, organizations representing materials producers, and professional organizations like the Urban Land Institute, the National Association of Real Estate Boards (NAREB), and the NAHB, but it apparently did not go far enough for the newly elected Republicans.

For five months in 1947–48, Senator Joseph McCarthy oversaw public hearings concerned with the issue of who would provide relief for the country's housing crisis: the government, through public housing, or private interests.[13] While severely censuring the state of affairs in the building industry, in particular traditional building-craft processes and labor unions, the Senate committee ultimately rejected any notion of government-funded housing for middle-income earners, paving the way for a solution centered on private business. Not surprisingly, given its chair, the committee linked public housing and the professed threat of socialism or, even worse, communism.

The subsequent bipartisan legislation—the Housing Act of 1949—was introduced by a Republican and passed by the newly elected, Democratic-controlled Congress. The act unambiguously depicted the government's role in the construction of postwar housing: "Primary reliance has been and must continue to be on private enterprise. [The Housing Act] provides that private housing enterprise shall be encouraged to serve as large a part of the total need as it can and that governmental assistance should be utilized to the extent feasible to enable private enterprise to serve more of this need."[14] While a great exercise of the lobbying strength of the building industry, the rejection of public housing for middle America was also part of a broader reassertion of individualism over the mindset of collectivism that had been prevalent in the central programming and planning of the New Deal and the nation's wartime activities and cooperation.[15]

Perhaps the most ironic and inherently problematic aspect of the full implementation of the business solution for housing was the federal government's multifaceted, central role in the process. One West Coast builder admitted in 1950: "If it weren't for the Government, the boom would end overnight."[16] Instead of sponsoring residential construction fully and directly, a situation that, in concept, might have had a chance of benefiting all eligible citizens, the government endorsed the existing Serviceman's Readjustment Act of 1944 (better known as the GI Bill) and established the Veterans Administration (VA). The VA program paralleled the FHA in that it offered millions of former servicemen federally backed, low-interest mortgages with generous amortization schedules. In addition, veterans could attain such mortgages with little or no down payment, all of which increased the prospect of home ownership and lessened the potential demand for public housing.

At a 1950 meeting about real estate in the postwar economy, Philip Klutznick, the president of the Chicago development firm behind famed Park Forest, Illinois, stated: "I don't want to be understood as rejecting the idea that there is not an area in which public housing serves a function, but . . . in the absence of long-term amortization and low down payment, the amount of pressure for public housing will multiply, and the amount that will be built (even to one such as I happen to be, who favors a certain amount of it) will be too much."[17] In the end, the public-private partnership resulted in an unprecedented expansion of home ownership that was almost wholly limited to white middle-income Americans.

Access to new houses was grim for nonwhite purchasers under both the FHA and the VA, but the existence of roadblocks for veterans stands as a particularly low point for government programs. Minority veterans were technically eligible for VA assistance; however, relatively few builders engaged in new construction for nonwhite buyers. At its best, FHA policy made obtaining approval for the development of minority housing extremely difficult, yet FHA policy was even more deeply and purposefully flawed. The FHA did not, as is commonly held, develop racially neutral policies that were then applied in a racist manner. Rather, FHA policy itself was purposefully written in a way to exclude nonwhite Americans, using the abstract notion of "market demands" as blanket justification for discrimination in sales.[18] A prejudiced appraisal system for mortgages passed over existing houses that were believed by officials to pose a risk for devaluation—those in mixed-race subdivisions, for example, or properties in older urban neighborhoods—which further reduced access to the financial windfall that became available to white veterans and their families.[19]

From the standpoint of the building industry, the calculated racial discrimination by the FHA and the VA widened the pool of prospective buyers without challenging segregation, which they thought might jeopardize the business of white consumers. These policies elevated the expansion of home ownership to a previously excluded and numerically greater swathe of white, middle-income earners over all nonwhite Americans regardless of their class. With reduced or eliminated down payments and the lower monthly mortgage bills of longer loan-repayment periods, builders had plenty of new business and could ignore the needs of nonwhites. Over time, the sustained demand generated by the newly suburbanized middle-income working class, by white residents already living in older middle- and upper-class suburban developments, and by any white suburban household with the increased resources and desire to trade up to something bigger or better, permitted tens of thousands of builders to prosper without any consideration of the ethical ramifications of their confined outlook. These actions excluded both nonwhite Americans and the less prosperous of all races.

Even while they profited from the government's largesse, postwar builders sidestepped the issue professionally and personally by claiming that they were caught "in the middle of a social-political struggle" much larger than the sale of houses and that the prejudiced white buying public held them back from more inclusive practices.[20] The hyperconsumerism of the postwar period gave the building industry a blanket excuse for discrimination that, it was often claimed, operated independent of a builder's personal feelings about race relations—integration, it was argued, did not make business sense. White Americans, both builders and buyers, were able to ignore the built-in discrimination of the system and even their own personal prejudices by focusing on the supposedly color-blind forces of the market.[21] The outcome of the FHA's emphases and biases further strengthened the links between race and wealth.[22] It would not be until the passage of specific legislation aimed at leveling access to new housing in the mid- to late 1960s that these iniquities were officially called into question.

The federal government was not a victim of pressure and circumstance in the matter of housing, as it participated fully and continually in its relationship with the building industry. The government even deepened aspects of inequality with a tax code that favored single-earner couples who owned their houses at the expense of nonconventional families, unmarried Americans, and renters.[23] The prejudicial unwillingness of the government and private industry to design, fund, and sell new houses for nontraditional, nonwhite, and nonprivileged households was far more complex than a lack of access and opportunity. This particular inequality had greater potency because it occurred at a time when a long-standing suburban ideal in the United States was reformulated and reissued as a central part of postwar middle-class consumer culture. Builders on all scales of business were intimately involved in this transformation; a builder selling even a single house was marketing a way of living as much as his skill.

THE CHARACTER OF THE POSTWAR BUILDING INDUSTRY: QUANTITY AND QUALITY

Building industry experts estimated in 1947 that "approximately 75,000 builders of all classes are active currently in attempting to solve the most critical housing problem in the history of the United Sates."[24] The largest builders of wartime defense housing—men such as William Levitt on the East Coast and David Bohannon in the West—were best positioned to begin meeting demand and in fact excelled, with massive developments built at a rapid pace. Their businesses were the latest chapter in the story of large twentieth-century residential developers who, in a time before zoning existed, attempted to maintain neighborhood stability and property values in new suburban developments through a variety of land use, occupancy, design, and discriminatory social restrictions.[25] These developers were integral players in the creation of the FHA and, seeing the potential for millions of new homeowners, used the agency's policies to assist them in their transition to the lucrative new role of builder-developer.

Furthermore, by expanding their concerns to the full realization of a given sub-division, builder-developers eliminated the guesswork in how to manage the design and siting of new houses—they now controlled the entire project.[26]

The immediate results of this shift are among the most enduring images of postwar suburbia—uniform rows of "ticky tacky" boxes. The FHA could not directly finance loans, nor did it design actual houses or neighborhoods. Rather, the agency provided guidance and reviewed proposals, and if the design and construction specifications of a subdivision and its houses were found to be sat-isfactory, it provisionally agreed to back all of the future mortgages for qualified buyers. With such backing, a developer or builder could then obtain a private loan with relative ease.[27]

This process could result in large, well-known, fully engineered residential developments filled with hundreds of identical or near identical houses, but at its core, the agency was only agreeing to back mortgages on individual houses. This meant that builders putting up even a single new house on an improved lot in an existing suburban subdivision could benefit in the same way. With an approved design, the individual builder might also gain access to private loans necessary to fund projects in the absence of a specific buyer.[28] Indeed, only a handful of builders among tens of thousands conducted business on the scale of Levitt and Bohannon. The great number of builders, their variable scales of business, and the breadth of methods and practices make it nearly impossible to describe an "average" business in the postwar industry. As one small-volume builder explained in 1956: "To me there is no such thing as the 'typical' builder. We all do things a little differently and each operation has its own peculiarities."[29]

The postwar expansion of the residential building industry complicates sim-ple categorization. Between 1947 and 1968, the number of active builders con-structing houses for people other than themselves in the country's metropoli-tan areas increased by about twenty-five thousand, from roughly seventy-five thousand to one hundred thousand.[30] Many of these new builders got their start in the heady seller's market of the late 1940s, emerging from an array of back-grounds, both within and outside the building trades. For example, after World War II Frederick W. Dreier decided to supplement his income as a farmer in Glenshaw, Pennsylvania, by constructing houses.[31] Located six miles from

downtown Pittsburgh, Glenshaw had been founded as a Victorian railroad suburb and enjoyed modest, though persistent expansion as a semirural automobile suburb during the 1920s and 1930s. Dreier possessed no formal education
in either architecture or construction, nor had he been formally apprenticed in
any of the building trades. He nevertheless wanted to build houses and taught
himself the basics.

Dreier subcontracted the wiring, plumbing, and plastering, but he did all the
structural and finish work himself, ordering supplies from the local lumberyard
and charging his clients twenty-five cents per hour. Relative novices like Dreier
and slightly more knowledgeable entrepreneurs emerging from the building
trades learned most of their skills through experience, yet there were many publications available that could assist them. The author of *The Business of Home
Building: A Manual for Contractors* (1950) expressed his book's purpose this way:

> Where can the small builder learn the rudiments of his business? Books written
> specifically for him are few and far between. Magazine articles seldom deal with the
> business of building. His only alternative has been to learn by trial and error. Unfor-
> tunately for the reputation of some builders, there have been too many business
> errors and too many failures. The editors have therefore planned this book to help
> the small builder, the man whose ambition and initiative have led him to make the
> jump from a skilled craftsman to a builder and businessman.[32]

The book covered such topics as land purchase and development, financing,
business organization, and sales. Similar publications, often directed to people
building their own houses, included practical illustrated discussions of excavation, framing, plumbing, heating, and wiring.[33]

Relying on his own ambition and practical know-how imparted by experience, and perhaps also books, Drier simply built houses. He replicated designs
found in publications or elsewhere in the neighborhood and built on lots
already hooked up to municipal water and sewer systems. Drier constructed
fewer than twenty dwellings in his lifetime, yet despite this modest output, the
varied forms and styles of the houses he constructed, on lots in proximity to
the intersection of Scott Avenue and Herron Lane in Glenshaw, contributed
to the architectural variety that characterized this small slice of suburbia. The

postwar period found thousands of such motivated individuals, most having a background in one of the building trades, starting their own house-building businesses. An NAHB survey of builder-members in 1959 found that the typical American builder had been in business for approximately eleven years, having gotten a start immediately after the war.[34] Whether these businesses remained small or grew into large merchant building companies, they all produced the character-defining feature of suburbia—the detached, single-family house.

It is difficult to generalize the building industry when its universe ranged from William Levitt to Frederick Drier (fig. 3). A 1949 Bureau of Labor Statistics report defined some of the more common descriptors used in the industry. It dubbed "those who build for a living or profit" as "professional" or "commercial" builders and divided these further into two essential groups. "Those who build housing to order, on someone else's land and to another's specifications," were "general contractors" or "custom builders," and "those who build housing on their land to their own specifications, for unidentified future buyers or renters," were "operative" or "merchant" builders.[35] Divisions based on business methods could be further separated into output-based categories. In the 1950s, the NAHB detailed differences between small- (one to nine houses per year), medium- (ten to forty-nine houses per year), and large-volume builders (over fifty houses per year).[36] The fourth category—the custom builder—was qualitatively rather than quantitatively defined and, standing apart, was retooled as a marketing strategy later in the period.

FIGURE 3. Individual builders and building companies within the industry had quantitative and qualitative divisions that were not absolute and often overlapped. 1946. (Photograph by Preston B. Reed; courtesy of Roger G. Reed)

Custom builders contracted with specific clients prior to planning and construction and, by default, were almost always small-volume builders. Unlike merchant builders, custom builders relied on more direct and personal business approaches, which meant that in addition to marketing a product, they had to establish and market their own reputation. In 1954, the *NAHB Correlator,* the member journal of the association, explained that the custom builder "builds his product, the house, after sale rather than before sale. He builds his product for a known customer, and the house reflects the customer's requirements."[37] Some self-identified custom builders at times also engaged in limited speculation, in order to, in the words of one builder, "keep the operation rolling" during slow construction periods; others were hired to construct houses for clients who had architect's plans in hand.[38] Custom builders also built speculatively to have a tangible product to show potential clients; this practice, according to one Minneapolis builder in 1953, "also keeps our crews busy."[39] Custom builders bridged the divide between mass-produced development houses and houses designed individually by a commissioned architect.

In the first decade following the war, the distinction between a custom-built and a merchant-built house was easy to discern because very few houses, whether constructed on contract or speculatively, were "built to order."[40] One real estate columnist observed in 1948: "The war put an end to persons building their own homes on contract. . . . Since the war most contractors have built homes on speculation. That is, they build a number of homes and [then] sell them."[41] A merchant builder allowed few, if any, substantive changes. For nearly a decade these conditions did not hamper sales, and it was estimated in 1956 that fewer than 15 percent of houses nationally were custom built.[42]

Savvy merchant builders, however, soon came to understand the exclusivity (and premiums) associated with the term *custom* and began to capitalize by allowing customized options for their tract models. In 1965, Tom Cameron, the real estate editor for the *Los Angeles Times,* wrote about customization: "It isn't so long ago that the average tract house builder would decline to trifle with his plans and specifications, at any stage of the project. But more and more, builders are not only willing to change floor plans and designs but even advertise their readiness to do so."[43] The marketing advantage of a customizable model was evident in two *Chicago Tribune* advertisements from 1965. A development called Capitol Hill was said to offer "gracious new homes" with "custom-character."[44] The houses themselves were not custom, yet the builder had shifted himself closer to that prestige category through use of the term *custom-character.* Another ad for a title insurance company conveyed that in its opinion, "far too many Chicagoland families . . . buy a house that was designed for a mythical 'average' family." The ad highlighted what the company saw as an in-process resolution to this problem, with builders now "designing and building houses to fit families. Even non-custom houses come in a variety of floor plans and configurations."[45]

The differences between a "custom-built" house and a "customized" one became less distinct over time. The merchant builder's inclination to offer more choice and consumer control brought him closer to the practices, and potential client base, of the custom builder, but it also reflected growing uncertainty about what the consumer wanted. One builder in a 1967 feature on custom building explained that "every production builder would like nothing better than to turn out standard houses and have people standing in line to buy them. . . . But the average buyer in the $25,000-to-$30,000 price range expects to make changes, particularly if he's bought from a model."[46] A second builder deepened the dialogue: "Any given model . . . could be hotter than a firecracker or it could be a dud. There's no way to know."[47] Buyer expectations for greater involvement in the design process, coupled with builder uncertainty about what constituted saleable design, caused the builders interviewed for this article to allow what might be considered the extreme in customization—greatly altering facades, adding rooms, and changing roof pitch.

The services advertised by many custom builders, however, were less extreme. For example, Frank Bozzo Jr., a medium-volume builder based in the same part of Glenshaw as Frederick Drier, constructed between ten and twenty-five custom houses per year in the 1960s. Bozzo offered his clients a selection of three or four generic prototypes created by a contracted designer. They could make any "reasonable" change they wished to a chosen prototype, such as dimensions, material, or mechanical upgrades, and minor spatial adjustments, so long as they agreed to pay for the time related to reworking the construction drawings, as well as additional or substituted materials.[48]

Still, a builder's success did not necessarily rely on customization, even at the end of the period. Ryan Homes—the nation's second-largest residential builder by the 1960s, only surpassed by Levitt and Sons—offered limited choice among interior fittings and finishes, but it did not allow "a single structural change, no matter what [a buyer was] willing to pay for it."[49] Ryan Homes offered more house for the money because of standardization of building components, and any deviation from this would significantly increase costs and the time it took to complete a house. Instead of a limited number of models that could be radically customized, the company crafted distinct, cost-differentiated product lines composed of a number of different models—with a total of upward of twenty available in an area at any given time. Consumer choice was met through the simultaneous development of multiple subdivisions, each featuring the models of a particular line within a narrow price bracket.[50]

The strategies for product variation used by all builders in the 1960s were intended to return a sense of control and choice to prospective buyers and lessen gambles on new designs. The domestic space and amenities contained in comparable custom-built houses and customized merchant-built houses did not vary all that much. Custom builders were still builders, not architects. The houses they produced might contain a bit more square footage, be more robustly constructed, and be finished with higher-quality materials and mechanical equipment than comparable merchant-built ones, but all were produced by an industry that existed, more or less, along a single product continuum.

A THREE-PRONGED MARKETING STRATEGY

"A builder today must be [an] expert in many fields." So professed the *Pittsburgh Press* in 1960, an indicator that the role of builders had been considerably altered since the years immediately following the war. The article relayed that a successful builder "wears many hats" and must simultaneously "be a contractor, designer, land planner, mortgage expert and market analyst."[51] Such complexity was not an entirely new condition. Kansas City, Missouri's, J. C. Nichols and Cleveland, Ohio's, Van Sweringen brothers are among the best-known developers of the early twentieth century, and most major cities boasted one or two residential suburbs that approached the cohesive planning of the Country Club District and Shaker Heights.

Large residential subdivisions also dotted the landscape for people further down the socioeconomic scale, especially as the automobile became more affordable and widespread. Yet overall, the interwar building industry was predominately defined by small-scale craftsmen and contractors building only a handful of houses each year, generally for actual clients and not on mass speculation. Except for the largest and most heavily advertised middle- and upper-middle-class subdivisions, residential builders generally devoted the bulk of their energies to construction and found clients within their own communities by word of mouth. This business environment changed considerably after World War II.

The building industry was able to re-create itself, first, as it relieved the acute housing shortage and, then, through comprehensive marketing strategies. With vast resources on hand, large-scale merchant builders were able to implement and refine these marketing techniques to the greatest extent, yet all successful builders utilized them to some degree and found profitable ways to tap into the consumer revolution in housing. A marketing professional explained as early as 1949: "With the nation entering a buyer's market in virtually every category of business, effective publicity now is more vital for sales than during the plush postwar period. . . . Until now, too many land developers and builders have not indulged in sustained publicity because sales were on an order-taking basis and they did not think they needed it."[52] The three key areas—extensive print advertising, "model" or "display" houses and closely related annual housing celebrations, and frequent and perceptive product design—were the principal parts of a full marketing program.

Builders had to become knowledgeable about marketing but did not necessarily have to be active experts in all areas since portions of the real estate and advertising industries specialized in the market for new houses. Some builders maintained full control of their marketing strategies. Others made decisions based on formal and informal relationships with advertising and sales professionals. At one extreme, when they planned the large subdivision of Bar Harbour in the early 1950s, located within the very competitive Long Island, New York, market, Irwin Chess and Nat Siegal embraced a holistic view of project development. They established a "planning board" composed of the builders, sales agent, architects, engineers, a landscape architect, a decorator and color consultant, and experts in advertising, publicity, and display.[53] Chess and Siegal felt there were distinct advantages to calling in outside professionals but still "coordinated" the various aspects of planning and implementation. Even more massive, Levitt and Sons created a number of in-house marketing divisions and hired and trained their own salesmen for placement in model houses at the company's sales centers. Large-volume merchant builders possessed the resources to secure the multifaceted expertise needed for massive developments whose success depended upon broad and sophisticated marketing.

Smaller-volume builders mainly turned to outside professionals for sales assistance. In the late 1950s, Walker & Lee, a realty company in Lakewood, a suburb of Los Angeles, directed sales for forty-two Southern California residential developments. The firm provided its builder-clients with trained salespeople to be stationed at model houses but did "not perform such auxiliary merchandising jobs as preparing advertising copy, furnishing model houses, and landscaping them." Indeed, the negotiated percentage of commission contracted by the realty company relied in part on whether a builder was "a good merchandiser."[54] Small-volume builders were more involved with day-to-day construction and, when trying to sell a house built on speculation, would either need to open the house on appointment or have realty companies staff regular hours.

In 1960, William Eichenlaub, a small-volume custom builder in Glenshaw, Pennsylvania, completed a handful of high-quality speculative houses on an existing road that became part of a new subdivision called Lyndhurst Estates. At the time, Eichenlaub was working to market the houses with the Benz Realty Company, self-described in an advertisement as "exclusive consultants."[55] The most recently completed houses were open daily for prospective buyers, from one to nine each afternoon and evening, a generous schedule that Eichenlaub could not have managed on his own while he was overseeing the construction of other houses. Two years later an advertisement for one of Eichenlaub's newest houses in the same subdivision noted that is was open from "1 P.M. until Dark"; however, he appears to have separated from the Benz Realty Company by this point, as the only telephone number listed was the one for the builder.[56] The attractive contemporary house with many custom features highlighted in the ad languished on the market until 1964, when George and Judith Kisak purchased it for three thousand dollars less than the original asking price. George Kisak recalled that Eichenlaub said he had fired his realtor because of slow sales and had taken on the task of selling the house himself.[57] Eichenlaub's experience demonstrates variety not only across the industry but also from year to year for the same builder or company.

The builder made an investment on speculative ventures and was most concerned with seeing a return, and whatever their capacity, outside experts were ultimately the clients of the builder. In 1947, an Evansville, Indiana, builder explained that his houses were "sold as completed through a realty organization which we control in the same fashion as we do other subcontractors."[58] A decade later, "Mr. Average Builder" offered a slightly different arrangement:

"I try to handle all my own sales and for the most part have been successful. *(Two out of three builders surveyed handle their own sales.)* Occasionally I call upon a real estate firm to sell one of my speculative homes but my local reputation and a little advertising are usually all that is necessary."[59] In addition to utilizing realty companies, builders frequently entrusted the content and dissemination of their message to outside advertisers as well.

PRINT ADVERTISING

Newspaper advertisements were the primary means of drawing prospective buyers to far-flung subdivisions. There was nothing particularly groundbreaking about using this medium to announce the sale of new houses, but it retained appeal because no other print form or affordable promotional alternative reached as many people as frequently or directly. One of the principal differences between postwar print campaigns and earlier advertisements was their number, so many that most major American newspapers created "real estate" or "home" sections or significantly reformatted existing sections and devoted them almost exclusively to new residential construction. There was also an increase in the size and graphic components of ads. Previously, newspaper listings for houses had taken more of a classified form, with a few small descriptive lines augmented at times by a

FIGURE 4. Visually exciting newspaper advertisements became a major marketing strategy for new houses. Ca. 1957–60. (Ryan Homes Collection; courtesy of Carnegie Mellon University Architecture Archives)

small photograph of the property. Within a few years of the war's end, however, sizable block ads featuring not only houses but also characteristics of a subdivision's overall environment appeared more frequently. Advertisements included a varying mix of text, photographs, and architectural drawings (fig. 4).

Strongly evocative text matched the persuasion of images even while it became formulaic across time and geography. In 1947, the *Pittsburgh Press* featured a new suburban development described as "nearly ready—for families able to enjoy fine living! There's always a demand for extra fine homes by Pittsburgh families able to afford distinctive residences. . . . Residences which these families have come to expect in Rolling Hills. . . . They are all built on large lots, and most boast virgin oak, walnut, maple, dogwood, and other fine trees surrounding the homes!" Ten years later, in 1957, the *Los Angeles Times* included this description for Palisades View Homes: "You'll marvel that such suburban magnificence is yours without even leaving the city limits of Los Angeles. 2,200 square feet of fashionable home design. . . . A nature-blessed setting overlooking the ocean and free from smog—sweeping sea views by day, jewel-like city lights by night. . . . Palisades View Homes . . . [are] a joyous discovery in happier living." In 1965, the *Chicago Tribune* highlighted a new "prestige" community: "Arrowhead in Northbrook is for those who understand the meaning of community spirit . . . who feel the need for residence among those who regard their homes, their families and their style of living as something special and apart from the ordinary."[60]

Slightly more verbose than typical, these examples convey themes often seen in advertisements: rarified living for the lucky few, locations bearing great natural beauty, and well-designed and well-crafted houses. Such ideas had particular appeal for more affluent middle-class buyers. A 1961 study by Community Builders, an advertising agency for builders in Washington, DC, found that 82 percent of its budget went to newspaper ads because the "newspaper display is the basis of our advertising to high-income buyers. . . . The best prospects for our higher-priced houses are second-time buyers who are actively looking for a new house. They read the real-estate sections carefully—this is one place where readers come to the advertiser."[61]

Community Builders worked with companies building houses that were somewhat more expensive, yet hardly opulent, intended for "government people and military personnel." A glance through a weekend real estate section

FIGURE 5. Furnished display houses encouraged prospective buyers to imagine themselves living in the house. 1962. ("Belair at Bowie, Maryland," 1962; author's collection)

anywhere in the country showed that print advertising was used by builders of all types of houses, for prospective buyers in a range of incomes. With greater resources at hand, large merchant builders could run big, polished, and eye-catching ads almost weekly, but the frequency and design of the advertisements also responded to the centrality of speculation to their business. Engaged only modestly in speculation, if at all, small-volume custom builders needed newspaper advertising on a far less regular basis. Regardless of their size or the rate at which they appeared, newspaper advertisements enticed prospective buyers to visit open models and furnished display houses in often far-flung subdivisions.

THE OPEN MODEL AND THE FURNISHED DISPLAY HOUSE

Opening a newly completed model or a furnished display house at a sales center for a large development intended for public visitation was a particularly potent element of marketing and sales strategies. In 1953, marketing specialists stressed the need for more innovation by builders in the sale of new houses, observing: "Many years of study have gone into developing the best display and sales methods for all retail businesses, but there are still no generally accepted procedures for selling houses. The truth is that in a seller's market a builder has not had to merchandise."[62] The article presented the model house as one way to help standardize sales methods among builders: "A model house, furnished or unfurnished, is a builder's show window. It can either attract or scare away customers, depending on how it is used" (fig. 5).

As with newspaper advertisements, the use of models did not originate after World War II, but it did become more prevalent. In the last decades of the nineteenth century and the early decades of the twentieth century, builders encouraged the public to inspect new model row houses in urban residential districts. Generally, these houses were a builder's most recently completed dwellings and were ready for sale and conveyance, devoid of any movable furniture or decoration. Similarly, the housing shortage in the years immediately following World War II meant that inventories of empty houses were kept low, and model houses tended to be the most recently completed units. They were singular products for immediate sale, rather than elements of a longer-term sales approach that highlighted the type(s) of house available in a particular subdivision.

A 1949 *Chicago Tribune* ad for "new 6 room homes" in Linden Manor commanded readers: "DRIVE OUT. See this model home at the S. W. corner of 3rd St. and Laurel Ave." The caption under the house's photograph contained additional information: "The home pictured above has been sold and [is] now occupied by [the] owner. 8 new additional homes have same floor plan with different exteriors and will be finished within 10 to 30 days."[63] The advertisement suggests that any of the models, save the one depicted, could be immediately purchased. Because the houses all had the same floor plans, the builder would not have been compelled to have a new house photographed each time the model was sold. Builders of subdivisions like Linden Manor, having houses with nearly identical floor plans, had no real need for a furnished display house. The most recently finished was representative of their available product, and the model changed every time one was sold. Furthermore, brisk sales late in the 1940s precluded spending the time, energy, and money needed to furnish a model that could otherwise be easily sold to turn a profit.

As the seller's market of the late 1940s and early 1950s transitioned into a buyer's market, furnished "display houses" joined open models in the marketing of a builder or subdivision; together, these approaches were employed by a little over half of American house builders in 1959.[64] Furnished display houses were viewed as "cheap advertising" from the beginning, and industry leaders admitted early on that "good decorating hides shortcomings [in design], makes small rooms look bigger, [and] any room look better."[65] Modest-sized rooms seemed larger with smaller-scaled pieces, and the thoughtful arrangement of living room furniture could create an entry area where none existed. Such pragmatic and relatively straightforward conceptualization of the furnished display house took on a more sophisticated role as merchant builders appreciated and had the means to act on the knowledge that the stage-set quality of the display house could have a positive influence on prospective consumers.

Industry leaders emphasized that the best display houses were not designer showcases, but decorated in a way that prospective buyers could "see themselves living in it."[66] Keeping the furnishings, accessories, wall art, and tableware within conventional norms made the tableau relevant to prospective buyers' lives and put them at ease. At the same time, the spotlessness and cohesive decorating schemes of the display houses provided not just a familiar but, importantly, a perfected domestic vision. Accelerated and unchecked consumption defined the postwar domestic economy, and its success depended greatly on the interplay between "illusion" and "reality." Daydreaming about idealized conditions, often because reality was either limiting or no longer stimulating, became an important motivation for pursuing and obtaining goods.[67]

By not only furnishing but also accessorizing the display house with wall art, magazines, tableware, toys, and games—even the wonderful smells of something baking in a shiny new oven—builders presented visitors with images of a prosperous and comfortable life (fig. 6). This approach astutely responded to the reality that more and more Americans were able to consider, literally buying into the now accessible fantasy. The postwar behavioral economist George Katona stressed the appeal of the broader phenomenon early in 1963: "*Today, in this country, for the first time in history, the majority of families own, wear, drive, live in, eat, drink and otherwise use a vast variety of consumer goods far beyond what is necessary for subsistence.* Nothing like this has ever happened in the past."[68]

Builders across the country presented their interpretation of the American "standard of living" or "way of life," with efforts ranging from a single furnished display house to an engineered sales center like that employed by famed merchant builder Levitt and Sons for its Belair at Bowie, Maryland, development outside Washington, DC.[69] The company opened sales at Belair in October 1960 with eight furnished display houses, models that were also available in new sections of Levittown, New Jersey (fig. 7). Resembling the alternating pattern of models that would be found along Belair's streets, the houses were lined

FIGURE 6. A split-foyer display house with contemporary furnishings that complement the house's overall style. Ca. 1966. (Ryan Homes Collection; courtesy of Carnegie Mellon University Architecture Archives)

up along one side of Sussex Lane, facing a broad lawn that extended between it and the parallel Route 450. The houses would have been clearly visible as a three-dimensional billboard from cars passing on this principal east-west roadway connecting Washington and Annapolis.

The "Levitt and Sons Decorating Department under the direction of Alice D. Kenny" worked with Mayer and Company of Washington to furnish the houses' interiors, whose décors contained a placid and inoffensive mixture of traditional and modern.[70] The *Washington Post* favorably commented on the outcome, noting that the rooms were "calculated to appeal to those of conservative but discerning taste."[71] This description of the taste level of Belair's prospective buyers would have been true for many in the relatively affluent metropolitan area. Younger first-time buyers likely had more modest conceptions of a domestic environment, and the scene presented to them in the display houses had a more powerful effect. For Jacqueline Federici, one of Belair's first residents, the display houses at the sales center seemed "just like heaven."[72]

The widespread use of display houses had some comparatively minor drawbacks. They required a builder to spend more money up front, both in dedicating an entire, completed house to visitation and in outfitting it with the best finishes and options available at the development and with modish, and costly, furniture and accessories. Heavy visitation meant that smaller items frequently disappeared under coats and into handbags and needed to be regularly replaced.[73]

The occasional loss of an ashtray or hand towels was far less of an annoyance than confusion about which features, amenities, and finishes came standard in a house and which were optional upgrades for the model or display house. A Ryan Homes internal sales bulletin from 1956 announced the opening of its new Harmony House model, which was fully decorated by Sears Roebuck & Co. Directed to Ryan salesmen, the bulletin explicitly stated that "copies of the Harmony House model on Firwood Drive will not include the following: draperies, furniture, dryer & outlet, painted laundry, carpeting, washer, finished game room, wallpaper, [and] smooth plaster except in kitchen & bath."[74] In the

FIGURE 7. Furnished display models were often grouped together to give prospective buyers a sense of a completed street. Ca. 1960. (Author's collection)

end, theft of objects and misinterpretation of standard features and amenities were relatively minor drawbacks in a sales and marketing method that became the most compelling means for generating curiosity about and maintaining consumer interest in new housing.

The attraction of models and furnished display houses was so strong that weekend visitation even became a leisure activity for families not necessarily in the market for a new house. A real estate journalist noted in 1963:

> Baseball is still the "official" national pastime. But now there's a newer and cheaper family diversion that's surely cutting the gate at Sunday double-headers—house shopping! The Sunday art of house looking (called "tire-kicking" in the trade) has developed into a rollicking recreation for Mom, Dad and the children, too. On the first day of every week, throngs of rubber-necking, never-buying, happy home inspectors pile into the family car for a look-see at what the latest model house has to offer. It's fun! And you don't have to buy—just look.[75]

While in part tongue-in-cheek, the article did not exaggerate the trend. When the Belair sales center opened in Bowie, Maryland, in October 1960, an estimated twenty to thirty thousand prospective buyers and curious locals visited the first weekend, backing up traffic for over a mile.[76]

The upbeat, festival-like atmosphere that materialized across metropolitan areas each weekend around crowded open models and sales centers could even encourage a random passerby or casual "house looker" into buying. In the summer of 1961, Ellis and Sally Yochelson chanced to drive by the Belair display houses, were intrigued by the crowds, and decided to stop—and moved into the three-bedroom version of the two-story Colonial model one year later.[77]

Industry leaders logically became interested in devising ways to further capitalize on the favorable consumer energy around open models and display houses. Builders frequently constructed and promoted "idea homes," regularly devised by utilities companies, in particular electricity companies, and appliance and materials manufacturers to highlight their new products. Many shelter magazines and research centers also sponsored the design of this type of model house as a means of exhibiting the latest developments in domestic planning and construction. They not only disseminated this knowledge through extensive and heavily illustrated print features in magazines and journals but also frequently made full sets of construction drawings available for purchase to the general public. Builders often constructed such houses as another opportunity for publicity. The underlying concept behind the "idea home"—creating a three-dimensional manifestation of domestic design and construction trends—also fostered the creation of entire festivals of new housing: "National Home Week" and the "Parade of Homes."

FESTIVALS OF NEW HOUSING

The most ambitious and widely observed housing festival was National Home Week (NHW). Early in 1948, the editor of *American Builder* suggested the idea of "simultaneous demonstrations of homes in every major center of the Nation" to the president of the NAHB, an idea that was apparently favorably received.[78] The *NAHB Correlator* announced and promoted the inaugural celebration to its builder-members in April 1948: "*Our Own 'National Home Week'—September 5th thru 11th.* That's what home builders throughout the country are going to have—come September. . . . The big week will encompass the greatest promotion ever undertaken for home builders. It will be *YOUR* opportunity to come in on national and local promotion and to show what you have been doing. It will be *YOUR* houses, *YOUR* projects, that will go on display. It will be *YOUR* big chance to tell your own story to your community—and you can tell it with your own products" (fig. 8).[79]

From the outset, leading builders understood that NHW had the potential to strongly concentrate consumer attention and encourage the purchase of a new house. It could also provide an ideal opportunity for defining an industry

FIGURE 8. The National Association of Home Builders launched National Home Week as a demonstration of the ways the industry had modernized its practices and products. 1949. (*American Builder,* April 1949, 102; courtesy of Simmons-Boardman Publishing)

composed of many different types of builder. "Because National Home Week is co-ordinated public relations by thousands of large and small business establishments scattered in every nook and crossroad of the nation," as observed by *American Builder* in 1949, "it has the effect of spotlighting all these units as a unified industry with a single purpose—to build more and better houses more economically for the nation's citizens."[80] What began in part as a branding exercise for a disparate industry soon became seen as a learning opportunity for the public, which would, as through the annual auto shows, be introduced to all the industry's newest features, trends, and amenities. This education was a sophisticated marketing tool that builders used subtly, and sometimes not so subtly, to create dissatisfaction among visitors with their present abodes and increase the likelihood that they would consider buying a new one.

Seventy-five cities participated in NHW the first year.[81] The earliest NHWs amounted to little more than extra print and radio publicity. Newspapers published special sections describing real estate trends and highlighting specific developments, sometimes with locational maps.[82] Most builders kept their models and display houses open for longer hours than normal and permitted the public to visit houses still under construction, a level of access intended to demonstrate the "progress made in building materials and techniques."[83] The event, held in most places in the same week in September, was sponsored at the local level by participating local Home Builders' Associations (HBAs), and its reach quickly expanded to include interested members of the National Retail Lumber Dealers Association, the NAREB, and other organizations with a focus on housing.[84]

Paralleling the rising importance of the model and display house for marketing, NHW became a vastly popular and much-enlarged event during the 1950s. In 1957, its tenth year, 185 communities participated, and builders completed and opened approximately ten thousand models for an anticipated ten million visitors nationwide.[85] Newspaper coverage was heavy in most metropolitan areas, and special sections on the event were greatly expanded. NAHB "Suggestion Bulletins" distributed to local HBAs reveal that for the 1957 NHW, the national organization issued participating local sponsors a copy of the insignia for promotional materials; encouraged television home shows to include spots and features; brokered agreements with appliance and utilities companies for additional promotion; oversaw newspaper contests judging the best NHW supplements; and published a booklet titled "How National Home Week Is Carried Out," providing examples from around the country.[86]

House builders were not the only people interested in the publicity surrounding NWH. Appliance and utilities companies affiliated themselves with particular builders to display their most up-to-date mechanical equipment. Most participating companies also issued informational signs, feature cards, and merchandising guides for their products.[87] NHW was a marketing coup for the housing industry, as it presented the industry and all its builders as a coherent whole and their designs as variations of a single product—the modern house. NHW established a supercharged period of self-promotion for a mass consumer culture increasingly hooked on the act and emotions involved in buying.

The industry and popular appeal of NHW encouraged the development of a second type of event, called the "Parade of Homes." The NAHB initially developed the Parade of Homes (PoH) as a feature of NHW, believing it enhanced public enjoyment and provided a centralized venue for promoting builders. Organizers selected one or more empty sites in a metropolitan area or a street in a subdivision already under development. Upon paying a participation fee, builders received a lot on which they could construct a model house representative of their product line or more inventively showcasing their design ingenuity and construction ability. "Everybody loves a parade!" asserted a promotional poster issued in 1954 by the NAHB. "In many cities, Home Builders erect special exhibit houses side-by-side on a selected street. This is a 'Parade of Homes'—and people swarm to see it. Here, in one convenient area, the public can inspect the finest houses it is possible to produce—replete with the latest and best equipment. It's a show-case of homes! And it's all part of National Home Week!"[88]

Unlike NHW, the PoH existed as a more controlled event—organizers charged admission for access to the street of models, refreshments were often available, and a general fairlike atmosphere prevailed (fig. 9). Some HBAs were so enamored of the PoH that they sponsored multiple sites in the same year. In 1956, Dallas observed NHW with five PoHs containing seventy-one houses visited by over two hundred thousand people.[89] The PoH became such a successful promotional tool that local HBAs began holding similar events at other times of the year.

MAKE SURE EVERYONE SEES YOUR HOUSE

Bob Markow

Put your model in the best location you can

FIGURE 9. The
Parade of Homes
was a self-contained
event that featured
the very best prod-
ucts by local build-
ers. 1957. (*House &
Home*, April 1957,
132; photograph
by Bob Markow;
courtesy of Paul
Markow)

The allure lay not just in the control of the event and the creation of an environment that was essentially a shop window for the building industry. This was
also, importantly, the one time in the year that small-volume custom builders
had visibility on par with large-volume merchant builders. For example, a 1963
advertisement for the "Home-O-Rama," a PoH-type housing festival established
by Pittsburgh's North Suburban Builders Association in 1957, gave equal bill-
ing to all participants. At the Swan Acres location, custom builders like William Eichenlaub were no less represented in the advertising or at the parade site
than were merchant builders like Ryan Homes.[90] For the price of the entry fee,
small-volume builders lacking their own subdivisions and limitless advertising

budgets gained essential public exposure. More significantly, this was a venue where the products of skilled custom builders might outshine those of merchant builders. This type of visibility could sustain their businesses for the remainder of the year—"Small builders often make all of their sales for the coming year from a single house in a Parade."[91]

The appeal of NHW and POHs for the building industry, prospective buyers, and the merely curious remained steady through the 1960s; however, the unabashed exuberance about new houses and developments eventually seemed trite for a nation of savvy consumers and serial house purchasers. *House & Home* observed as early as January 1960 that buyers "know more—more about houses, more about the equipment that goes into them, and more about the importance of good location. Many of them are already homeowners who are now in the market for their second, third, and even fourth houses."[92]

The widespread perception of a particularly informed prospective buyer caused building-industry leaders to reevaluate their recommendations for every step of the sales process. They advised local HBAs to eliminate the overly celebratory environments at the opening of new models and in the observance of NHW. Industry leaders leveled with builders in 1962: "DON'T put on a carnival. Balloons, popcorn and brass bands sell circuses, not houses."[93] The same sentiment was expressed again two years later: "Gone almost completely are the CARNIVAL TACTICS—balloons, clowns and costumed hirelings—that do little more than attract the curious."[94] Marketing experts and building journal editors also encouraged builders to reduce the quantity of furniture and accessories in their display houses—"most model houses become department store salesrooms"—so that the features inherent to good residential design would read through clearly.[95]

In time, popular interest in NHW and PoHs disappeared almost entirely, although furnished display homes remain popular sales and marketing tools for new residential developments. Created, or at least perfected, during the postwar period, the model house, furnished display home, and structured housing celebrations were an integral part of the building industry's attempt to redefine its purpose and place in American culture. In the process, these efforts also helped to transform new houses into marketable goods. This change in perception offered the tantalizing possibility of even greater business success for motivated builders. Such builders knew that clever newspaper advertisements, knowledgeable sales staff, and tastefully decorated display homes would be a waste of resources if their products were badly designed or did not present consumers with something perceived to be better. Only a seemingly superior product that was competitively priced would turn casual lookers into serious buyers.

PRODUCT DESIGN AND REDESIGN

No element of a marketing strategy was more important to the success of a builder's business than the development of a salable design; indeed, only the selection and negotiations for the purchase of land had more weight.[96] Whether constructing houses speculatively for an unknown buyer or working with a specific client to customize a generic prototype, someone, somewhere, was responsible for developing the design of a new house. Influences on the design process were myriad and its exact structure highly changeable. Aside from experience and personal insight, the ideas of other builders, architects, homeowners, government agencies, marketing firms, and housing research groups were widely disseminated in newspapers, popular publications, trade and professional journals, and published and unpublished reports and surveys. The millions of houses constructed each year also represented a major source of ideas. In one example from the late 1940s, James and Margaret Funk's builder replicated a new house they liked a few blocks over from their lot in suburban Pittsburgh.[97]

This type of direct design copying was not limited to small-volume custom builders working with specific clients. An expert in merchandising, participating in a design clinic held at Stanford University in 1960 that was cosponsored by the American Institute of Architects and the NAHB, admonished merchant builders about their product development schemes: "Builders have a lot of contempt for the buying public. If you didn't have contempt you wouldn't do what you are doing—buying blueprints from draftsmen or photographing your competitors' houses and having them copied."[98]

Builders were certainly aware of what the competition was constructing in any given market, particularly taking notice of successful models. Nevertheless, the similarities between their products were another outcome of the FHA.

Underlying the design of all houses were the guidelines issued by the FHA, which stipulated the minimum expectations for new houses in order to receive FHA backing. The FHA's *Technical Bulletin No. 4: Principles of Planning Small Houses* contained standards that established a "national program" of residential design with regard to expected rooms, layout, and built-in features that strongly influenced the design and construction of houses after World War II.[99]

The FHA's interest in design was a financial one—it wanted to be certain that the houses coming under its review were wholly modern and appealing and would hold their value over time. A revised version of *Principles of Planning Small Houses,* released in 1937, explained that the FHA "has emphasized its disapproval of . . . [design] standardization through insistence upon the localization of its own minimum standards and through its encouragement of the use of architectural and other professional service[s] by builders and owners of low-priced dwellings."[100] Even in instances where builders employed architects, the houses did not depart drastically from the FHA prototypes. Herman York, a well-known architect in the arena of mass housing, reflected in 1958 on the atmosphere immediately after the war: "When housing sales were booming and a 'desperation' housing shortage existed, we were pretty much confined to designing homes which readily lent themselves to mass production and economy construction. Little time was devoted to creative or constructive planning."[101]

When the housing shortage abated early in the 1950s and the last of the materials restrictions were lifted with the end of the Korean War, builders began concerning themselves with "a new *rehousing* market . . . to help Americans not only maintain but raise their standard of housing."[102] The FHA minimum standards alone could no longer provide the direction needed to develop salable design. By this point, consumer conditions required builders to regularly and critically assess their product and the new housing needs of the area in which they were planning to build. They had to keep an eye on trends and incorporate them without significantly driving up costs. Large merchant-building companies with in-house design teams constantly tinkered with their models and frequently offered new and improved versions. In contrast, small-volume builders might go through the trouble and expense of developing new prototypes only after observing what types of rooms and features clients were requesting as part of a customized design.

Although materials and labor costs were a significant part of retail pricing, prospective buyers generally expected that a new dwelling would be decently constructed. Unless a builder had a spotty reputation for quality, most consumers considering a specific house cared less about the type of wall construction or the technical elements of an electrical system than the number of bedrooms, the floor finishes, and the kitchen appliances. Buyers wanting higher-quality construction gravitated toward a more costly relationship with a custom builder and a situation where they had more control over the outcome. The fundamental elements of location and construction quality had the greatest effect on the pricing of a new house, yet both operated more or less independently of domestic space planning. The type of space and amenities offered in a new house most preoccupied prospective buyers and, because of this, was the focus of most product redesign by builders.

A 1979 retrospective of the postwar housing industry published in *Public Interest* concluded that the key thing builders "did right" was to regularly update their designs. The residential building industry "was able to improve the product, trade-up the product, give details to that product, and impart tremendous value to that product. These were values that the consumer could see, taste, feel, and use; they were not hidden values but consumer values. They were not great planning values, maybe not great elite values, maybe not esthetic values, but they were consumer values."[103] Postwar builders, of course, could not have forecast this, and they cautiously yet steadily increased the average size of a new house, added rooms, introduced novel plans, and incorporated the latest appliances and equipment. When asked in 1962, "Why change models at all?," an architect who frequently worked with builders tellingly responded, "It's the only road to more business: you anticipate demand, create a new market,—get a best seller. I don't mean taking reckless chances: keep testing new ideas a little at a time."[104]

Builders had a number of places where they might learn about "must have" features. A 1967 article on a study of buyer motivations related to the house and home found that a residential builder "traditionally has relied on meditation and prayer to determine what makes the home buyer tick."[105] While there was a degree of truth to this statement, postwar builders found themselves more and more awash with sources of feedback about consumer desire as it related to houses. It might be attained passively through experience with either briskly or poorly selling models. There were also more formal sources of information and insight, such as market research conducted by the builder or contracted firms; information generated through university and other research programs, such as the University of Illinois Small Homes Council or the Housing Research Foundation of the Southwest Research Institute; knowledge gained from visitors to model houses and through postpurchase interviews; or local government offices.[106] Industry leaders exhorted builders and salesmen in annual marketing issues to be more diligent in listening to and taking advantage of cues offered by prospective buyers and, toward the end of the period, of industry and nonindustry studies and surveys.[107] Builders were even instructed to pay more attention to widely circulated popular periodicals.

Wherever builders ultimately found their information, they often needed expertise in translating trends into new or improved models. An NAHB study of its builder-members conducted in 1959 found that about half of the respondents utilized outside design assistance, with 34.2 percent relying on a contract or in-house architect; 12 percent hiring a "designer," most likely a skilled draftsman; and 6 percent purchasing blueprints through a commercial plan service.[108] While it is impossible to know for certain, the builders seeking professional design services were in all likelihood involved in the construction of larger and more ambitious houses that incorporated new rooms and features. In contrast, the 38.3 percent of builders reporting that they designed their own houses probably kept their business focus on minor updates to tried and true models with which they were completely familiar.

Large builders had the greatest amount of resources either to contract with independent architects or to establish their own in-house design offices. In California, collaboration between Eichler Homes and two different architectural firms, Anshen & Allen and Jones & Emmons, produced some of the most lasting images of affordable contemporary design.[109] Eichler is best known for work within the trend of postwar "tract-house modern" design, but the collaboration between builders and architects espousing Modernism occurred throughout the United States.[110]

Other large firms established internal design departments with a makeup similar to period architectural offices. While Alfred Levitt has been given general credit for the initial postwar house designs constructed by Levitt and Sons, the company also had a "chief architect," John Sierks, on staff as early as 1948. Sierks had received his degree in architecture from the Pratt Institute in 1938 and was still working for Levitt in the late 1950s and early 1960s, when Levittown, New Jersey, and Belair at Bowie, Maryland, were being designed and constructed. At the company offices in Levittown, Sierks headed an architectural department of uncertain size, but his position title, the workload for the massive company, and its level of vertical integration meant that there were probably a number of architects under him who worked in the collaborative manner typical of large midcentury design firms.[111]

Builders with smaller businesses did not generally have the luxury of hiring a licensed architect or a standing design team to update or create new models. One Minneapolis custom builder explained in 1953 that he kept a "designer" on retainer who would translate plans devised by the builder into detailed construction drawings based on the input of "buyers and prospects." He avoided architects because they "usually over-design for the price and try to beat the builder over the head to deliver more house for less profit."[112] Hiring an architect was not a priority for most builders, because they frequently believed they had a better handle on consumer desire. "We know what the public wants," said one builder in 1960, "the architect doesn't. And if we make a mistake we suffer for it."[113] Small-volume builders, particularly ones engaging in modest speculation, needed to be somewhat more cautious when updating designs, since their finances would be more impacted by a poor model that did not sell. On the other hand, small-volume builders were more often in direct contact with prospective buyers and their housing needs and wants; custom builders would have had even greater knowledge of the latest trends as they worked with clients to alter plan prototypes.

The houses built in suburban Pittsburgh by Frank T. Bozzo Sr., versus Frank T. Bozzo Jr., demonstrate the insight that small- to medium-volume custom builders gained over the course of the postwar period. Frank T. Bozzo Sr. began building houses in 1945. Upon his death in 1963, his son, Frank T. Bozzo Jr., came into control of the business and consciously repositioned his client and product focus.[114] Whereas Bozzo Sr. had mainly constructed six-room houses aimed at people with comparatively modest incomes making their first move to the suburbs, Bozzo Jr. decided to build a smaller number of larger houses and target higher-income entry-level buyers or second- or third-time homeowners. He made this change based on the belief that Americans had moved well beyond the "house as shelter" idea, and he sought to create a more enhanced and, hopefully, more marketable and competitive product. In translating this idea into a business activity, Bozzo Jr. hired a "designer" to devise new generic prototypes based on popular ideas about domestic space that could in turn be customized by a specific client. Regardless of how a builder arrived at a final design for a particular house or model, its plan included rooms, and standard and optional features, that held a significant influence over the eventual lifestyles of their clients.

CONCLUSION

During the postwar period, residential builders moved themselves from a relatively limited function as skilled craftsmen constructing houses to central and prominent players in the construction of a new way of life in the American suburbs. In the process, their industry attained a new and high level of national prominence and cohesion through unrelenting self-promotion and energetic product promotion.

Builders commenced their postwar business activities in a manner closely circumscribed by government policies put into place by the FHA. The agency's far-ranging policies reduced the financial risk of conducting business, massively increased the number of prospective buyers through a softening of class- and income-based exclusion at the expense of racial inclusion, and raised the design and construction standards for new houses. These publicly funded economic safeguards permitted builders of all types and scales of business to assertively engage domestic consumer culture by, depending on one's viewpoint, either anticipating consumer demand or generating it in order to stay in business.

With eye-catching advertisements, the modish interiors of furnished display houses, annual housing festivals, and regularly introduced new and improved models, builders marketed a suburban lifestyle that appealed to a large number of Americans. More important, they convinced buyers that this lifestyle was not only desirable but also easily attainable through the purchase of a new house. Whether constructing speculatively for an unknown buyer or developing prototypes that would be customized with the input of a specific client, postwar builders needed to design with someone in mind—a generic prospective buyer. The cultural commentator Russell Lynes observed that by 1957 builders were designing houses "not for *the* family but for *a* family."[115]

The Imagined Consumer

IN 1968, the sociologist Bennett Berger reflected on the general shape of the suburban narrative in the United States: "The myth of suburbia fosters an image of a homogenous and classless America without a trace of ethnicity but fully equipped for happiness by the marvelous productivity of American industry: the ranch house with the occupied two-car garage, the refrigerator and freezer, the washer and dryer, the garbage disposal and the built-in range and dishwasher, the color TV and the hi-fi stereo. Suburbia: its lawns trim, its driveways clean, its children happy on its curving streets and in its pastel schools. Suburbia . . . is America."[1]

Berger's thoughts were included in a new preface to the 1968 printing of his groundbreaking study, *Working-Class Suburb* (1960), one of a group of suburban cultural critiques ranging from satire to academic investigations that began appearing in the 1950s.[2] These books were primarily intended to counteract the enshrinement of the dominant narrative limiting suburban residence to white, home-owning households composed of upwardly mobile nuclear families. Residential builders were among the principal contributors to the tenacity of the association between this demographic and the suburbs. They designed and marketed detached, single-family houses almost entirely to this core type of imagined consumer who had actual, presumed, and constructed traits determined through government intervention, tastemaker advice, and long-standing and modified conceptions about an "American way of life" on the metropolitan periphery.

The robustness of the suburban narrative upheld by builders and consumers alike extended from social, political, and economic traditions passed on from generation to generation. These familiar traditions primarily include: ownership of a detached house set within a garden in a neighborhood of like properties on the edge of a city; the view that such an environment is the only appropriate one for family life, in particular for raising children; and the separation of income-producing work from the daily activities of the home, a condition that fostered distinct female and male spheres of operation and influence. Relative homogeneity is also a cornerstone, and its numerous meanings affect all of the others to some degree, whether considering race, socioeconomic standing, or stage of family formation. Interestingly, even as strides were being at least superficially made toward the goal of racial desegregation, and ownership restrictions based on ethnic or religious background also lessened considerably for those considered "white," postwar suburbanization heightened socioeconomic separation.[3]

Surpassed in importance only by the nuclear family unit, the building industry's steadfast belief in the pervasiveness of upward mobility sustained its long-range product development and marketing strategies, resulting in an unremitting progression of upgrades and enhancements to existing models as well as entirely new ones. Builders were not alone in this outlook. The longtime *Fortune* writer and editor Daniel Seligman remarked in 1959 on the nature of consumerism as a component of upward mobility or at least the appearance of upward mobility: "If most 'workers' still cannot afford $110 suits, boats, Thunderbirds, *and* trips to Florida," noted Seligman, "they have at least enough discretionary income so that they can have some of these things some of the time."[4]

What is particularly interesting is that by 1959 Seligman and many of his contemporaries had already moved beyond merely owning a house in the suburbs as a mark of comfort, success, or status, ascribing these things to other types of consumer goods. The ownership of a suburban house had become ordinary, an expected event in the life cycle of even a moderately prosperous family. Still, there were gradations of suburbs and the isolation of suburbanites in new neighborhoods lacking not just the very rich and the very poor but also, frequently, even a varied mix of middle-income earners. This phenomenon permitted all of them to view themselves and their neighbors as "typical" middle-class Americans, a situation that actually and perceptually contributed to the vast postwar expansion and reformulation of this class. Of course, the relationship among consumerism, a new house in the suburbs, and middle-class identity almost fully excluded nonwhite Americans even though they were very much influenced by the same images and aspirations as their white contemporaries.

Mobility within metropolitan areas and between regions also contributed to a neighborhood's economically homogenous character. The nationwide codification of long-term, amortized lending created an economic structure that affected all house purchases, not just the initial one, which made movement from one house to another much easier for consumers. A household seeing a significant increase in income might move to a new house in another neighborhood; such a salary increase was often tied to a job offer or transfer elsewhere. "Americans are almost too ready to abandon one thing for another," noted the sociologist David Riesman in 1958, "provided they are persuaded by the media or friends that the other is somehow 'better' or, preferably, 'the best.'"[5] These moves suggested to many contemporaries that a predictable and smooth process of upward mobility was sweeping the nation, and the idea quickly became an integral part of the postwar suburban ideal that was a primary motivator for builders and their house designs.

House builders, individually and as an industry, became especially skilled in using the concept of upward mobility to their benefit. By truly and deeply believing that upward mobility was widespread among households, builders fashioned and sustained a housing boom that might otherwise have wound down as soon as shelter needs had been met. In 1960, the Chicago merchant-builder Harry Quinn repeated a widely held belief in the residential building industry: "There are thousands of dissatisfied homeowners who have the equity and income to trade up to a better home. The reason they don't is because we've never gone after them the right way."[6] For roughly two decades following the war, builders— having clear government backing as well as popular participation—were able to educate and induce millions of American families to trade up to a product, and a life, believed to be of higher quality than what they already enjoyed.

HOME OWNERSHIP

The postwar embrace of home ownership was widely understood by contemporaries to be a positive economic and social goal. It had become a basic objective much earlier but attained an urgency after World War II as it rose to be the defining requirement in the quest for an idyllic suburban life. The expense of a detached house set in a private garden of a leafy suburb, and mortgages

that were both difficultly obtained and strictly termed, assured that for its first
century American suburbanization was predominantly the realm of the prosperous. The FHA and VA mortgage programs later normalized the long-term,
amortizing home loan, which so completely changed the environment and
structure of all residential financing that home ownership not only emerged as
a key part of the postwar suburban ideal but became more or less synonymous
with middle-class identification.[7]

Government approval of house and subdivision plans reduced risk in speculative construction among builders and provided relatively easy mortgage terms
for millions of home buyers. As a result, the postwar period saw an unprecedented swelling in the number of American households occupying a building
that they owned. Rates of home ownership shot up sharply, from about 40 percent in 1940 to near 63 percent by 1965.[8] As home ownership became a reality
for greater percentages of Americans, the house itself became a vital indicator
of middle- and upper-middle-class status. Late in the nineteenth and early in the
twentieth centuries, this status was based less on actually owning a house: general residential location, white-collar work, education, family ancestry, and religious affiliation all strongly informed class identity. Indeed, as early-twentieth-
century rates of home ownership appear to have been higher among certain
tiers of the working class than among the middle class, it is possible that the
postwar emphasis on owning a house might have been due in part to segments
of the middle-income working class "becoming" middle class at that time.[9]

Despite its widespread popularity and ideological dominance, the call for
generalized home ownership was not accepted without question. In 1945, Miles
L. Colean, a respected expert on housing issues, in particular the economics of
housing, expressed a widely held worry about returning to the rampant foreclosures of the 1930s: "As an ideal state to which every family may aspire, home
ownership has been seriously questioned since the last depression."[10] In the
foreword to John P. Dean's *Home Ownership: Is It Sound?*, published the same
year, the renowned sociologist Robert S. Lynd reflected on the "strong American
tradition in favor of home ownership" and observed: "This problem of knowing when it is wise to exercise one's freedom in following American tradition
in such a major venture as buying a home is complicated, as Dr. Dean amply
reveals, by the fact that not only does business organize itself to keep alive the

unequivocal sentiment of the rightness of home-ownership, but even our government lends itself to the ends of the real estate and home-selling interests."[11]

Home ownership's dubiousness was particularly evident in the early postwar years as many returning veterans, enticed by houses requiring no down payment or, because of the housing shortage, having no rental options, got in "over their heads" by not considering all the additional expenses associated with a house.[12] Some literature immediately following the war—before the full scale of the postwar suburban expansion could be grasped—even asked Americans to discern what sort of lifestyle they wished to maintain when deciding whether to rent or to purchase a dwelling.[13] There were also questions about the essential character of long-term loan amortization. One merchant-builder participant at a 1950 real estate conference queried the panel of experts about whether the system of thirty- or forty-year mortgages would "take us back to feudalism. . . . Doesn't the government, in effect, become the landlord if we have forever to continue to make payments, which the average American in his lifetime can never pay off?"[14] Even the more affluent needed to think about how to transform domestic ideals into something tangible. In 1948, Colean cautioned readers of *House Beautiful* that *"house-dreaming is good fun, but talk to your banker before you cut loose."*[15] An accompanying illustration tellingly depicted a couple's dream house greatly reduced with each successive visit to the banker, the architect, and the contractor.

Despite the many earnest questions, by the mid-1950s most popular and trade literature ceased questioning home ownership, and it became a widely accepted goal and, for many middle-income white Americans, a reality. In 1951, Janet Levritz and her husband did not ponder the concept of home ownership at all when they purchased a new house in Arlington, Virginia. She reflected: "It was the thing to do. . . . [It] didn't take a lot of thought or consideration."[16] Prospective buyers needed only to calculate how much of their monthly income could be reasonably applied to mortgage payments. Most articles directed toward consumers encouraged them to disregard popular formulas, such as the one holding that the purchase price of a house should not exceed your annual income doubled. Or, as explained in *U.S. News & World Report* in 1950: "Families are finding . . . that there is no single rule to fit the situation of every family. For those who are planning to buy or build, there must be an assessment of how

FIGURE 10. Frame from the cartoon "Jane and Bill Learn How a Mortgage Works." 1957. (Ryan Homes Collection; courtesy of the Mortgage Bankers Association)

secure are job and income, of other obligations that have been assumed, of the number of children to rear and educate, of many other factors."[17]

Instead of providing formulas, articles throughout the postwar period usually encouraged readers to set up priority lists, along with considering their monthly expenses.[18] They reminded prospective buyers that, in addition to the down payment, they needed to have ready cash for such things as surveys, appraisals, title insurance, deed and mortgage recordation, attorney fees, and items and services related to closing.[19] Lending institutions also distributed explanatory publications, such as the Mortgage Bankers Association of America's "Jane and Bill Learn How a Mortgage Works" (1957). Its comic book format gave the serious topic of loans and mortgages a quality of ease and portrayed the purchase of a house as a simple decision and action (fig. 10).[20]

Ownership of the best house possible became ordinary enough that a household might stretch its budget to buy in a certain neighborhood or to purchase a particular house model. During the planning and construction of their second new house, early in 1971, Albert and Shirley Robick did not enhance their custom builder's prototype because the standard version was both "enough" house and all they could afford after purchasing and specially grading their lot.[21] While most prospective buyers thought a great deal about their budgets, they do not appear to have consciously thought about home ownership and its meanings. Recalling two successive new house purchases, one couple in the Pittsburgh suburbs noted: "At that time, I don't think we thought much beyond needing space. I can't remember isolating the single thought of 'ownership' and being motivated by that. It was sort of assumed that we would have (own) our own house. It was part of the trip as opposed to a destination."[22] The concept became such a standard expectation among middle-income whites that it was essentially taken for granted as a central element of the American way of life.

An often blasé approach to home ownership could translate into major mistakes. A 1967 issue of *Good Housekeeping* featured an article titled "What Went Wrong in Dreamland?" The article explained that buying in Larkdale, Illinois, was made to seem uncomplicated through FHA and VA loans, but many buyers did not include taxes, utilities, and transportation costs in their budgets; said one former resident: "Our only sin was being naïve."[23] From late in 1962 until the article's preparation, an average of one person per month had gone bankrupt in the 415-house subdivision, with one hundred foreclosures by 1967. Tales like these worked to reinforce the importance of the learning processes that occurred in tandem with an all too often vastly understated purchase.

In less than a quarter century, owning a house surrounded by a grassy plot had moved from being an ideal, out of reach for most Americans, to being a reality that was attainable for many. Of all the factors shaping the popular manifestation of the postwar suburban ideal, home ownership was the one most clearly reflected in reality even if the actual situation was, at times, less than ideal. Indeed, while the national rate of home ownership impressively increased overall by roughly a third during the two decades following the war, rates of (mortgaged) home ownership in a majority of newly constructed suburban subdivisions would have been upward of 100 percent at the time of their completion.

THE NUCLEAR FAMILY

Like ownership of a single-family suburban house, the belief that such a dwelling was designed for the nuclear family was another fully realized element of the postwar suburban ideal. Period literature and later scholarship have dissected nearly every aspect of expectation and reality in postwar family life; however, none of these critiques and assessments have ever seriously questioned that the postwar suburbs were at the outset overwhelmingly, if not entirely, devised for a specific type of family (fig. 11). It follows closely then that postwar suburban houses were always created with some sort of nuclear family in mind and are a concrete record of how idealized family life continually impacted the postwar version of the suburban ideal.

Suburban houses were indisputably designed for families and are evidence of how postwar society expected them to operate.[24] The link between behavior and roles and architecture was not lost on contemporaries. A thirty-year retrospective on housing appearing in *Parents' Magazine* in 1956 opened with a simply stated thesis: "To the Average Family—that indescribable but extraordinarily powerful influence—the changes in housing over the last three decades would add up to something like this: thirty years ago they somehow had to fit themselves into the house; now the house is planned to fit them."[25] It was "planned to fit them" only if it were the industry's prototypical household.

The evolution of postwar domestic space paralleled and was dependent on changes in how families were popularly envisaged over time. No element of postwar culture held more sway over the dreams and realities of families than their houses. In the years following the war, couples viewed a new suburban house as the concrete manifestation of a better life, fantasized about during the stressful, straitened, and tragic war years. Later in the period, a new house in a new suburban neighborhood was also a persuasive force maintaining an extremely confident and optimistic societal outlook, which centered on the possibility that American society might reach an ideal state.[26] The suburban house was also a demonstration of family unity, comfort and leisure, and a more equitable division of national wealth.[27] The rooms and layout of detached suburban houses and widely promoted characterizations of "typical" family life evolved together, and one could not help but impact the other. A home-centered existence with a "high valuation on family living" was a driving force for how houses changed in the postwar period.[28]

FIGURE 11. Builders designed for what they believed to be the typical American family. 1956. (Author's collection)

Houses were constructed by the millions, and there were few alternatives at a time when the government, industry, and society favored a certain lifestyle. There was essentially one mode of living being made available to Americans. When queried, they often expressed satisfaction; however, it is impossible to know how many would have chosen another option had a viable one existed.[29] It seems that not until the later years of the postwar period—as even the upwardly mobile members of the middle class who were inclined to "trade up" seem to have tired of the process—did builders began to catch on to how they had been limiting consumer choice even while they believed they had been expanding it. Chet Tomlin, a builder-developer from Winter Park, Florida, observed at a 1968 housing round table: "We are making a serious mistake in equating what our customers really want with what they take, simply because it is the only thing available to them."[30]

As millions of families relocated to the metropolitan fringe, emerging patterns of suburban living affected all members of a household. The reasons for

FIGURE 12. Children were an oft-cited reason for moving to a new suburban house. 1959. (Courtesy of the Jewish Museum of Maryland)

moving to the suburbs were many, but it was still widely claimed that suburbs existed, first and foremost, for children and often at great personal sacrifice by their parents (fig. 12).[31] Harry Henderson, a widely read journalist, writer, and social activist, mused in 1953: "Children love living in these towns, the first large communities in America which have literally been built for them; everything from architecture to traffic control takes into consideration their safety, their health, and the easing of their parents' worries."[32]

The suburbs—with open spaces and good schools—were a major draw for postwar couples thinking about current and expected children, and the houses there were designed for a single type of family. For George and Judith Kisak, the purchase of a house in a Pittsburgh suburb in 1964 "meant we would have a place to raise a family and create a home for the children in a nice area."[33] This emphasis on a specific type of family structure—married couple with children—was exclusionary; however, contemporary Americans— possibly even excluded ones—would have agreed that such a household was the basic building block of a strong society. Far more troubling than this particular emphasis was the lack of access to these idealized places by nonwhite Americans.

RACIAL HOMOGENEITY

The desirability of home ownership and the appeal of a more stable family structure can be effectively debated outside the context of postwar consumer culture as it relates to suburban houses; not so the real and apparent homogeneity in newly constructed subdivisions. This homogeneity resulted directly from such things as levels of purchasing power; the stage of family formation; and the self-fulfilling, race-based actions that were claimed would maintain property values against the nebulous threat of "market forces." The geographic relocation and social transformation of white working-class households were reinforced and legitimized by images of houses and gardens in newspapers, the shelter press, and elsewhere. These sources presented a vision of suburban life in such a way as to make viewers believe that their newly achieved level of economic well-being or social standing might be more solidly projected through the purchase of a particular house.[34] In contrast to the white working class, nonwhite Americans were absent from these visions and largely denied participation through restricted access to goods, housing covenants, and other means of housing segregation, geographic isolation, and economic marginalization.

In a cultural environment where rising incomes and the obtainment of an array of domestic goods became an idealized norm, the reality of life for nonwhite Americans became increasingly trying. A 1968 report titled "Business and the Urban Crisis" argued that "deprived people feel most frustrated when their hopes and expectations have been raised but not completely satisfied."[35] Occurring at the tail end of a generation obsessed with new dwellings, the urban riots of the 1960s had as one of their key backstories a lack of equal access to the suburban houses that were praised in virtually every forum.

The restrictions barring nonwhites from purchasing new suburban houses is what most tarnishes the suburban ideal in postwar America. The enduring popular vision of happy families in newly constructed subdivisions is essentially a white one, and postwar suburbanization dramatically intensified residential segregation in the United States.[36] While seemingly universal and certainly the dominant narrative for most new residential developments, this exclusion was never total. Early on after the war, some builders began seeing the "minority market" for housing as a profitable emerging sector. The national racial discourse of the period was almost exclusively presented in terms of "black" and "white." Use of the term *minority* in contemporary publications usually referred to black Americans, although depending on the city and region, racism was often directed toward Asian Americans and Latino Americans. Though some builders—both black and white—were successful in creating new subdivisions for minorities, they were comparatively few and far between, and when constructed, these neighborhoods were segregated.[37]

Although this segregation is not justifiable, it is not hard to comprehend why small-volume local builders were unwilling to blaze a trail with regard to integration—they were raised within a culture of segregation and knew that the viability of their business depended on commerce within already segregated communities. In contrast, for most of the nation's larger builders, decisions to employ race-based sales restrictions at new subdivisions are revealing, given the size and comparative anonymity of their operations. These decisions mirrored the depth of white racism, overt or covert, and exposed the deep divisions that undermined the building industry's rhetoric about "creat[ing] for every man a home for the good life."[38]

For most of its decade of construction, sales, and initial occupancy after 1960, Levitt and Sons' Belair development in Bowie, Maryland, remained a segregated project, despite the fact that it was constructed by the nation's largest merchant-building company.[39] When civil rights activists protested the race-based sales restrictions at Belair in 1963, the company claimed a blanket justification: "[We] obey the law and follow local custom. To do anything else would be, for us, economic suicide."[40] This public statement was an attempt to exonerate Levitt and Sons from its discriminatory sales practices by using the idea of the market as a smokescreen and also passing off responsibility to the prospective buyers at Belair. The statement also indicated that Levitt and Sons viewed its target market as a white one. Despite the fact that metropolitan Washington had the nation's largest concentration of black middle-income earners, the company calculated that its profit gains from selling to black buyers would not offset what it thought would be its profit losses from prospective white buyers who would not purchase a house in an integrated development.

Levitt and Sons was hardly alone among large builders when it came to barring the sale of houses to black buyers. Ned Eichler, whose father was a large-scale builder in California and a pioneer in the integration of new subdivisions, admitted: "There is no question that almost all merchant builders refused to sell homes to blacks in their projects."[41] In early 1954, the NAHB began "a campaign to spark greater construction of housing for Negroes and other minority groups."[42] The timing of the campaign is not surprising, as the overall housing shortage had been largely alleviated, and builders were keen on finding new marketing angles. The NAHB expressed social "satisfaction" in constructing minority housing, but it was not promoting "philanthropy": "If housing for minorities does not pay its own way, a basic requirement for improving the lot of minorities has not been fulfilled."[43] For reasons ranging from immediate and outright racism to long-standing economic realities that resulted from racist limitations placed on access to education and job opportunities, only a scattering of builders constructed houses for black purchasers, and almost none devised integrated subdivisions.

Builders cannot shoulder the entire blame for segregation, as few members of white, middle America, many of them recent arrivals to that income class, sought to buy houses in integrated communities. The feelings of most prospective white home buyers ranged from outright hostility and violence toward black suburban pioneers to ambivalence about desegregation. The Californian Gordon Chittenden was the stand-in for a "typical white suburbanite" in a 1965 article in *Ebony:* "All we want to do is live in peace. We don't want any trouble, that's why we're living in suburbia."[44] One year later, a staff writer for the *Washington Post* explained that metropolitan areas in the East were possibly less accommodating than the West: "Open housing is a sensitive subject in the Northern cities of white suburbs and black ghettos. Many whites reject the 'love thy neighbor' philosophy when a Negro moves in next door. Open hotels, open restaurants, open employment, yes; open housing, no."[45]

Social prejudice against blacks provided the foundation for the widespread desire of whites to keep the suburbs segregated; however, these feelings were considerably amplified by the even then long discredited belief that the mere presence of nonwhites would depress property values.[46] This idea was not new; it had been explicitly present in restrictions tied to most suburban development during the first half of the twentieth century and was enshrined by the FHA in its appraisal practices. However, whereas earlier suburban development had been enjoyed predominantly by the truly affluent, postwar suburbanization included many people who were investing significant percentages of their household worth in their houses and stood to suffer serious losses with any reduction in property values.[47] For most of the postwar period, active discrimination by builders—always unethical and increasingly illegal—was accepted

by most white buyers, keeping whites and blacks apart in the American suburbs and thus severely limiting minority attainment of a suburban ideal that was endlessly trumpeted as the American way of life.

While the difficulties in buying a house were immense, they did not stop black families from moving to the suburbs. Between 1940 and 1960, the number of blacks living in the suburbs rose from 1.5 to 2.5 million; by the end of the 1970s, the number would nearly double, to 4.6 million.[48] In contrast to earlier black suburbanization, which drew significantly from the working class and centered on semirural enclaves, the postwar increase corresponded with an expansion of the black middle class, a cohort that very much aligned its aspirations with other middle-class families throughout the nation. The role of housing in the configuration of class identity was just as strong for middle-income black families as it was for their white counterparts. As blacks attained higher levels of education and income and began entering white-collar professions in greater and greater numbers, they, too, desired to live among similar households in new houses in middle-class subdivisions.[49]

As the residential building industry maintained segregation within new subdivisions, for a majority of members of the burgeoning black middle class, a move to the suburbs frequently meant an older house in an existing neighborhood (fig. 13). A 1975 study of black home ownership in the three decades following World War II found that "the upwardly mobile black middle class, aspiring to homeownership and anxious to leave the central cities, provides a source of demand for the older housing of the inner-ring suburbs."[50]

Whether dating from the 1920s or the product of the early postwar construction boom, such houses were made available as departing "white families sought new and better accommodations in the [segregated] suburbs" further out from the metropolitan center.[51] Such neighborhoods frequently became available for black ownership through blockbusting, a process structured by the purposeful use of racial anxiety and panic to undermine the residential housing market, ultimately for the profit of real estate brokers.[52] These agents convinced white residents that they should sell their properties at below-market values because blacks were beginning to buy in the neighborhood, and their property values were bound to fall even more. Agents then turned around and sold the properties to black buyers at inflated prices. The process provided agents with immediate profits from the flip and also benefited builders and developers because the departing white families often ended up in a new house on the suburban periphery.

The difficulties facing black Americans desiring to move to the suburbs were myriad; more often than not, regardless of class standing, such a move was an emotionally debilitating process, with houses, neighborhoods, and frequently whole sections of metropolitan areas made unavailable to them.[53] A journalist wrote in 1954: "Despite their ability to pay, Negroes still find themselves unable to buy homes available to others."[54] Even in the few places where new houses in segregated or integrated subdivisions were available, black families were often unable to make a purchase because they lacked equity as first-time buyers or owned a house in a depreciating urban neighborhood.[55] This became even more of a problem later in the postwar period, when purchasing a newly constructed house was even more costly and generally required either a very high income or equity in another dwelling.

With the overall market for houses restricted, and many of the suburban houses that were available being older, black suburbanites were frequently dissatisfied with the suburban houses that they purchased.[56] This dissatisfaction is logical since black middle-class families possessed the same desires for new houses as their white contemporaries. Reporting on the black middle class in 1966, a writer for *Fortune* magazine found that "most middle-class Negroes also share with the white majority the nation's traditional values. . . . The consumption pattern of Negroes as they move into the middle class increasingly duplicates that of the larger society's majority."[57] Around the same time, the mortgage industry also acknowledged the need for new and up-to-date houses for the black middle class: "Part of the American style of life includes residence in accommodations of more recent vintage and architectural design."[58]

Middle-class black families had long desired the same type and quality of housing as their white contemporaries, and this trend continued in postwar America.[59] In one of the best-known cases of suburban desegregation, Bill and Daisy Myers encountered a tense and dangerous scene when they moved to Levittown, Pennsylvania, in the summer of 1957. In Daisy Myers's memoir of the period, a narrative started while the nationally publicized events were still unfolding, she explained why they were drawn to Levittown despite the expectation of trouble. Her young family had "outgrown" their attached, single-family house in nearby integrated Bloomsdale, which they had purchased new a few years earlier, and now they "needed another bedroom to separate the girl from the boys [and] . . . wanted a [detached] single-family residence with more yard space. . . . The cheerful, pink, three-bedroom ranch house on the corner of Deepgreen and Daffodil Lanes in Levittown had everything we could want."[60]

Almost a decade later, the Sullivans, a black middle-class family in New Jersey, also had difficulty in finding a new suburban house to purchase on account of their race. Still, the type of house they desired was closely comparable to that of their white counterparts. The Sullivans had "their hearts set on a single-story, modern ranch house" and, in 1965, were able to purchase, after much difficulty, a newly constructed stone-clad ranch house on a spacious lot, featuring such expected middle-class rooms and features as formal and casual dining space, a basement recreation area, a two-car garage, and a patio in the backyard.[61] For both the Myerses and the Sullivans, the desire for a modern suburban house was realized through processes charged with frustration, disappointment, and fear, but the tangible, material goal was no different from that of other middle-class families.

At the same time that northern and western cities were embroiled in open occupancy situations or the integration of existing neighborhoods, southern cities for the most part continued to follow a path of complete residential segregation. The establishment of "sanctioned 'Negro expansion areas'" acknowledged the need for new houses, while it controlled how existing black neighborhoods expanded and where new ones would be established.[62] These conditions, ironically, led to a greater number of new detached single-family houses made available to black buyers.

In one black suburban community in the South, not only were housing expectations within the middle-class mainstream, but prospective buyers also exhibited a level of consumer control over their purchase that is usually not associated with blacks in postwar America. The one-story, two-, three-, and four-bedroom houses in Hamilton Park in Dallas were similar to those found in subdivisions throughout the country. The model offerings appear to have also been regularly upgraded through product redesign, keeping pace with the rapid changes in postwar domestic architecture and a more knowledgeable and selective buying public. One original homeowner reflected: "'I was not at first really impressed with [Hamilton Park] because I did not want a carport, and most of the houses were smaller than what I wanted. Then, as I continued to come out here, they continued to improve the houses,' making them larger, with enclosed garages, and discarding the wall heaters in the early homes in favor of central heat. 'So I came out in February of 1959 and decided to buy one.'"[63] Pontchartrain Park in New Orleans, developed as a segregated community beginning in 1954, not only contained houses indistinguishable from those in adjacent white subdivisions but also included such amenities as playgrounds, ball fields, and an eighteen-hole golf course.[64]

Situations like these were admittedly rare when one considers the entire landscape of postwar suburbia; black buyers were denied geographic and financial access to new houses or, in cases where they were able to buy, were forced to compromise by purchasing an older dwelling. These difficulties meant that a suburban house and home ownership symbolized something different for black Americans. They were proof of hard-won success and a family refuge, not just from the real and perceived perils of the Cold War but also from the daily turmoil characterizing the America of the civil rights era. Black families accepted and desired the popular, mass architectural ideal of the postwar suburbs, and when given a relatively uncommon instance of full or expanded agency in house buying, white and black class equivalents generally sought similar types of houses.[65] One Virginia house builder perceived in 1962: "White or Negro—all buyers want essentially the same things. . . . As we move up the price scale, we find they all want more baths, a complete kitchen, a family room, a fireplace, more brick on the exterior, and air conditioning. The chief differences between buyers appear at different economic levels."[66]

The Virginia builder's observation reinforces the notion that black and white concepts of an ideal house were most solidly based on economics and mass-culture portraits of middle-class life. Instances where black families were actually able to purchase suburban houses provide evidence that consumer desire, in contrast to the realities of the housing market, seems to have been the same across color lines. Home ownership as a desired state was a given, as was the idea that new suburban houses would be occupied by nuclear family units. Government programs and private-industry policies privileged white buyers, yet the desire of a middle-income family, white or black, to own a modern house in the suburbs was extraordinarily potent. Builders took this one step forward and did not just design for and market to a generic nuclear family, but to an upwardly mobile one.

UPWARD MOBILITY AND THE IMPETUS TO TRADE UP

The short period between World War II and the Korean War saw an unprecedented amount of residential expansion, primarily aimed at relieving an acute housing shortage. Builders could have rested on their laurels after eliminating this shortage or could have done more to provide up-to-date single-family houses for minorities or those lacking a middle-income salary or wage. Whatever the nature and extent of the "community building" rhetoric, however, this was a private industry, and despite the government's assistance, it never saw itself as anything near public in nature. The direction of the housing industry for the remainder of the postwar period did not primarily center on translating the basic elements of the suburban ideal into reality for as many Americans as possible, but rather on crafting a business model that enshrined the concept of upward mobility.

A May 1955 editorial in *House & Home* declared that the publication was "dedicated to helping the homebuilding industry move in faster on a vast new market—a new market as big as the [basic] shelter market the builders have served so well in the past ten years."[67] Among the emerging market's highlighted characteristics, a widespread rise in incomes was thought to be the most important. *House & Home*'s builder-readers were tasked in no uncertain terms: "You can't sell them a new house unless you first make them dissatisfied with their present housing by offering them something new and different and excitingly better."[68]

In the early decades of the twentieth century, the productive capacity of the United States grew immensely, and the associated material abundance and rising affluence among workers transformed the advertising and marketing of products. With the basic needs of many citizens increasingly met, the "urge to consume" was not only encouraged by producers but also positioned as a virtuous act that benefited society as much as the individual.[69] Before the postwar period, the most substantial goods that could be considered key parts of this transformed economic system were durable goods, such as refrigerators and automobiles. Expanding national wealth and favorable government programs during the postwar decades extended the mass production-consumption equation to new houses.

Postwar builders used fast-evolving notions of house, home, and idealized suburban family life as a means of convincing consumers they should trust the long-term viability of a housing investment and expect a continued rise in their standard of living. Russell Lynes attempted to describe aspects of these conditions in 1957, observing the typical American past and present: "As a believer in progress both material and cultural he has hesitated to lag behind the advice that was given him. So he has been partly the victim and partly the purveyor of the notion that to make up one's mind about the dimensions and accouterments of the good life is 'bad for business,' that change and growth are synonymous, and that as a consumer it is part of his duty not to know his own mind."[70]

Comfortable and confident in comparative prosperity, middle-income American consumers found themselves bombarded with conscious and unconscious suggestions to at least consider buying a new house, or a second or third, in a suburban locale in a process known as "trading up" or "buying up." In 1962, for example, Robert Anderson and his wife, Frances, hired the custom-building firm of William Miller & Sons to construct a new house for them outside Pittsburgh. This house was the third they had owned during their marriage and their second new house, all of them located in the same portion of one suburban township.[71]

A study commissioned by the Housing Industry Promotional Operation of the NAHB in 1961 noted that 2 percent of their sample had moved into a new house purchased during the previous year. Outwardly small, the study sample represented an estimated market of over thirty million households; 2 percent of this total is a figure corresponding to roughly two-thirds of the total number of single-family houses constructed by the building industry in 1960. About one-third of the purchasers of new houses in the study had moved from ones they owned, a group numerically equivalent to a little over 20 percent of all purchasers of privately constructed, single-family houses in that year.[72] This cohort, intent on trading up, along with high-income first-time buyers, represented a significant amount of the building industry's business and profits. These groups became a large enough portion of individual house sales that industry leaders easily folded the idea of upward mobility and affluence into the makeup of their idealized consumer and the related design and marketing of houses.

Acknowledgment of builders' motivations and a conception of their idealized buyer do not refute studies arguing for a more inclusive and heterogeneous understanding of suburbia. In *Working-Class Suburb,* Bennett Berger discusses the "myth of suburbia," a key element of which was upwardly mobile families.[73] He was among the vanguard of scholars who helped to launch a whole tradition of suburban literature furnishing a virtually endless march of real alternatives to the popularized vision of postwar suburbia. In time, the sociological studies of the 1950s, 1960s, and 1970s gave way to a growing corpus of academic literature that has repopulated the suburbs with the nonwhite and non–middle class or pointed to ways that inhabitants departed from popular visions of perfect family life. All of these studies, both period and contemporary, are extremely important to understanding the diversity of both the historical and the current social, economic, and cultural landscapes of the suburbs. Still, although more realistically populating suburban neighborhoods, they give only a cursory glance at the original design intents for individual houses in those neighborhoods.

The houses making up a new subdivision in the postwar period were most often created for and marketed to a generic family who builders believed, by the mid-1950s, possessed the economic means through increased income or equity to buy another new house. The growing number of postwar families who had attained middle-income status and held discretionary funds forced most other types of manufacturers to diversify their product range to meet the widening spectrum of consumer expectations.[74] This was less the case with the residential building industry. Over time, comparatively few builders appear to have had a strong interest in the lower end of the market, in large part because it was already served by an existing stock of reasonably well-built suburban houses. The builder Ned Eichler clarified that the "gradual market rejection of [the] minimum was simply a function of the millions of [more modest] housing units built since the war."[75]

Industry leaders urged builders to regularly, even annually, upgrade their models with new features such as larger rooms, zoned plans, additional bedrooms and bathrooms, new spaces such as the family room, and an array of standard household appliances. While a 1958 article listed a number of practical reasons why current homeowners might consider buying a new house having all the bells and whistles, the final one best represented the tone of industry opinion: "People trade up because they are moving up."[76]

A sustained process of model upgrades contributed to sharper class distinctions in the suburbs, even while the intense promotion of houses thought to be new and improved made it seem as if all Americans were "moving up." In the late 1940s, new suburbs displayed a greater degree of class heterogeneity because the housing shortage limited consumer choice, but it did not take long for the suburbs to resegregate by class, as many prospering middle-income residents continued to trade up to new and larger houses, leaving their lower-income or merely contented neighbors behind.[77]

The "pioneering stage" of new suburban neighborhoods built in the 1950s and 1960s exhibited very high levels of homogeneity since similarities in the type and cost of housing created a built-in economic filter.[78] In 1959, the popular writer Daniel Seligman further observed that the desire and ability to move might be defined not just by income but also by other outlooks and considerations: "The young white collar usually regards his first suburban home as a temporary lodgment on the way to a better one. The blue collar sees it as security for his old age."[79] Even as housing costs spiked toward the end of the 1960s, the *Chicago Tribune* reported that the upgrade market contained the vastest group of prospective buyers, and this was where builders' attention remained fixed.[80] Over time, the building industry's sustained promotion of new and improved models underscored an incorrect characterization that all suburban dwellers were upwardly mobile.

Builders publicly passed off the upgrade trend as being predominately consumer driven, as if they were solely responding to demand. As claimed in a *Time* magazine article in 1956, "Better houses abuilding because buyers demand them."[81] The design and construction, and sale and purchase, of new houses, as with all other products, reflected the complex negotiations, motivations, and realities of consumer-based domestic economy. For the uninitiated, periodicals and newspapers furnished concise, user-friendly advice related to such topics as design, construction, financing, choosing the "right" neighborhood, the sales process, interaction with builders, and even how to care for a new house. As the postwar period proceeded, builders conceded that the average American home buyer had become increasingly more knowledgeable, sophisticated, and formidable. The situation required that builders remain diligent in their product design and make sensitive refinements to their marketing techniques.

Who, then, was most responsible for the steady enlargement and enhancement of newly constructed houses in the postwar period—builders or buyers? Both groups made decisions within a domestic economy on a scale never before experienced. A close, and in some cases very personal, interaction between builders and buyers spawned a producer-consumer relationship that, while extending from established trends in early twentieth-century consumerism and marketing, was new to the postwar world. The motives of builders in maintaining demand and profits and the desire of consumers for additional rooms and amenities incubated a coordinated, but never fully codified, system of mutual response that fueled a rapid evolution in the design, marketing, and sales of new houses during the postwar period.

CONSUMERISM AND THE DISPOSABLE HOUSE

During the quarter century following World War II, the detached single-family house attained preeminent status among consumer products available for mass consumption in the United States. While its immense relative expense when compared to other goods was generally acknowledged, the milestone step of purchasing a house was frequently likened to the selection and financing of a washing machine, lawn mower, or automobile. This transformation occurred as part of a renewed and much-altered consumer world where commercialized urban economies, widespread during the first half of the twentieth century, reemerged after fifteen years of depression and war as metropolitan economies that increasingly operated on a national scale.[82] Consumer products went from being merely desirable and enjoyable to a status where many viewed the purchase of certain goods as vital to personal fulfillment and familial joy.

The emergence of this distinct domestic economy was fully noted, if not comprehensively understood, by contemporary commentators and critics who felt it represented the rise of a peculiarly "American" mode of living. Awash with resources—savings, high incomes, and personal credit—and consumer goods, many postwar Americans enjoyed a record level of comfort and an extraordinary amount of choice in their lives, giving rise to a distinct style of living in the suburbs.[83] A spreading sense of intense desire for and gratification through the consideration and purchase of consumer goods was the linchpin in the development of this novel way of living. In 1960, Vance Packard wrote about the widespread character of contemporary consumer culture: "New pressures are causing ever more people to find their main life satisfactions in their consumption role rather than their productive role. And these pressures are bringing forward such traits as pleasure-mindedness, self-indulgence, materialism, and passivity as conspicuous elements of the American character."[84]

Government policies favoring home ownership and steadily rising incomes for many reshuffled priorities and expectations as they related to houses and home ownership. In 1926, among the principal reasons for buying a house, Sears, Roebuck & Co. stressed: "Be independent in old age."[85] For the minority of Americans then able to buy a house, it was more often than not something astoundingly significant and generally seen as a stopping point, a secure haven for the owner. Later, a "sense of security" remained a compelling reason to own a house, but not necessarily to stay in it.[86]

Perry Prentice—the "founder, editor and publisher" of *House & Home*—offered, quite expectedly, a different scenario in 1959: "Yesterday's house is as obsolete as yesterday's car, but not enough people seem to know it. By yesterday's house, I mean almost all the houses built before the war, perhaps half the houses built since the war, and too many of the houses being built right this year—new houses built to yesterday's standards, new houses built without benefit of all today's new and better materials, today's new and better construction economies, today's new and better design for easier, pleasanter living."[87] By the mid-1950s, discussion of the shortcomings of existing houses, even dwellings built within the previous decade, had become widespread, and those with equity in existing houses and rising incomes could consider trading up.

The essential conditions nurturing a climate of serial home purchases included continued economic expansion and stability, equity in existing houses, and growing and aging families, with stages of family formation being the most often cited reason for considering a new home.[88] A popular news magazine concluded in 1955: "Apparently people do not buy homes for a lifetime but to meet the needs of a few years, with the idea of trading for some other kind of house when their needs change."[89] Indeed, as the answer to changes in lifestyle over time, trading up was understood as a normal action. Kiplinger, the personal finance advisers and business forecasters, argued for the social and financial benefits of trading up as early as 1953: "The ideal solution, of course, is to change houses as family needs change. You may be able to do it by buying several times during your life if you buy wisely enough each time and get a decent break on the fluctuations of the real-estate market."[90] Social status and class identification surely contributed to many decisions to trade up. These concerns related more to issues of overall location (development or town) and lot size, rather than to interior room arrangement, a factor more relevant to family size and age.

The phenomenon of trading up resulted in a further stratified suburban landscape with relative socioeconomic homogeneity within subdivisions. Such homogeneity was a favored target of cultural commentators, but residents were generally satisfied with the situation. Indeed, too much socioeconomic diversity within a development could be a liability for builders. Levitt and Sons dropped its most expensive model at its Belair development before it even went into production because it had few orders, and the company even struggled with slow sales of the next most expensive model until it created a section composed exclusively of these houses.[91]

The reasons for trading up covered a range of ideas about families and human nature. A housewife from Washington, DC, commented in 1964: "Really you need more than one house. When the children are little you need one type of house, and when the children get older, you need another type of house. You can't answer all the questions with one."[92] The NAHB's Housing Industry Promotional Operation consumer survey found that "one should always improve himself" and "can get a better house" were the top two reasons given for moving, if a family was financially able and inclined to do so.[93] Support for the trading-up trend was not universal, for reasons ranging from construction quality to family stability. An architect writing for *Ladies' Home Journal* in 1963 claimed that "few people, escaping from one inadequate house to another house they do not really want, will invest in quality. The house needs to be only good enough to last a few years."[94] Acceptance of the idea that a house might be disposable and replaced because of a change in family life cycle or desired lifestyle fed into the notion of trading up.

Another motivation for trading up was the nature of consumerism itself. Since the turn of the twentieth century, the instant and often ephemeral pleasure found in commercialized leisure and through the purchase of mass-produced goods at department stores had transformed how Americans viewed themselves and interacted with each other. In the 1920s, business owners began applying production techniques pioneered by Henry Ford's automobile assembly line to the manufacture of a variety of consumer goods, making household appliances, radios, and phonographs available to an unprecedented number of Americans. This initial, and comparatively modest, venture into the mass purchasing of durable goods altered notions regarding the consumption of "wants" in addition to basic "needs," or increasingly the transformation of many "wants" into "needs." Consumption moved from being seen as self-serving and not necessarily useful to the greater good to an action of utmost importance for the country's economic expansion and well-being.[95]

A legitimized and insatiable hunger to purchase propelled the postwar economy from the war's end through the early years of the 1950s. A backlog of demand, steady-to-rising wages, and high levels of available consumer credit sustained spending. This situation allowed for indulgence in both necessities and luxuries, as well as a formidable retention of wartime savings. An article about buying trends in 1946 found: "The whole picture is not by any means on the side of frugality. Whereas relatively few intend to use wartime savings to buy goods . . . many millions are in the market this year for cars, houses, and other things, and want to finance the buying by other means."[96] Two years later neither craving nor resources had diminished—the "market for consumer goods is growing, not shrinking."[97]

By early in the 1950s, the initial spate of delayed demand for durable goods, automobiles, and other home-related purchases began to slow, but consumer spending remained brisk, and commentators noticed marked changes in consumers and their spending habits. The promise of technology and the continued modernization of daily life replaced a backlog of needs as an impetus to buy.[98] "A new, strikingly different way of life is emerging in the United States," offered *U.S. News & World Report* in 1953. "The country is moving, little by little, into an era of easy, push-button living. New products catering to modern tastes are springing up everywhere. Old stand-by products are falling by the wayside. In the process, the country is going through a kind of modern industrial revolution."[99] Whatever the consumer good, many Americans continued to buy and were particularly enthralled with anything new.

In the postwar period, "new" often meant "novel," meaning that the item had not been previously owned or experienced on a personal level. As time passed, "newness" compelled Americans to desire the latest appliances, furniture, or houses, and they eliminated existing possessions in order to make room for them. In many analyses of postwar culture, the orgy of postwar buying was described as fulfilling a desire to acquire as many material goods as possible. An active feature of midcentury consumerism was also the omnipresent drive for something *novel* and not always something *additional*.[100] "The American consumer *expects* new and better products every year," claimed J. Gordon Lippincott in a 1947 book chock full of buoyant prose about the importance of industrial design and the frequent consumption of goods in the American domestic economy. "His acceptance of change toward better living is indeed the American's greatest asset. It is the prime mover of our national wealth."[101] The replacement of the existing with the new more often than not was directed toward home or family life, including houses, cars, home furniture and appliances, and even vacations.[102] Speaking about houses specifically, Russell Lynes provided this outlook: "To many an American the ideal house is a disposable house like the log cabin—warm and comfortable while he is in it, but easily got rid of when opportunity or whim or tragedy beckons him to move on."[103]

Within this atmosphere, producers of American goods nurtured a world of product obsolescence in terms of both quality and visual design, where "a [product] standard based on changeability and not on permanence" reigned.[104] Vance Packard conveyed that a primary result of this environment was that in postwar America, "anything 'old,' 'used,' or 'permanent,' was to be disdained" and replaced as quickly as possible.[105] *Consumer Reports* chronicled the changes in American consumer life between 1936 and 1956 and found that appliance manufacturers now aimed to "build in obsolescence. . . . People buy new cars every two or three years. There is no reason why the kitchen should last forever."[106] In characterizing this obsolescence, the article focused as much on visually outmoded model styling as on functional quality. Through a fiercely marketed regular turnover in models, producers of goods created a foundation for sustained profits by fostering consumer demand, a concept that merged the "ability to buy" with the "willingness to buy."[107] Encouraged by manufacturers, advertisements, and articles, postwar Americans engaged in a cycle of purchase and replacement, not only supporting the national economy, communities, families but also their own personal appetites for unique experiences.

THE KNOWLEDGE AND EDUCATION OF PROSPECTIVE BUYERS

The initial turn to suburban home ownership was a relatively easy one for Americans to make because of the housing shortage, government enticements, the focus by builders on single-family houses in suburban locales, and the psychological need for stability after fifteen years of dislocation and uncertainty that resulted from the Great Depression and World War II. Despite all of these factors, many people had no idea how to select and purchase a house. A writer for *American Home* ruminated in 1947: "For some odd reason, people who think twice before making a $10 purchase will plunge headlong into buying a home costing thousands of dollars with little or no forethought. Probably, the reason is that most of us lack everyday experience in home buying, and we are not accustomed to thinking in thousand-dollar terms."[108] The learning curve was fast. American consumers became knowledgeable and comfortable in the process, so much so that builders believed only new models and sales approaches could satisfy prospective buyers, who were described in 1960 as "more serious, more cautious, more critical, and more demanding than at any time since World War II."[109]

How did Americans make the jump from complete novices who were prone to falling for gimmickry to expert, even sophisticated buyers comfortable in the process and able to closely scrutinize the products? Part of the answer is that many Americans acquired practical knowledge through the purchase of one, two, three, or even more houses in their lifetimes. This experiential knowledge was further compounded because a house buyer's friends, family members, and neighbors were also engaged in the same activities. Overlaid on this was an astonishing number and variety of books and articles in newspapers and popular magazines. These sources did not just tout home ownership in general terms or implore readers to be financially cautious in creating a comprehensive budget. They provided easily accessible, digestible, and applicable knowledge about nearly all facets of buying and building a new house and, in the process, also nudged buyers into believing they needed to upgrade. In the postwar era, America learned to be a nation of house consumers.

The extent and structure of the learning process can be thematically outlined based on common topics in books and articles. The first stage focused on translating a budget figure into physical options for consideration. Location was the bedrock of this stage, since much of the cost of a new house was in the land. For most people, location trumped all other concerns: proximity to transportation routes and networks; distance from a workplace; the nearness of schools, shopping, churches, and recreational facilities; and less tangible aspects of prestige and the social appropriateness of a suburb. Some people simply sought a new house in their own communities or might be drawn to areas with good, established reputations. For others, particularly those living in cities, a relocation to the new suburban developments at the metropolitan fringe was very likely a move into unknown territory.[110] Some articles cautioned readers about problems with buying in a far-flung subdivision because of its immediate affordability; taxes would surely go up as public services and schools were added, and if a development was located amid farmland, a household could never know what might be constructed on the land next door.

Having pinpointed an area that looked desirable, the consumer needed to decide whether to build a new house on contract or to buy one already completed in a speculative subdivision. In 1945, when the scope and scale of the postwar housing industry were not wholly ascertained, prospective buyers were warned about purchasing an already completed house: "The house may have defects hidden behind a shining surface. Its basic structure may have been compromised in order to permit greater allowance for the eye-catchers so often considered by builders as an important adjunct to marketability."[111] Articles favoring having a house built on contract still cautioned the reader that there could be cost and time overruns, and the finished product might not exactly be what was imagined when the buyer looked at the plans.

By the mid-1950s, as more people were purchasing houses in subdivisions and developments—three out of five new houses were constructed in subdivisions with at least twelve similar houses—articles appeared specifically detailing how to approach the purchase of a "development house."[112] Shelter magazines advised their target female audience to investigate the builder's reputation by visiting other subdivisions and, in terms of the house, to "look around until you find a builder offering the floor plan that fits your family."[113]

Consumers seeking to buy or build a new house faced three principal options in terms of the quality of the location: a subdivision that was fully engineered by a single builder-developer; a subdivision in which a developer sold lots to both builders and individual home buyers; or an infill lot in an older subdivision. The first category took in large- and medium-scale builders who developed or "improved" land with roads and utilities, created the subdivision, and then constructed and sold the houses on lots apportioned from the improved land. The Levittowns are a primary example of this type of subdivision, although their scale was so much larger and more comprehensive that they occupy a special group of comparative developments nationwide. Merchant-built subdivisions were far more likely to be large enough for just an elementary school and recreation facilities; others might constitute only a handful of streets inserted into an existing road network.

Regardless of its size, a set number of models or variations of a single model repeated along the streets characterized this type of subdivision, and they were

completed all at once or, for larger developments, in a consecutive series of "sections." The control inherent to the design of these subdivisions lent itself to the establishment of an underlying theme. This was introduced by the development's name and often carried through street and model names, highlighted in advertising, and sometimes extended to the exterior styling of the houses. This type of subdivision allowed for economy of scale in design and construction and is most associated with postwar suburbia (fig. 14). It ordinarily offered more house for the money, appealed especially to young and first-time buyers, and tended to result in homogeneity "both in housing and in the characteristics of neighbors."[114]

Fully engineered subdivisions did not excite all people wishing to buy a new house. Prospective buyers might be turned off by the visual repetitiveness of the streetscape, the quality of the housing, or the perceived social homogeneity of the neighborhood. These buyers had two alternatives: a subdivision where a developer or builder-developer improved the land and then sold lots to other builders or individual prospective homeowners or an infill lot within an existing neighborhood. Either alternative provided the opportunity to build a custom design. The pattern of ownership and the involvement of custom builders resulted in visually diverse subdivisions. This type of buyer tended to be more experienced and confident about what they wanted and familiar with the industry's products. They were also sometimes reacting to their own prior experience with a fully engineered suburb.

Albert and Shirley Robick purchased a new six-room ranch house in 1960 in Ridgeway Heights, a merchant-builder subdivision north of Pittsburgh. A decade later the house seemed too small for their family of four, and they had also tired of the neighborhood. The couple sought a quieter place where they would have more privacy to raise their sons without the distraction and input of a neighborhood awash with children. They began looking around for options, including subdivisions where a variety of custom builders were active. In the end, the couple drove past a lot in an existing neighborhood with a mix of houses and residents, "fell in love" with it, tracked down the owner, and made an offer that she could not refuse.[115]

Once decided on a location and type of subdivision, prospective buyers needed to make sure that they knew, exactly, what came standard with the house and what would cost extra.[116] They were also encouraged to have the best possible finishes, fixtures, and equipment options put into the house from the beginning, as this action would save money later and set the house apart from its neighbors. By 1965, in contrast to earlier in the period, *American Home* dissuaded first-time buyers from having a house custom built and encouraged them to purchase a completed house in a development: "Most first-time buyers aren't experienced enough in selecting a house to know what they really want, what they find essential, and what they are willing to omit. Only after living in another house for a couple of years are they ready to plan the final house that they won't wish had been a little different, after they've moved into it."[117] Many of the suggestions presented in reference to houses built in larger subdivisions mirrored what consumers were told to look for before purchasing any new house. Other considerations included a neat neighborhood that was fully hooked up to utilities and possessed paved roads; a house that contained quality materials,

featured name-brand appliances, was fully insulated, and had a workable plan catering to the needs of a specific family; and having everything put into writing and reviewed by an attorney before signing.[118]

Regardless of whether they were contracting with a custom or a merchant builder, if deciding to build a house on contract, consumers needed to be aware of appropriate interaction with the builder during construction. "There are two ways to view your builder," explained *American Home* in 1955. "One is to think of him as a shifty, dishonest, and incompetent woodbutcher who drives a high-priced car, never seems to know what's going on, and acts as if he were doing *you* the biggest favor of your life by taking your money. The other way to enter into this relationship is to think of your builder as he really is (in most cases)—a combination of designer, mechanic, and businessman who runs a pretty complicated and successful business, and who is a respected member of the community."[119] Of the two options, the article encouraged trusting one's builder and set ground rules for consumer-builder interaction, including: "Assume that your builder is both honest and capable"; "Get everything ironed out and *on paper* before the work begins"; "Don't try to be a part-time foreman and give orders to your builder's men on the job"; "Be sensible about the progress on the job"; and "After you move in, be patient about details that need adjusting."[120] Stressed more often than interaction with the builder before and during construction were pragmatic requests: "Keep a cool head while your new house settles down" (fig. 15).[121]

CONCLUSION

The search for a new house, and its consideration, purchase, and care, became familiar activities for members of the expanded postwar middle class.

Their consumer confidence resulted from knowledge gained through both personal experiences in this process and an education obtained through a variety of media. These sources—reinforced by government policies and generally held popular beliefs—were not just objective primers about different types of houses or how to go about purchasing a house. Rather, they permitted builders to limit their focus to meeting the needs and aspirations of comparatively affluent nuclear families with the prospect of an even more comfortable future. The building industry's belief in widespread upward mobility—partly reality and partly self-delusion—drove a process of design and marketing that remained steadfastly preoccupied with ever larger and better-appointed houses and constant in the belief that with them builders would "raise the whole standard of American life."[122]

An aggregate rise in the standard of living provided the primary backdrop for public discourse about national democratic identity and perceived economic equality and consumer opportunity for all. "More people are finding more money to buy more things than ever before," touted the *Washington Post* in 1949, an outlook echoed by the *Los Angeles Times* thirteen years later: "American families are enjoying a steadily mounting standard of living as income gains continue to outstrip price increases."[123] From newspapers to magazines, radio, and, increasingly, television, domestic economic gains seemed to be everywhere, and the nation's economic health and, indeed, its claimed superiority on the international stage was more and more interpreted in terms of buying power and consumer freedom. Business owners, workers, and the government focused on developing policy centered on the ability to buy things, and the success of this approach contributed to the vast expansion of the socioeconomic middle—a 1965 Curtis Publishing Company travel magazine reflected that during "the fourteen years beginning in 1947, some 14,000,000 American families came crashing into the Middle Class."[124]

This extraordinary expansion fueled claims that class divisions in America had disappeared and was further reinforced in the burgeoning suburbs of the late 1940s and early 1950s. In them, builders quickly and efficiently constructed millions of minimum houses, which relieved the intense pressure of the housing shortage facing middle America. While initial consumer satisfaction would only be temporary, these houses became the foundation for building a generation of equity enjoyed by the burgeoning white middle class, regardless of whether they stayed put or traded up. The byproduct, however, had more than a financial dimension, in the form of social change and class cohesion. Over time, the limitations of the minimum house for postwar families transcended background, origin, and personal economics, and its relative decline was a step in the formation of a new type of middle class in the postwar suburbs.

Livability in the Minimum House

DURING THE DECADE following World War II, the minimum house dominated new construction from coast to coast. This type of house was primarily an outcome of the minimum standards for design and construction required by the FHA in order to receive the administration's backing of homeowner mortgages. With the economic uncertainty of rising costs and periods of limited consumer credit and materials all lingering until the end of the Korean War, builders relied on the uncomplicated minimum house as the best and quickest way to meet the nation's housing needs.

Physically constrained by modest building envelopes, minimum houses contained four, five, or six small rooms arranged in uncomplicated plans with reduced or nonexistent circulation spaces. Their laudable attributes were mainly ease of construction, cost-effectiveness at a time of housing inflation, and a full complement of modern systems and equipment. Builders turned to minimum houses with enthusiasm as a way to efficiently and inexpensively provide technologically up-to-date dwellings for millions of families. The tight quarters did not allow much in the way of functional separation, formality, or privacy. The houses' livability depended more on equipped kitchens, modern bathrooms, and integrated utility systems than the extent or character of their domestic space. Industry leaders believed that consumers could enjoy "tomorrow's homes today" through the purchase of houses with floor plans that "must embody the basic principles of efficient layout including maximum livability and economy in a limited area."[1]

The term *minimum house,* derived from *minimum standards,* is a relative one that appropriately characterizes the simplicity of such houses when contrasted with the larger models with more spatial components and amenities, which later became widely available to middle-income buyers. The reduced dimensions and stripped-down plans of even larger minimum houses undoubtedly fell short of many expectations held by members of the existing middle class who purchased them anyway, given the initial dearth of options among newly constructed houses in suburban areas. It should not be overlooked, however, that many purchasers of minimum houses were also improving their living conditions. Information collected as part of the 1940 census revealed that the median number of rooms among all "dwelling units" in the United States—single family and multiple, urban and rural—was 4.73, meaning that some purchasers were getting not only a fully equipped, modern house but also an equivalent or even more spacious living environment.[2]

A 1955 investigation of housing and consumer expectation commented on variation in how different socioeconomic classes might experience similar trends. While focused on the size and value of houses relative to other consumer goods during a much longer period—1890 to 1950—the conclusions are applicable to the minimum house, which would have affected data for the final years of the study in any case. The housing economist who authored the article found that changes in consumer behavior had shrunk typical houses for the comparatively well off: "It is probably among the middle and upper classes that housing has suffered its greatest decline." In contrast, easily obtained mortgages meant that "the lower income classes [had] substantially bettered their living accommodation."[3]

Minimum houses were the smallest ever marketed to middle America. They became so prevalent in the years immediately following World War II that at no other time in the mid-twentieth century did the houses built for the great economic middle more closely resemble each other. Many members of the existing middle class would have found them inadequate from the start. Over time, members of the newly suburbanized, middle-income working class also found minimum houses in their original form an impediment to family enjoyment and the smooth functioning of a postwar household.[4] No matter the speed with which that dissatisfaction manifested, minimum house owners made the choice to stay and expand or to begin the search for another new house. Whether trading up or adding on, negotiating life in a minimum house became one part of the shared experience that powered the postwar expansion and reformulation of the middle class.

AN UNCERTAIN ECONOMIC OUTLOOK

The postwar era is popularly portrayed as a steady period of optimism about domestic economic growth. Such an outlook, while not incorrect, shadows the uneven translation of confidence tied to the recent military victories of World War II into confidence tied to the economy. Everyone who was an adult at the end of the war had also lived through and had memories of the traumas of the Great Depression. Americans were not certain whether the postwar economy would grow, contract, or collapse. At the National Conference on Family Life held in Washington, DC, John Corson, the chair of the "Economic Welfare Committee," explained in a report that "stabilization of the basic economy" was "essential" to safeguarding the lives and livelihoods of Americans. Corson further noted that since the end of the war many families had "consumed their savings": "The situation today . . . is not like that of the postwar twenties, when optimism ran high. Uncertainty . . . is now the rule and even home ownership is no anchor."[5]

Many families used their wartime savings as down payments for new houses, and others went into installment debt buying consumer goods. These purchases mostly replaced older durable goods or allowed households to buy them for the first time. The initial postwar consumer boom was not frenetic in the same way the period is characterized as a whole, with prosperous and excited consumers trading up to goods perceived as better. At first, Americans merely enjoyed purchasing and using basic new durable goods that had remained out of reach for many years, houses included. They were willing and also able to buy. Nevertheless, the transition from a wartime to a peacetime economy was hardly a smooth shift.

Americans purchased or aspired to purchase houses despite the strong disconnect between their expectations and the realities of the cost of a new house at a time of high demand, rising labor expenses, and scarcity of some key building materials (fig. 16). A 1946 consumer survey noted that the "average [respondent] counted on getting a house of six and four-tenths rooms—but not [the] lot—for $7,300."[6] To this expectation an architect replied: "Stop kidding. A house of five and eight-tenths rooms costs more." Materials and labor expenses for a

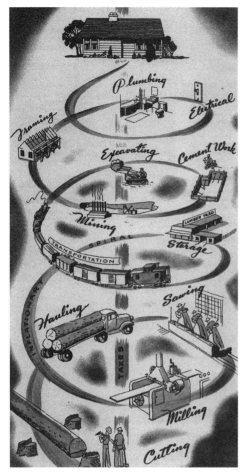

house costing $10,778 in 1947 had been only $6,040 six years earlier, around the time that the private construction of new houses had for the most part ceased for the duration of the war.[7] Certain building materials—in particular steel and copper—remained in short supply, with restrictions renewed after the outset of the Korean War. Such restrictions required builders to spend considerable time and design energy calculating the exact amount of structural steel (I-beams) and nails, steel and copper water-delivery and -distribution piping, metal ducting, and copper electrical wiring necessary for new construction.[8]

The expansion of domestic materials production did not necessarily mean that more were available for residential construction, as schools, hospitals, and highways were given preference in a commitment to defense readiness. Leonard G. Haeger, the NAHB's research director, explained the shift in national priorities in 1952: "We in the United States have made the decision to embark on a definite, long-term plan to increase the level of our military strength. . . . Gradually there has come about the thinking of the 'dual economy,' under which the needs of the defense are added to the needs of a strong civilian economy."[9] The flush postwar years were ultimately able to provide for both parts of this "dual economy"; however, at the outset civilian expansion and defense expansion were viewed as vital yet competing interests.

Worry about housing inflation was not limited to individual builders and buyers but also reached the U.S. government. If left unchecked, inflation threatened to be a drag on the economy. In October 1950, the Federal Reserve began to limit credit for residential and commercial construction through a policy known as "Regulation X," which was devised "to restrain inflationary pressures and conserve defense-needed materials."[10] Regulations limiting credit existed for other consumer goods as well, but private construction was understood to be the principal competitor for materials. For nondefense residential building, Regulation X significantly increased down payments required for new houses, with two schedules developed, one for conventional loans to nonveterans (FHA and conventional financing) and one for loans to veterans (VA). Because more expensive houses were generally larger and required more materials, Regulation X also stipulated that down payments for both groups would increase sharply for pricier houses. Down payments under Regulation X started at a low of 5 percent for veterans and 10 percent for nonveterans and rose to a high of 45 and 50 percent, respectively, for the most expensive houses.[11]

Regulation X slowed building starts in 1951, but 1952 started much more strongly and ultimately became the second biggest building year in U.S. history. Some of the reasons for the record year given by "surprised experts" indicate why Regulation X was mostly ineffective: low unemployment and high personal savings and the maturation of war bonds meant that families were still able to meet the steep down payment requirements.[12] By September 1952, the Federal Reserve relaxed credit controls on most types of mortgages. Taken alone, then, the impact of Regulation X was inconclusive; however, its creation and implementation fueled continued uncertainty about the capacity and priorities of the national economy.

As much as labor and materials, demand for new houses during an acute shortage drove costs upward and acted as an encumbrance on national optimism. New residential construction fell 95 percent between 1928 and 1933, with starts in the latter year dipping below one hundred thousand for the first time since such statistics were first recorded, in 1889.[13] The industry showed recovery by the end of the decade, but the war stopped nearly all nondefense housing at exactly the time when cities were flooded with industrial workers from rural areas and, later, at the war's end, with returning veterans. By 1947, six million families shared housing with extended family or friends, and another half million lived in temporary dwellings such as Quonset huts.[14]

Despite these quantifiable realities, the shortage was also one of perception and desire. An administrator of the National Housing Agency estimated in 1946 that of the approximately thirty-four million nonfarm dwellings in the United

States, fully ten million of them were "in such bad shape they need either major repairs or replacement."[15] Years of deferred maintenance, wartime crowding, and industrial pollution had soured Americans' opinions of urban housing. A 1944–45 consumer housing survey conducted by the Curtis Publishing Company, publisher of such popular magazines as the *Ladies' Home Journal* and the *Saturday Evening Post,* found that 91 percent of respondents, comprising both owners and renters, desired a "single family, detached" house.[16] Instead of reinvesting and rehabilitating existing houses and neighborhoods, Americans were ready to abandon crowded cities for new suburban neighborhoods.[17] Builders lacked the resources, know-how, or available materials to inexpensively devise a wholly new type of dwelling or significantly enlarge the size of a typical house. Working under the FHA's design guidelines, they turned to minimum houses and constructed them by the millions in new suburban subdivisions.

THE ORIGINS OF THE MINIMUM HOUSE

The minimum house, or less frequently the "economy" house, looked conventional, was rich in technology but not gimmicky, and was modest to the point of being confining. It was sometimes referred to as a "prewar house," a term that nodded toward its genesis: the FHA's technical bulletins first issued in the 1930s and then frequently revised.[18] Addressing such items as square footage, mechanical systems, and the number of closets and other amenities considered essential for the modern house, these technical bulletins and the system of mortgage insurance they reinforced were the starting point for postwar residential design. Importantly, the FHA and its bulletins concretely established, for the first time ever, a baseline for new housing in all metropolitan areas coast to coast. Published designs had previously allowed people everywhere to be conscious of trends, but the translation of these into an actual house was subject to the abilities and limitations of the builder; the input of the buyer; and local codes, restrictions, and traditions. The FHA became the mechanism that created a national standard for new housing and set up the framework for a housing market that could, for the first time, be understood as national in scope.[19]

Through the FHA, the Roosevelt administration championed policies that positioned home ownership and the modernization of houses as central components to both social and economic revitalization and the future stability of the United States.[20] Title I of the National House Act of 1934 provided a system overseen by the FHA that offered modernization loans for existing dwellings. Title II addressed mortgages for favorably appraised new construction that, along with the FHA's design, construction, and planning guidelines, would ultimately bring up-to-date houses within reach of millions of Americans after the war. The FHA's *Principles of Planning Small Houses* set baselines from which the form and character of the postwar house emerged.

These technical bulletins were one of the tangible outcomes of the Central Housing Committee, an advisory body to President Roosevelt established in 1935 "for the purpose of pooling housing information and experience."[21] Committee members included a range of design, construction, and finance experts drawn from the FHA, the National Bureau of Standards, the Public Works Administration, the Resettlement Administration, and the Federal Home Loan Bank Board. Its first meeting was held on September 11, 1935, at which time the committee noted the need for "a vast program of technical research" to produce "reliable data" on such topics as building materials, construction methods, costs, building codes, and "factual data on which to base minimum standards of housing requirements."[22] The committee's varied makeup and the direction of their work were very much a part of a decade-long interest by business, philanthropy, and the government in utilizing objective, scientific approaches toward the goal of creating an acceptable minimum level of housing.[23]

Within a year, the "reliable data" called for by the Central Housing Committee appeared in the FHA's *Principles of Planning Small Houses,* affording a flexible discussion of basic accommodations, domestic technology and equipment, and construction methods. The generators of the publication intended the guidelines to be "a starting point from which amplification and improvements can be made as circumstances permit or as local conditions demand."[24] Regardless of how the depicted prototypes were "amplified" or "improved," the creation of a universal "starting point" for the design of houses was unprecedented.

The residential prototypes advocated by the FHA represent the culmination of decades of structural and technical modernization and spatial simplification in American houses. The opening of the twentieth century saw middle-class Americans abandoning the large, spatially differentiated dwellings that supported the nuanced social framework of Victorian America. Among other functions, these houses helped resident households manage interaction among groups of people, such as family and nonfamily, servant and served, men and women, and young and old.[25] After 1900, changing social and familial norms, continued suburbanization, and an expanding industrial economy made many of these distinctions and associated rituals increasingly extraneous.[26] Cultural changes made smaller houses acceptable, but new domestic technologies like central heating and electrical systems, kitchen appliances, and complete bathrooms made them possible and, because of cost, necessary. In the early twentieth century, utility systems and rising materials costs increased the price of a new house by at least a quarter; to keep houses within range of middle-class buyers, builders had to construct smaller ones.[27]

Builders, architects, and consumers quickly came to understand that smaller houses were just as difficult, if not more difficult, to design well. In the 1920s, private organizations, such as the Architects' Small House Service Bureau (ASHSB, established in 1919) and Better Homes in America, Inc. (BHA, established in 1922), sought to improve the design of houses.[28] Backed by the American Institute of Architects (AIA) and, later, by the U.S. Department of Commerce, the ASHSB desired to see more architects involved in the design of small houses, which had largely been the domain of builders and, in the absence of an architect, were thought to be poorly conceived. The greater involvement of architects would have the practical outcome of providing professional designs for builders and landowners and at the same time educating the public about the value of their services. Distinct from concerns about architecture specifically, BHA was organized and led by women interested in defining and endorsing middle-class notions of modern domesticity with fresh designs for small houses. An outgrowth of Progressive reform, it eventually included a variety of government agencies and private organizations dealing with housing, health, and social welfare.

The intentions of such groups as the ASHSB and BHA, however favorable, dictated a narrow middle-class view of domestic life in the United States. While aspects of their underlying motives were questionable, these campaigns did have some positive outcomes. Improvements in domestic technologies that both saved labor and increased comfort were occurring at a rapid rate and could not be easily understood or fully implemented without guidance and explanation. Indeed, the draw of mail-order dwellings in the 1920s, most famously those of Sears, Roebuck & Co., Radford, and Aladdin, stemmed from their comprehensive services related to housing, which considerably lessened burdens related to house construction by providing working drawings; building instructions; and high-quality precut, prefitted, and precounted materials and fixtures. The purchaser only had to choose a model, stipulate the desired options and extras, and then build it or find someone else to do so.[29] Even for people not having a new house constructed, the promotional materials issued by the ASHSB and BHA, and other types of commercial sales catalogs, educated the viewer in the latest available designs, features, and mechanical equipment (fig. 17).

The published plans of these houses hint at a more variable view of domesticity. Even the definition of what might constitute a "small" house invited a high degree of interpretation. The ASHSB defined a small house as having "no more than six major rooms and a maximum of 30,000 cubic feet. (Using a 10ft ceiling height, this is a house of 3,000 square feet; an 8ft ceiling height would equate to 3,750 square feet.)"[30] A cap of even 3,000 square feet in floor area might seem excessive against the idea of a small house. It makes more sense, however, contrasted with the houses for the middle class that had been built in previous decades, which easily exceeded that total; few of the plans published by the ASHSB came close to this square footage.

Most of the houses in ASHSB's *Small Homes of Architectural Distinction* (1929) had five or six rooms and modest dimensions.[31] Yet even when focusing just on average-sized houses and ignoring the spectrum of architectural styles and forms, the arrangements of domestic space do not suggest the presence of underlying principles. Varied planning inefficiencies included jogs in hallways that consumed valuable square footage, front doors opening directly into living rooms, and kitchens with only one point of interior access. One-story houses and bungalows frequently lacked effective zoning or buffers between zones, bedrooms opening onto public rooms, for example, or shared walls, which increased the likelihood of noise disturbances.

HOME BW-4235

Sloping Roofs Delight-
fully Employed

Size: 26-6 x 34-6 ft.

I

T has been the custom in the past to associate the use of brick with large pretentious houses or commercial buildings, but we are glad to see the trend slowly but surely turning to homes of moderate size. The design pictured above follows the English type of architecture, with steep roofs and symmetrical peaks, duplicating in brick what is being done in stucco or frame. It is both artistic and distinctive. The interior is cozy and attractive with large living room, and plaster arch purposely wide entering the dining room to give you full use of the two rooms together for entertaining. The kitchen although small, is very compact and contains everything necessary for efficient work. Two bedrooms and bath with a roomy attic complete a popular little plan.

*Stucco, Shingle or Siding could be substituted
with just as pleasing an effect.*

FLOOR PLAN

BILT-WELL
MILL-WORK

The shortcomings in residential design in the United States would eventually move beyond the private sector and become a key concern of the federal government in the 1930s, yet in a much more limited way than in Europe after the destruction of World War I, which saw notable, even radical design achievements. In contrast to the United States, where the creation of modern small houses in the 1910s and 1920s was largely directed toward the middle class and articulated through predominately conservative stylistic modes, European developments mainly targeted workers and fixated on the possibilities of standardization, mass production, and modern aesthetic tenets and engaged designers in a sociopolitical dialogue.

In France, Le Corbusier expanded on his Maison Dom-Ino prototype (1914) as he further examined the potential for structural and spatial simplicity in domestic design. These efforts ultimately led to his Maison Citrohan, developed between 1922 and 1926. The Maison Citrohan balanced dramatic open-plan public spaces at one end of the unit with multiple stories of private spaces—kitchen, bedrooms, and bathroom/toilet facilities—at the other end. Le Corbusier's clear passion for modern domestic environments led to his invitation, one of only a handful received by non-Germans, to participate in Stuttgart, Germany's, influential Weissenhofsiedlung in 1927.

The Stuttgart Weissenhofsiedlung was a special exhibition of cutting-edge residential development sponsored by the Deutscher Werkbund, an organization founded in 1907 to explore the potential of the fusion of traditional craft and mass production. Although it was a demonstration event that included the work of many prominent architects, including such notables as Walter Gropius and Mies van der Rohe, the Weissenhofsiedlung was part of a larger movement that was in the process of reshaping cities across Weimar Germany, with especially notable outcomes in Frankfurt.[32] Favorable political, social, and economic factors merged in Frankfurt during the second half of the 1920s and led to the construction of modern housing developments, known generally as *siedlung,* in the singular, collectively made up of thousands of attached single-family houses and smaller apartments. Ernst May became the city architect for Frankfurt in 1925 and oversaw the creation of what was called "New Frankfurt" over the next five years. This initiative merged architectural Modernism with garden city planning principles, introduced a generation earlier by Briton Ebenezer Howard.

With the collaboration of a number of architects who had a strong interest in Modernism and residential design, Ernst May established standards
for the design and construction of spatially, technologically, and aesthetically
modern housing units. May publicized his efforts and new types of residential
development in Frankfurt in an architectural journal titled *Das Neue Frankfurt*
and through other means.[33] The work became well known within the progressive design community in the United States, mainly through the architect and
planner Catherine Bauer's book *Modern Housing* (1934) and her participation
in New Deal housing initiatives.[34] European precedents in housing, however,
ultimately did not make serious inroads in the United States for a variety of
reasons, ranging from the role of real property within the domestic economy to
the federalized government structure and the high value placed on the ownership of a detached, single-family house.[35] The various strains of Modernism
predominately remained outside the realm of residential design in the United
States. Even Frank Lloyd Wright's homegrown efforts to rethink domestic architecture for middle-class suburban families were not directly replicated on any
large scale. Elements of his well-known Usonian houses eventually appeared
in many postwar houses—indoor-outdoor connections, efficient kitchens, and
integrated covered parking for automobiles—but most often as parts of far
more conventional designs than the ones produced by Wright.[36]

As the economy ground to a halt in the 1930s, even more visionary concepts
than Wright's emerged. The construction of smaller houses responded to the
cost of integrating new domestic technologies into the fabric of a house. These
systems and appliances were largely subservient to a conventionally designed
and constructed house. A parallel vision arose in tandem with a revolution in
the aesthetics of product design. A number of inspired architects and designers sought to use technology as a platform on which to more fully integrate the
space, structure, aesthetics, and mechanical equipment in a house.

The sometimes fantastical outcomes of their experiments became exceed-
ingly popular as stand-alone exhibits or parts of world's fairs and expositions,
heavily covered by the press. Few people envisioned themselves making a home
in Buckminster Fuller's coldly mechanical Dymaxion House (initial design
1929) or George Fred Keck's House of Tomorrow (1933-34), created for Chicago's Century of Progress Exposition. During the 1930s and the first half of the

1940s, materials manufacturers and corporations seized on the "dream house" tradition in American culture and created the futuristic "miracle house."[37] During the war, architects promoted themselves and their modern visions of the postwar world as they collaborated with both business and advertising.[38] The Depression and the wartime economic climate allowed dreamy and technology-rich domestic images to flourish, but builders ultimately and pragmatically turned to more conventional-looking, cost-effective construction, since they knew there were absolutely no affordable avenues in the construction of a miracle house for the mass market.[39]

Consumers understood and accepted this decision. The Curtis Publishing Company's *Urban Housing Study* of 1944–45 found that participants "do not want or expect miracles in postwar houses and they hold no particular brief for unusual and untested housing innovations."[40] They were content with the products that "the industry [was] equipped to supply now." Elizabeth Gordon, the editor of *House Beautiful*, summarized this viewpoint in 1945: "People want sensible things . . . [and] are more interested in how houses work than how they look. . . . *They want the function of modern architecture, without the look of modern.*"[41] Modern bathrooms and kitchens, and utility and mechanical systems, seemed futuristic enough to many buyers and offered them a lifestyle of comfort and convenience only recently limited to the affluent. The design, marketing, and sale of a fully equipped, move-in-ready house occurred, in the 1949 opinion of Carl G. Lans, the technical director for the NAHB, "with an eye to more gracious living."[42] Undeniably comfortable in many ways, the minimum house nevertheless had spatial shortcomings that severely curtailed the pursuit of "gracious living."

With consumer expectations for space in new houses already checked by the economic distress of the Great Depression or by personal experience in small or substandard housing, the FHA issued minimum standards that valued technologically up-to-date and fully equipped houses over spacious ones, in the full realization of the minimum house. The standards offered simple, modern accommodations, while also stabilizing values in the housing market, both of which lifted the national psyche. *American Builder* optimistically reported on the effects of the FHA's policies in 1936, just two years after the agency's creation: "The feeling now is one of assurance instead of anxiety, and the make-up of the house will reflect the feeling of the owner . . . [who will] insist that he be emancipated from any state of discomfort. . . . He, and the thousands of others like him, are going to raise our living standards."[43] The creation of the FHA not only inaugurated a shift in outlook but also provided the requisite institutional framework from which the scientifically derived minimum house, long the goal of public and private interests, could be dispersed throughout the country.[44] The widespread rise in living standards and the associated optimism only came later, as millions of minimum houses materialized in the suburbs.

THE MINIMUM HOUSE TAKES SHAPE

While not daring in design, the minimum houses that dominated new construction in the years immediately following World War II were entirely modern, or up to-date, and met notions of livability. Modernity in these houses was not expressed so much through radically different plans, forms, and details, but rather through the latest mechanical systems, utilities, and appliances. Svend Riemer, a prominent researcher studying the sociological and psychological dimensions of housing, proposed in 1946 that in order to be livable, a dwelling needed to "accommodate a family life free of friction," a challenge for families living in a minimum house, with its small rooms and simple floor plans.[45] The revised edition of the FHA's *Principles of Planning Small Houses,* issued in 1946, addressed livability directly, commenting on its components and goals: "[The] livability of any house is dependent upon the adequacy of room areas, relationship of rooms to afford privacy, circulation within and between rooms, room exposures, and equipment that provide for the convenience and comfort of the occupants."[46] Standing at the intersection of domestic space, plan, equipment, and function, the degree to which a house embodied livability was at its base a subjective concept. The FHA's minimum standards and their graphic representation were an attempt to bring a level of objectivity to the notion of livability through the rational quantification and codification of "good" design.[47]

With a goal to maintain future property values, the FHA concerned itself with the livability of the minimum house and the quality of its construction but maintained relative silence on the topic of aesthetics. In contrast to earlier publications promoting the small house movement, the FHA's standards were conspicuously quiet on issues of style. A summary of the FHA program at its establishment in 1934, issued jointly by *Time* magazine and *Architectural Forum,* merely observed: "Designs which are faddish . . . and which in general smack of stage scenery, will be turned down by the Housing Administration [for mortgage insurance]."[48] With moldering late-nineteenth-century row houses and Queen Anne suburban dwellings in mind, the FHA felt that only cleanly articulated houses would contribute to maintaining value in the long term.

The 1946 revision to *Principles of Planning Small Houses* presented "exterior design" near the end, perhaps an indication of its perceived unimportance to the design process of a modern and livable house. In its relatively brief discussion of the topic, the bulletin stated: "Simplicity in exterior design gives the small house the appearance of maximum size."[49] It also condescendingly elaborated in a more qualified explanation directed toward builders or prospective homeowners who might possess a less sophisticated sense of aesthetics: "Refinement, sometimes termed 'good taste,' is characterized by freedom from ostentation and by restraint in design."[50] Per this outlook, the bulletin discouraged "unnecessary gables and dormers, over-elaborate cornices and other nonessential items." The perspective renderings in the bulletin depict simply massed forms with pitched roofs and a conventional, even humdrum appearance that pleased real estate appraisers and were attractive to many consumers because of their conventionality. The housing economist John P. Dean and the architect and housing expert Simon Breines elaborated on the FHA's minimum standards in a 1946 publication: "Most of the structures shown [in this book] have traditional styles because most of the homes you will find for sale are traditional . . . and the chances are you prefer these kinds anyway" (fig. 18).[51]

The FHA's minimum standards were intended at the outset as "standards to be *built up from* rather than to be *built down to*": in other words, they represented a solid starting point in a flexible process of design for modern housing, not an outcome resulting from the reduction of existing designs to bare essentials.[52] *Principles of Planning Small Houses* cautioned: "As presented herein, these plans have not been sufficiently developed to serve as drawings from which to build."[53] It is true that the plans and renderings in *Principles* were not construction drawings. Still, the work's graphic depictions of the minimum standards

were detailed enough that a competent builder or draftsman could easily produce working drawings based on them. The simplicity of the minimum house, in any case, meant that even if a builder were not looking specifically at the technical bulletins for design inspiration, the end result was closely comparable.[54] The NAHB simply defined this type of house in 1948: "a home that the average man will and can buy, pay for and live in. It must not be a 'stripped down' shell. It must be durable, livable, sturdy, healthful and safe at a price the average man can afford. It must be a complete living unit" (fig. 19).[55]

For a decade or so following World War II, minimum houses remained the most widely available for purchasers, whether existing members of the middle class or rising members of the middle-income working class. Cost variations related more to region, materials, and location within a metropolitan area than to the quality of space in houses available for purchase. On the whole, these houses were even more simplified versions of those built at the end of the 1930s under the then-new FHA guidelines. A late-1930s "National Archives Exhibit" provides some understanding of the general character of houses receiving FHA loan guarantees.[56] The initiative brought together "case files" for individual houses submitted by FHA insuring offices from throughout the country. Although handpicked, the projects still provide a fair indication of the types of houses being constructed under the new, and unprecedented, national design guidelines.

Overall the submissions indicate that five- or six-room, detached, single-family houses predominated, with somewhat better-appointed ones appearing in large metropolitan areas. Perhaps one in five might be considered a minimum house, more frequently submitted by insuring offices in smaller metropolitan areas away from the coasts. The houses nearly all contained a single multipurpose living room and a separate dining room as the principal living spaces, with a modern and efficient kitchen set off as a work area. Many had such desirable enhancements as multiple bathrooms, separate entryways or vestibules, and plentiful closets, but the plans were also compartmentalized, and circulation was segmented and choppy. These houses are the descendants of the small houses promoted in the 1920s and, with the economy still fragile, were largely intended for the same market: solidly middle-class buyers. They also embraced the spirit of the FHA's minimum standards through mostly architect-conceived "amplification and improvements" above and beyond the illustrative prototypes included in the agency's guidelines.

A majority of new houses constructed after the war did not exhibit many, if any, meaningful spatial enhancements above and beyond the FHA prototypes. The nationwide average square footage in new houses fell from 1,177 in 1940 to 983 during the first half of 1950.[57] This drop of roughly two hundred square feet, equivalent to the combined loss of a small bedroom and a modest dining room, is reflected in the figures about the number of rooms. In 1940, 22, 47, and 26 percent of new houses contained four, five, and six rooms, respectively, in contrast to 46, 35, and 17 percent during the first half of 1950.[58] This was a significant decrease, even with lowered buyer expectations.

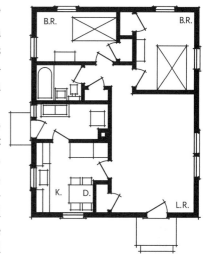

FIGURE 19. A majority of houses constructed immediately after the war did not depart significantly from the FHA's depictions of its minimum standards. 1946. (Drawing by Paul Davidson, after original in *Principles of Planning Small Houses,* [1946], 19)

Rising costs and high demand conspired to make the FHA's most basic minimum house prototype an industry favorite (fig. 20).[59] The fact that 46 percent of new houses started between January and June 1950 contained four finished rooms, as opposed to 22 percent in 1940, demonstrated builders' affinity for these houses. They featured two bedrooms and one bath, a living room, and a kitchen on a single floor. The dining area was either a portion of the living room or accommodated in the kitchen. Utility needs such as laundry and heating equipment were sometimes grouped in a small room near the kitchen or located in the kitchen itself.

Architectural professionals concerned with "planning the postwar house" in 1944 offered an apt description of the minimum house and its appeal as they disparaged it and misrepresented its prewar predecessors built under the auspices of the FHA: "Remember the house of 1939? Small, squarish, built on one floor, it was a true child of the depression. It never really lost its pinched, poor man's look. It was labeled 'Cape Cod,' but resembled its prototype only in the rarest of instances. . . . Darling of the FHA, pride of the builders, it converted very easily into war housing: all that was needed was the elimination of those items which gave it what little quality and convenience it had."[60] Familiarity of design, ease of construction, and an economical use of materials meant that for the first years after World War II, the "darling of the FHA, pride of the builders," remained exceptionally popular and, more than any other form, typified new houses in the suburbs.

Four-room minimum houses appeared nationwide almost exclusively as one-story houses or as "expansion" story-and-a-half "Cape Cod" versions, made famous in the first Levittown and widely copied throughout the country. Expansion Cape Cods offered a fully finished house downstairs and competitively added value with bonus space on the half story upstairs (fig. 21). This combination was one of a number of reasons for the "maturation" of the minimum or economy house observed in 1949: "The roof is high enough to add two chambers on the second floor."[61] For builders, the Cape Cod form was an easy one to turn to: "Because of the almost unbroken foundation lines of the true Cape Cod and the simplicity of framing, with which most carpenters are familiar, it is to be expected that the prewar popularity of this style will enjoy still greater acceptance."[62] While one-story houses dominated both buyer preference and the actual houses built and bought immediately following the war, houses with more than one story remained a significant minority of new housing starts. For example, three-fifths of new housing starts in the Pittsburgh area during the last quarter of 1950 were one-story houses, yet "a third of these [had] expansion attics," indicating a Cape Cod form.[63]

The scale of widely publicized and written-about communities like William Levitt's Levittown in the East and David Bohannon's San Lorenzo Village in the West contributed to the idea that all of the new suburbs teemed with thousands of the most basic minimum houses. In truth, nearly half of new houses included either a dedicated dining area or a third bedroom, or both. Yet, even with inclusion of these spaces, such houses were still appreciably smaller than their counterparts in 1940. Minimum houses having more than one story, for example, were more likely to have five or six rooms, but their predecessors from 1940 had

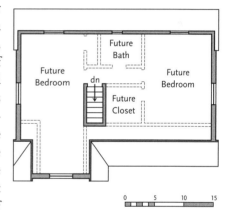

FIGURE 21. The Cape Cod with expansion possibilities on the upper half story remained an economical housing option into the 1950s. 1956. (Drawing by Paul Davidson, after a plan in the Ryan Homes Collection)

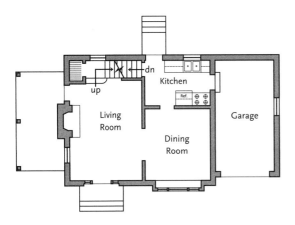

FIGURE 22. Compar-
atively spacious two-
story houses in the
late 1940s intended
for solidly middle-
class buyers also
exhibited minimum
characteristics, such
as small rooms, a
lack of meaningful
circulation spaces,
and cramped stor-
age. 1947. (Drawing
by Paul Davidson,
after a plan in *Amer-
ican Builder,* May
1947, 95)

slightly less than three hundred additional square feet of finished living space.[64] As with the most basic of minimum houses, homeowners still had to contend with rooms having small dimensions and patterns of circulation where rooms doubled as entries and corridors (fig. 22). A five-room house presented in *House Beautiful* in 1946 as a "bad" example of domestic planning was typical for the time and described as "a cramped rectangle of poorly related cubicles" that could only allow for "cramped living."[65]

Faced with the lack of space in minimum houses, the popular and trade presses cheerily presented such ideas as open planning and dual-use rooms as solutions for attaining a livable environment. Open planning referred to either the reduction of walls between rooms or the elimination of rooms altogether, in both cases requiring the remaining integrated space to support numerous and sometimes competing functions. In 1947, John Normile, the building editor for *Better Homes & Gardens,* enthusiastically interpreted open planning as a liberating force: "We still seek privacy, but not to the extent that we hide every facet of our personal life from those outside our family. Only now is this emancipation extending to home design. . . . This emancipation has brought a new concept to home architecture—open planning."[66]

Similar viewpoints were widespread in the popular, trade, and professional presses, but the houses featured in these publications indicate that most did not incorporate open planning beyond combining living and dining functions into a single space or, in the most modest examples, folding the dining area into the kitchen. In either of these scenarios, the kitchen usually remained a physically separate space from the living room, which reflected the continuance of a more traditional division of domestic space into the postwar period. Even designs that more vigorously demonstrated the potential of open planning in the daytime use zone of the house still showed ambivalence about the role of the kitchen as a component of domestic space and domestic life. Houses in Enaco, Inc.'s Noble Grove subdivision outside Minneapolis, or in Nobel S. Clay and the architecture firm of Ringel & Grove's Cliffwood development in the Pittsburgh area, showed a marked reduction in the amount of wall enclosing kitchens, even while the work area remained screened from the living room (fig. 23).[67] In the toolkit of strategies to establish actual and illusive spaciousness in middle-class houses, the (partially) open plan joined such other design elements as extended eaves and glass walls.[68]

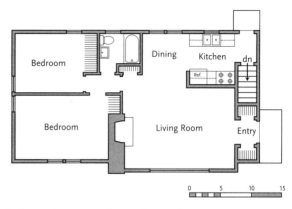

FIGURE 23. Open planning was one strategy for giving small houses an appearance of spaciousness. 1949. (Drawing by Paul Davidson, after a plan in *American Builder*, May 1949, 98)

Making provisions for "outdoor living" and creating a sense of spaciousness through large windows were also professed strategies for making modest houses appear more livable. The picture window began appearing in nearly every type of house, and no matter its overall form or style, the feature contributed to the understanding that a house was a modern one.[69] A prominent picture window became a standard component of houses constructed throughout the country, and its popularity was long-lived, even with the somewhat bemused criticism that the picture framed by the window was very often a similar house with its own picture window. *American Builder* called attention to the feature's questionable utility in 1948: "Most of the operative builders are using or have included at least one such window in each of their houses. This is done irrespective of whether the window overlooks an alley or a park."[70]

Although outdoor living became a significant selling feature of many postwar houses, and was situated early on by the trade, shelter, and popular press as a means for increasing the livability of small houses, porches and terraces beyond stoops and stairs were far from standard in new houses. In many cases, the secondary exterior door was located in the kitchen and opened to the side of the house, carport, or garage, indicating an intended use for domestic work rather than an inviting means of accessing and enjoying the rear garden. "Enjoying" a yard or garden in the East, South, and Midwest could be challenging with the summer's storms and bugs, without a roofed terrace or screened porch. Even in California, the state most associated with the establishment of outdoor living, new houses were not guaranteed to have outdoor living space finished at the time of purchase. An advertisement for Encino Park Homes, a large subdivision in the San Fernando Valley, depicted houses with a sheltered front entrance, whereas the rear opened onto a concrete stoop. The list of features noted that these houses were situated on "large, level lots. Plenty of room for patio, garden, and youngsters," signifying that these things would come later, after the time of purchase.[71] As with any amenities beyond the accepted standard, the chance that an outdoor living space would be completed at the time of purchase increased with the cost of the house.[72] Most minimum houses lacked such spaces, as well as the meaningful indoor-outdoor links that would become prevalent in the following decade.

Rooms and spaces with dual purposes were also a tactic for increasing livability in a minimum house (fig. 24). *House Beautiful* reported in 1948 on the "trend to make at least two uses of every room," an idea highlighted again two years later in a *Good Housekeeping* article describing how "rooms have a new job today."[73] The motivation to create multifunctional living spaces, or "rooms within rooms," had been part of domestic planning for middle-class houses since the beginning of the century, but the extreme dearth of total living space in minimum houses pushed the idea to its limits. Dean and Breines, in *The Book of Houses,* recommended such "convenient double-purpose combinations" as a child's bedroom or dining area also being used as a play space or other bedrooms functioning as places for study or sewing.[74]

The advice that rooms should be designed specifically for more than one activity resulted in the short-lived, dual-purpose bedroom/den or bedroom/study. This room usually appeared in one-story houses adjacent to the living room, separated by a curtained wall or sliding panel, but sometimes it was connected to the kitchen with a second, standard door. The bedroom/den/study

FIGURE 24. Multifunctional rooms and a kitchen set off from the rest of the daytime use rooms were typical in minimum houses. 1951. (Photograph by Preston B. Reed; courtesy of Roger G. Reed)

concept was intended to provide greater functional flexibility in the small house. In most cases, the space was more needed as a bedroom by growing families, and the permeable walls were abandoned for new houses almost as quickly as they had appeared. Rooms serving multiple functions were a part of daily life in a minimum house, and most did not include any meaningful design accommodations toward this end. Minimum houses remained a collection of small rooms whose limitations could initially be overlooked because of the houses' technological modernity.

THE STANDARD AMERICAN BATHROOM

The challenges to livability posed by a lack of space and design features were mitigated by the modernity of the systems and equipment in minimum houses. In no rooms were these components more integrated and evident than in bathrooms and kitchens. A three-fixture or "full" bathroom was the most widely shared component of minimum houses.[75] From the most basic of minimum

houses to dwellings that were considerably more spacious and expensive, nearly all contained a single full bathroom. By the 1920s, the accepted standard
bathroom in the United States was a simple square or rectangular space whose
overall dimensions ranged from a minimum of 5' x 5' to a more common 5' x 7'
or 6' x 8'. The modest size of the typical bathroom was in part accepted because
nineteenth-century houses that had been retrofitted for plumbing often had fixtures tucked into small, "incidental spaces."[76] The hotel industry's adoption of
private baths for each room around this time also influenced expectations about
the limited size of bathrooms in houses.[77]

The codification of bathroom size occurred at roughly the same time that a
full bathroom became an expected feature in most new houses built in metropolitan areas. A modern bathroom in a dedicated space, with matching fixtures
and modern finishes, would still have been a novel experience for many Americans purchasing houses immediately following the war. The housing census
taken in 1940 found that about half of all U.S. dwelling units (both single family
and multifamily) lacked a full private bath.[78] Given the virtual standstill in residential construction during the previous decades, many of the houses recorded
as having full bathrooms would have been older and cobbled together a generation earlier. Whether a familiar feature or a near luxury, the full bathroom was
an essential component of the modernity and livability of the minimum house.

The postwar bathroom typically included a sink or lavatory, a toilet, and a
bathtub-shower combination, housed in a single, uncompartmentalized room.[79]
Although building codes increasingly allowed for mechanical ventilation as an
alternative to an operable window, bathrooms in minimum houses were nearly
always situated against an outside wall fitted with a window. For plumbing efficiency, the fixtures were usually aligned on a single wall, with the toilet positioned between the sink, nearest to the door, and the bathtub located on the
exterior wall under the window. This commonplace arrangement flouted the
published prohibition against fixtures, in particular the bathtub, being installed
under the window to avoid unpleasant drafts and difficulty in reaching the window or blinds.[80] Another widespread layout situated the sink and toilet across
from the bathtub, with the door and the window on opposing walls. Both of
these bathroom plans shielded the toilet from view when the door was open.
This was a topic often covered by articles in the popular and trade press, which

underscores later analysis finding that the modern American bathroom was "physically clean yet culturally dirty."[81] The straightforward design and efficiency of the standard full bathroom remains in widespread use today.

The appearance, if not the layout, of the bathroom dramatically changed in the 1930s and 1940s. "Nothing dates a house so conspicuously as a bathtub with four legs or an old-fashioned 'water closet,'" offered a pair of experts on housing in 1946.[82] The functional modernity of the bathroom, coupled with its aesthetic modernization in the 1930s and 1940s, resulted in a space that "embodied" modernity, rather than one that merely "expressed" modernity.[83] The popular and trade press made many predictions about new bathroom features, such as in-the-wall hampers and heat lamps. Few became standard and, rather, were selectively utilized by builders as gimmicks intended to set their houses apart from others. Instead, new fixture shapes, brightly colored porcelain and floor and wall tile, and chrome elements created a sometimes-garish vision of modernity, even while the size, arrangement, and function of the bathroom remained unchanged (fig. 25).

FIGURE 25. The standard American bathroom was an important component of the minimum house. (*American Builder*, August 1948, 95; courtesy of Simmons-Boardman Publishing)

A single modern three-fixture bathroom was enough to ensure the livability of not just minimum houses but also, for a time, more expensive houses. Between 1940 and 1950, the number of new houses containing a single bathroom jumped from 80 percent to 92 percent of all houses, an outcome of the minimizing effect of the war on consumer expectations, the novelty of a three-piece bathroom for many Americans, the restrictions on copper and steel, and limits on the number of fixtures.[84] Writing for *Parents' Magazine* early in 1952, the NAHB's Leonard Haeger assured couples with growing families that despite controls on certain types of materials, "most builders feel that these amounts . . . will be sufficient, certainly for the great bulk of houses having three bedrooms, two baths, and the usual living-dining and kitchen areas."[85] The article was certainly playing to its intended audience—what household with children did not desire a second bathroom?

Despite the obvious appeal, very few new houses built between World War II and the Korean War contained more than one bathroom, primarily because of materials restrictions. The housing economist Edward Paxton explained in 1955 that Americans had developed a "very strong preference" for multiple bathrooms before "the war dampened the demand, driving it down to a bare majority or less," and that after the war shortages meant that "many a builder had to exercise all his resourcefulness to get the fixtures for even one complete bathroom in each of his houses."[86] The reality of a single bathroom operated independently of consumer desire, as Paxton also concluded: "The real desire for at least two bathrooms did not disappear. It only went underground."[87]

THE EQUIPPED KITCHEN

The kitchen was an especially significant touchstone in the development of suburban domestic life in postwar America. It instantly conveyed modernity and an increased standard of living, and its appearance was remarkably consistent from house to house, whether contemporary or more conventional in style.[88] From the marketing and sale of houses, to the purchase and replacement of household appliances, to the planning and preparation of meals, the kitchen was more closely tied to consumerism than any other room in the house.

In a world ideally structured around the nuclear family and traditional gender expectations, a well-designed and -located kitchen was seen as the physical manifestation of a woman's agency within the household. As the postwar period unfolded, women forced the transformation of the kitchen from a modern and "efficient" (read: tiny) room into one of the house's main centers for casual living. Postwar Americans thought the kitchen was a quintessential demonstration of national ingenuity and superiority. Mary and Russel Wright, outspoken product designers and cultural critics, observed as early as 1950: "In the kitchen, the combined genius of architects, engineers, designers, home economists, and manufacturers has dramatically lightened women's work and has provided one of the great technological contributions to home life in centuries—an American achievement as typical, and as impressive, as American skyscrapers, highways, and jazz."[89]

The kitchen was the most programmed room in the new postwar house; the most complex in terms of planning, equipment, and systems; and almost always the most expensive. Just prior to World War II, home economics experts, appliance manufacturers, and house builders had wrapped up a half century of intense reorganization and rethinking in regard to the kitchen. A 1954 publication titled *Inside Today's Home* summed up the widespread outcome of this process: "Twenty or thirty years ago there was a marked trend to make the kitchen as small and compact as possible—a highly specialized laboratory for cooking only."[90] Gas and electric stoves and ovens, iceboxes and electric refrigerators, and an increasing number of foods requiring little more than heating had reduced the somewhat chaotic nature of earlier kitchens. Home economics experts, most notably Christine Frederick, had engaged in "scientific" research concentrating on the motions and actions of kitchen-related work and come up with layouts to minimize steps and maximize efficiency.[91] Much of this early-twentieth-century interest in minimizing superfluous work in the kitchen extended directly from the falling number of households employing domestic help; between 1900 and 1920 the number of families with servants dropped by half.[92] At the end of World War II, middle-class women remained no less tied to domestic work in their role as housewife than their mothers and grandmothers had been—without the servants.[93]

Christine Frederick's work on efficiency in the kitchen was so consequential that it became widely known outside the United States, leading to a milestone in the development of modern kitchens with Grete Lihotzky's "Frankfurt Kitchen." In 1925, at Ernst May's invitation, Lihotzky relocated to Frankfurt to work with May on the development of new housing in that city. She soon devised the Frankfurt Kitchen as part of May's housing programs, exhibiting it in 1927 at an annual trade fair in Frankfurt.[94] Lihotzky's kitchen was a total design, in which all of the steps of meal preparation and other household tasks were taken into account. This small room was fully engineered to ease urban women's domestic work, through continuous countertops, thoughtful storage and layout, and modern technology.[95] The comprehensiveness of its design is startling for this date, as is its prefabricated construction. The level of integration exhibited in Grete Lihotzky's Frankfurt Kitchen would not be widely available in the United

States until well after World War II. Furthermore, although postwar kitchens are broadly comparable to Lihotzky's kitchen, rather than being total designs, these later rooms were assemblies of individually selected components whose combination was made possible through the adoption of standard depths and heights for cabinets, countertops, and appliances.

As the size of American kitchens continued to shrink in comparative terms through the 1930s and into the 1940s, there was more of a demand to make the best use of space and attempt to streamline the choppy nature of freestanding kitchen components. As electric and gas utilities lessened the size and messiness of work space, and the need for it to be removed from anything that could catch fire, the "continuous" countertop, with upper and lower cabinets and flush appliances, began to appear (fig. 26).[96] The idea of cabinets, countertops, and appliances spreading unimpeded across one, two, three, or more walls—pioneered by Lihotzky—required both dimensional standardization and modernization of utilities, notably electricity.

FIGURE 26. The continuous counter-tops and appliances in this combined kitchen-utility room helped to offset the isolation of a house's work area. 1950. (Photograph by Poist's Studio, Hanover, Pennsylvania; courtesy of Jeffrey Herr)

Electrification and *electrical modernization* are frequently presented as synonyms. In reality, *electrification* refers to the point at which houses were initially wired, principally for electric lighting. *Electrical modernization* standardized electrical components and provided adequate loads for the worry-free introduction and use of large appliances in houses. Popularly associated with the 1920s, the electrical modernization of most American houses in fact did not come until after World War II, through a combination of governmental direction and policy and an expansion of available consumer credit.[97]

Modern appliances and an engineered layout for kitchens ranked well ahead of size, partly because of the spatial limitations of minimum houses and partly because of notions restricting kitchens to domestic work alone. Well-publicized examples of kitchens that were more open to the front door and living areas—such as the redesigned Rancher (1949) in Levittown, New York—suggest that this was the dominant trend. Yet an overwhelming number of the houses described in trade journals, shelter magazines, and the real estate sections of newspapers show that even in cases where designers utilized open planning in a house's living and dining areas, the kitchen and its intended female occupant remained concealed or closed off (see fig. 24). The kitchen's isolation was a holdover of middle-class residential design in the 1920s and 1930s. The separated kitchen reflected a desire to keep the commotion of domestic tasks behind closed doors, rather than a strategy for distancing families from their servants, since the number of households with outside domestic help declined precipitously during those decades.[98]

A parallel and widening belief in the ability of technology to lessen the rigors of domestic work for women of all classes initially worked against moving kitchen design beyond a compact and isolated nature. For middle-class women an equipped kitchen offered the promise of rapid escape from the kitchen and its related work, and for working-class women it offered the suggestion of eased workloads.[99] Unfortunately, life's realities were not so simple. Technology merely facilitated middle-class women's increase in work and expanded the productive potential for working-class women. In either case, suburban women of all backgrounds and class divisions found themselves spending more of their days at work, much of which occurred in small kitchens located apart from the rest of the house but increasingly resplendent with modern equipment.[100]

Elizabeth Beveridge, an editor for *Woman's Home Companion,* explained simply in 1947: "Kitchen planning is fundamentally the process of organizing the fittings of the room around the pieces of equipment."[101] Home builders echoed this sentiment the following year: "The primary consideration in planning the kitchen—the 'workshop of the home'—is to determine what equipment to plan for."[102] The "completely equipped" kitchen became immediately desirable because it included labor-saving devices that conveyed to visitors the comfortable circumstances of a household, of particular appeal among the middle-income working class.[103] In the same way that the novelty of modern systems and utilities stymied dissatisfaction with the minimum house in general, the importance and desirability of kitchen equipment, and increasingly laundry facilities, outweighed significant and widespread spatial expansion in kitchens until the 1950s.

Relatively few new minimum houses came "complete" or "fully equipped" with appliances. A government report compiling data on new single-family houses built during the first half of 1950 found that while 100 percent of the new houses surveyed included "cabinets and countertops" in the kitchen, only 21 percent featured ranges, with 15 percent including exhaust fans, 10 percent refrigerators, and 5 percent in-sink disposers.[104] For refrigerators, at least, builders may have recognized that their inclusion would provide no marketing or sales advantage, because they had already come into widespread use as standalone objects, and purchasers would relocate with them.[105] The availability of consumer credit—mainly an expansion of installment buying—also allowed middle-income purchasers of new houses to buy household appliances that were not included in the sales price.[106]

The fully equipped kitchen remained a powerful marketing idea throughout the postwar period, and expectations for what this meant expanded and evolved, as did the space itself. For the minimum house, an efficient kitchen set off from other rooms typified what builders provided. These kitchens provided a segment of upper and lower cabinets and corresponding countertops, usually flanking the sink, with the range and refrigerator often standing in isolation. The space was highly utilitarian and intended for domestic work only, the preparation and cleanup of meals and, in some cases, the laundry. It would have been difficult to see the coming revolution in the role and spatial articulation of kitchens as they existed in most minimum houses.

THE NEED FOR MORE SPACE IN THE MINIMUM HOUSE

Middle-income consumers continued to accept the minimum house during the nation's transition out of war, a process that was beset with anxiety about rising costs and the need for sustained defense readiness. Nevertheless, the deficiencies of the minimum house became rapidly understood and increasingly untenable for expanding households with growing incomes and equity. An acute lack of interior square footage was the principal complaint of buyers, and builders initially responded in the early 1950s with modestly enhanced versions of the minimum house.

Regulation X required significantly higher down payments for even moderately priced houses; however, given the extremely small size of typical new houses at the outset of the policy, average square footage, even with the credit restrictions, could still be increased without pricing out prospective buyers. In just one year, from 1950 to 1951, the number of houses being built having at least one thousand square feet increased from about 40 to 60 percent.[107] This percentage held steady through the middle of the decade, and by 1955, the size of the average new American house had returned to pre–World War II levels.[108] Enclosing the same amount of space as the typical prewar house, the minimum houses of the 1950s were not, however, a clear throwback to the "enhanced" FHA designs of the late 1930s. Builders were understandably enamored of the planning efficiencies and construction economy inherent to the minimum house. They began building slightly larger houses, with an additional room or two, that still lacked the generous room dimensions, patterns of circulation, and domestic zoning that would soon become characteristic of a well-designed house.

One-story houses continued to dominate new construction nationally. These houses were often referred to as "ranch" houses, but the term was at first irregularly applied and adopted. Furthermore, many of the ideas and features popularly associated with ranch houses—space for casual living and meaningful indoor-outdoor connections—were not widely available until later in the 1950s, as the size and amenities of typical houses continued to expand. The origins of the modern suburban ranch can be traced back to the actual, functional ranch houses in the West and to traditional Spanish haciendas, but the evolution included a number of intermediate steps, such as the enlargement of the minimum house. The sprawling forms and rustic construction of the true ranch house appealed to architects early in the twentieth century. By the 1930s, the work of architects and designers such as Cliff May, O'Neil Ford, David Williams, William Wurster, and others had elevated "ranch style" design, and practitioners needed to be as familiar with it as with the various period revivals still popular throughout the country.[109] *Sunset* magazine heavily promoted ranch houses as an embodiment of the "Western myth," and their rising popularity was also based in a simultaneous embrace of America's historic architecture, not only high-style but also regional and vernacular traditions.[110] The ranch house's exposure in professional journals and shelter magazines in the 1930s facilitated its nationwide spread; however, these houses tended to be architect-designed or custom-built one-offs for relatively affluent clients.[111] This characterization remained largely in place when private residential construction began again after World War II, even while more builders turned to one-story designs, increasing numbers of which were dubbed "ranch houses."

Large builders in the West began marketing one-story minimum houses from the moment the war ended. These had very little in common with the high-end ranch houses of the 1930s, but they would become the seed for the postwar interpretation of the suburban ranch. The houses in David Bohannon's San Lorenzo Village in the San Francisco Bay area (1944), the Sandberg-Asbahr Company's development in Portland, Oregon (1946), and Fritz Burns and Henry Kaiser's Panorama City in Los Angeles (1948), typified widely available one-story houses in the West. Mark Taper, Louis Boyar, and Ben Weingart started Lakewood in Los Angeles County, California, in 1949, a development that corresponded in scale and basic character to the contemporary Levittown, New York. The roughly nine-hundred-square-foot houses in Lakewood adhered to prewar FHA guidelines, with their uncomplicated layouts.[112] Most of these houses were West Coast manifestations of the minimum house, small four- and five-room one-story dwellings. The feature most distinguishing them was an increasingly standard attached garage, made necessary in a region that more than any other at the time was dependent on the automobile.

A majority of the one-story houses featured in *American Builder* in the late 1940s were either minimum houses or larger custom-built ranch houses, then found throughout the country. The custom-built "modern ranch type house" was closely aligned with its 1930s California predecessors and easily demonstrated the style's pleasant characteristics, with "large, comfortable rooms, arranged in a manner to give the greatest amount of livability to the occupants, . . . [that have] captured the imagination of the public."[113] Whether considering a "wide-flung ranch-style house" in California, a house of the "South-western ranch type" in Oklahoma, or a "rambling modern ranch house" on Long Island, it is impossible not to grasp the allure of these substantial, expansive, and visually complex houses.[114] In contrast, the characteristics of the one-story minimum house were less effusively promoted: with their "ample closet space, minimum kitchen and bathroom equipment, privacy between the living-working area and the sleeping-dressing-toileting area . . . [these houses were] safe and easy to run . . . [and] might be very livable."[115]

Articles showcasing one-story houses having four or five rooms tended not to use the term *ranch,* instead stressing such things as construction quality, economy, and practicality. *American Builder*'s "All-American House of 1950" offered a fairly prosaic view of contemporary mass housing: "The most popular type of dwelling now being sold—will be a bungalow of no definite architectural type ranging in price from $8,000 to $10,000, with no dining room or basement and with smaller kitchens but greater closet space than prewar."[116] The sketch of this bungalow depicted a familiar-looking one-story dwelling with a cross-gable roof and traditional architectural features such as horizontal weatherboarding and double-hung windows set off by (likely nonoperable) shutters. Custom-built ranch houses remained the ideal for their room size and aesthetics, but most people buying any house—one story or multistory—had to be contented with minimum models enlarged by one or two added rooms.

The enlarged one-story minimum house had not quite yet reached the horizontality that has become associated with the suburban ranch house type; rather, this was a transitional moment in its development. The architect Rudolph Matern toured cities on the West Coast in 1948 and reported with "a firm conviction that a new American style of architecture is now being evolved" in cities throughout the West, not "through architects' abstract dreams, but directly across the salesman's desk."[117] The photographs included with the article make it clear that these houses all contained a single story. Matern went on to observe that most of them were not aggressively modern, but "a digest of the best of the old and the best of the new" that borrowed from more traditional forms and elements in the East.

As an architect familiar with the spread of large, architect-designed or custom-built "ranch houses" across the country, Matern did not apply the term to this new type of architecture; however, it was soon attached to the form in the public mind. In an article on the topic of the "modern house," Mary Davis Gillies, the house and home fashions editor of *McCall's,* expounded in 1950: "The ranch house is the true transitional form. It borrows from design motifs from both the Cape Cod house and the modern house and blends them into a familiar looking whole."[118]

The resulting architectural hybrid was highly marketable and spread quickly throughout the nation. Much of the coverage documenting this type of house itemized the ways the house looked different—one story, lower-pitched roofs, novel window arrangements, and new combinations of cladding (fig. 27). This transitional design phase for one-story houses was also the focus of modest interior changes that pragmatically met the most severe shortcomings of

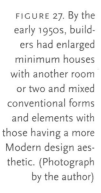

FIGURE 27. By the early 1950s, builders had enlarged minimum houses with another room or two and mixed conventional forms and elements with those having a more Modern design aesthetic. (Photograph by the author)

minimum houses and began to more truthfully reflect what American families desired in a house. The enlarged minimum house, or, perhaps more accurately, the emergent ranch house, was a tentative step toward the now-classic ranch house of the 1950s.

In 1954, *U.S. News & World Report* reflected on things having a negative impact on the livability of houses recently constructed in the United States: "Relatively few houses have been built since World War II with all the desired attractions."[119] The article reported that government studies had identified the fact that such elements as a third bedroom, a separate dining room, a second bathroom, and a porch were frequently missing from typical new houses; however, the "biggest complaint is with the size of rooms. . . . Many owners, when asked what they will look for next time they buy, say more rooms and bigger rooms." The deficiencies listed in this article described the plight of owners of basic minimum houses—those with few rooms, small rooms, and "efficient" plans lacking circulation pathways or meaningful zoning. As the realities of daily life in a house that was often no larger than an apartment or row house became strongly evident, consumers began thinking about the larger dwellings continually featured in newspapers and popular periodicals. Builders, perceiving a continued windfall and, under the system of FHA and VA loan guarantees, undertaking very little financial risk, were more than happy to begin the enlargement of the postwar suburban house.

In addition to their modest but steady increase in total square footage, more and more minimum houses began to incorporate a third bedroom. During the first half of 1950, only one-third of new houses contained three bedrooms; by the first quarter of 1955, over two-thirds did.[120] A June 1955 "progress report" in the *NAHB Correlator* discussed the houses of ten builders. In 1948, seven of the ten featured two-bedroom houses; in 1955, all ten of the highlighted models had three bedrooms (and two had four).[121] The increase in the number of bedrooms during the early 1950s documents the beginning of a long line of targeted enhancements in typical houses, resulting from builder-buyer interplay.

Newly formed households with no children or with young children could be content with two-bedroom houses; as the children aged, however, an additional bedroom was advantageous in maintaining livability. The trends were already in place and were hardly surprising—households with more children or older children were in the majority of those purchasing houses with three or more bedrooms.[122] These numbers significantly increased in the 1950s. In families with children of varying genders, a bedroom for each child was an imperative. The American Public Health Administration set standards for calculating bedroom needs and advocated no more than two people per bedroom, boys and girls in separate rooms unless very young, and children of drastically varying ages in their own rooms.[123] The general expansion of the American family also had a great influence on the trend for new bedrooms; by 1956, a baby was born once every twelve seconds in the United States, "more and more often as an addition to an old-fashioned-size family of three, four or more children."[124] The addition of a third bedroom was the most crucial of enhancements to the minimum house.

A dining room or defined dining area was also essential to augmenting the livability of a minimum house. In 1949, the *Washington Post* counted a combination living-dining room among the notable changes in the design of new houses.[125] Two years later, the *Chicago Tribune* pointed out that "the dining room has been sacrificed" not only in minimum houses but also in "many larger homes."[126] The widespread abandonment of the dining room was a nationwide phenomenon by 1950. *American Builder* explained: "The dining room in the House of 1950 is vanishing. . . . It is likely to be a mere indicated corner of the living room."[127] Viewed by many as superfluous and loudly touted by the building industry and shelter presses as expendable, a room or area primarily used for dining was not permanently lost for postwar households.

Mealtime and dining were a central part of life and, for families with children, often a messy and sometimes chaotic one as well. A collection of data presented in surveys dating from 1936 through 1950 concluded: "Families with children tend consistently to want separate dining rooms."[128] Owners of minimum houses found plans that placed dining functions in the living room pushed the concept of multiuse rooms beyond the limits of livability, and those that limited the dining area to the kitchen alone did not allow for enough separation from the main work area of the house. In an article about a recently released government study of housing, *U.S. News & World Report* concluded in 1954: "Most families also want a separate dining room or a dining ell off the living room. They don't like the idea of eating all their meals in the kitchen or at one end of the living room."[129]

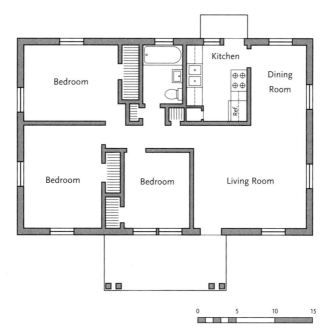

FIGURE 28. Builders enlarged minimum houses with dining rooms and a third bedroom. 1955. (Drawing by Paul Davidson, after a plan in *NAHB Correlator*, June 1955, 30)

Increased square footage in the form of larger rooms, a third bedroom, and a dedicated area for dining maintained the livability of minimum houses by addressing the most acute areas of consumer dissatisfaction (fig. 28). These new houses' floor plans remained unimaginative and inflexible. They stressed the efficient organization of rooms within a simple building envelope over a more nuanced approach that weighed how a room's location and its relationship to other rooms might affect the day-to-day activities of a household. An architect addressing the annual meeting of the American Home Economics Association in 1950 suggested that "the home buying public did not demand good house planning."[130]

Much of the "home buying public" had not yet had the opportunity to develop an opinion on what a trained professional might consider "good house planning." Having lived through a deep depression and world war, their only practical knowledge would have come from single-family and multifamily residences largely built before 1929 or from postwar minimum houses. "Good house planning" was too abstract a concept for consumers with a limited base of knowledge and few alternatives to consider. Consumers understandably and pragmatically sought more obvious and tangible ways to improve livability, such as more square footage and additional rooms. Builders met these demands with slightly larger minimum houses and could thus delay having to admit that their pinched character might pose as much a barrier to livability as too few rooms.

The daytime-public and nighttime-private zones in larger minimum houses, and the basic functions occurring in the component rooms, remained unchanged. Deane Carter and Keith Hinchcliff, professors at the University of Illinois, spelled out the functional areas within the minimum house in their 1949 publication *Family Housing*. The rooms for daytime use included the "public portion" or "recreation area" (main entrance, living room, dining room or area, and porch) and the "occupation" or "work" area (kitchen, laundry/utility area, and garage or carport).[131] These two functional areas accounted for a bit more than half of the diagrammatic plan used as an illustration, yet the minimum house depicted was so small overall and its plan so compartmentalized that it could not even begin to foster any degree of flexibility. Certain activities, such as cooking or entertaining, occurred in specific places, but a lack of rooms, and sizable rooms at that, would potentially turn every room into a multifunctional space. Carter and Hinchcliff admitted that this functional overlap occurred even with the nighttime use or private zone, which they called the "relaxation" or "quiet" area, explaining: "It is apparent that boundaries cannot be set to confine the activities of recreation, relaxation, and occupation within definite parts of the house. Bedrooms may contain lounge chairs, radio, and study table; sewing, mending, ironing, and other duties may be done in any one of several places; and relaxation is not limited to a particular part of the house."[132]

The potential for functional chaos in minimum houses was not limited to the multipurpose nature of rooms but also extended to a lack of divisions between spaces and daytime and nighttime areas, particularly in houses with one story (see fig. 51). The main entrance often opened directly from a small front porch or stoop directly into the living room. Living and dining areas also doubled as corridors linking the kitchen with the bedrooms and bathroom, which, in the great majority of minimum houses, were located off a small hallway entered from the living room. Kitchens were no longer buffered with closable doors, pantries, or hallways, and in houses without basements, the kitchen also often served as a laundry. The continued identification of an "occupation" or "work" zone in discussions of minimum houses demonstrated that long-established middle-class notions of domestic work and its location in the house lingered into the postwar years. This carryover occurred for a number of years, until casual living began to transform suburban life and suburban houses.

CONCLUSION

The uncomplicated organization of all minimum houses soon made it difficult to consider them livable, as the functional overlap in rooms and between zones made day-to-day life problematic for growing and maturing families.[133] In 1956, the United States Savings and Loan League "cautioned against the building of an enormous quantity of so-called 'minimum' houses" because the "incomes of American families will continue to rise in the years ahead, and . . . as these incomes rise, fewer families will want to buy 'minimum' houses."[134]

Builders began moving strongly away from literal interpretations of the FHA's minimum standards and started to use them as they were intended, as "a starting point from which amplification and improvements can be made as circumstances permit or as local conditions demand."[135] David Bowen, a real estate journalist for the *Washington Post,* explained in 1959 that the recent changes to the FHA's guidelines primarily influenced construction standards and elements of financing; it was up to the designer of a house to elaborate on and enhance the minimum house prototype in the manner the FHA intended at the time of its establishment. Bowen explained that in the opinion of the architect whose house design accompanied the article, a "house conforming exactly to the minimum standards, while providing adequate shelter, would not . . . provide for the living comfort modern Americans expect in a home."[136]

By the mid-1950s, industry and popular publications widely reported on and advocated for houses that were not just bigger but also perceived to be better designed. In 1956, *Time* magazine reported the most broadly stated reason for the quick turn away from the minimum house: "The demands for more attractive homes are all part of the rise in the U.S. standard of living."[137] A writer for *Time*'s sister publication, *Fortune,* concurred a year later, more explicitly severing the "good life" for the upwardly mobile from minimum houses: "American consumers are no longer content with minimum standards but demand the abundance, quality and style that used to differentiate the *good life* from *ordinary living*."[138]

Against a Cold War backdrop, the perceived superiority of the "U.S. standard of living" and its sibling the "American way of life" attained cultlike status in public discourse and in the self-identity of individual Americans. The nationalistic motivations and favorable economic realities underlying these concepts were real enough, but they also referenced a new and distinct pattern of life in the American suburbs, that of casual living. The New York architect Herman H. York, who worked frequently with the building industry on the design of houses for the mass market, was asked to comment about the direction of house design in 1957 as part of symposium sponsored by the *New York Times*. York launched his remarks by stressing that "casual living . . . is influencing our concepts of space use in new homes today."[139] The excitement over the American standard of living and way of life was moving prospective buyers not merely away from minimum houses but toward new designs that made clear, if experimental, efforts to incorporate space intended for the pursuit of casual living.

Casual Living

THE ADOPTION OF casual living by Americans in the middle decades of the twentieth century was the catalyst for rapid change in the design of suburban houses. Casual living was a purposefully laid-back, easygoing, and supposedly effortless lifestyle choice, whose simple appeal masked complex geographic, economic, domestic, and spatial factors that contributed to its formation. As advanced by tastemakers and builders, and quickly espoused by suburban households, casual living promoted togetherness for nuclear families no longer residing in proximity to their extended kin. It advocated a type of sociability and a level of consumption that bridged differences between neighbors of varied backgrounds. It challenged long-standing boundaries between "work" and "leisure" within the house. Casual living was so swiftly and fully endorsed by suburban households that it is impossible to now separate the concept from middle-class life at the metropolitan periphery. Consumer interest in space for casual living was strong enough to launch an essential rethinking of the American house. It remained the primary force in the design of domestic environments for the rest of the century and contributed to an increasing number of households feeling that they were "middle class."

Sustained economic growth, a burgeoning consumer culture, and the many shortcomings of minimum houses provided a platform for major architectural changes in the 1950s and early 1960s. If demand for a third bedroom was paramount during the first half of the decade, a space to accommodate and facilitate casual living dominated the second half, and it advanced quickly to become part of the housing ideal. Builders remained uncertain about how best to incorporate casual living—a new and still-evolving concept—into existing forms, within established regional traditions, and at a reasonable cost. A multiplicity of novel solutions appeared throughout the nation, and the resulting rooms, plans, and forms define a notably creative and inventive period of American domestic architecture.

Two principal design arcs for incorporating casual living into suburban houses emerged from the jumbled array of responses. In one, the kitchen was transformed, first into a living-kitchen through the addition of space for informal dining, and then into the somewhat larger kitchen–family room. This design arc was typical in ranch houses and dwellings in areas where slab foundations predominated. In the other, the basement recreation room was transformed into the lower-level recreation room of three new multistory house forms: the split-level, the bi-level, and the split-foyer. These distinctive architectural hybrids addressed a desire for more space, generally, and casual living, specifically, at a time when land costs were skyrocketing and Americans favored the aesthetics and livability of the one-story ranch house.

Independent of form, households also lived in a casual manner just beyond the dwelling's exterior walls, on patios, terraces, porches, and decks. These features were generally appended to a house rather than being integral to its design. Designers envisioned these elements, as well as sliding glass doors and interior brick feature walls, as blurring the distinction between indoors and outdoors, landscape and architecture. Outdoor living space was a widespread component of suburban life but fell short of becoming a nonnegotiable element of a house at the time of its construction or purchase. It could be passed over by builders in order to lower the base cost of a model, and the creation of such spaces after the time of purchase was entirely manageable by a homeowner within the "do it yourself" culture burgeoning in the suburbs.

CASUAL LIVING AND THE RANCH HOUSE

The ethos of casual living as practiced both within and between households valued friendly and easygoing domestic environments and downplayed inflexible social boundaries and rigid rules of conduct. A dynamic consumer culture provided the foundation for the acceptance of casual living in the postwar suburbs. With rising national wealth shared by unprecedented numbers of Americans, middle-income households could choose to participate in this lifestyle merely through the acquisition of certain material goods—with the house being the most consequential. Tastemakers, builders, and housing experts continually claimed that only modern domestic settings could effectively stimulate family togetherness and household harmony in addition to providing a backdrop for relaxed sociability between households of differing origins or ethnic backgrounds. Members of both the rising middle-income working class and the established middle class did not question this claim in any great numbers.

One cultural outcome of widespread enjoyment of a casual lifestyle, perceived by many observers at the time, was an unblemished veneer of homogeneity, unifying members of a vastly expanded middle class, that was as pointedly exclusionary as it was inclusionary. Frederick Lewis Allen, the longtime editor of *Harper's Magazine* and a popular historian, commented on suburban demographics in a posthumously released article in 1954: "A firm believer in diversity, who would like to see more, not less, mixing together on easy terms of people of different economic fortunes, different age-groups, and different occupations and pre-occupations, cannot help wondering if these larger new suburbs can escape being natural breeding grounds for conformity."[1] Racial diversity was not part of even a more liberal critique of suburban life, and the primary narrative of social development in the suburbs was class oriented and rested solidly on the consumer-based pursuit of a casual lifestyle.

In 1950, successful product designers and cultural commentators Mary Wright and Russel Wright observed: "A new way of living, informal, relaxed, and actually more gracious than any strained imitation of another day could be, is in fact growing up. . . . There is evidence all around that the hard shell of snobbish convention is cracking."[2] A "new way of living" was not just something predicted or noted by elite tastemakers, but a mass social revolution extending from the swift improvement in the life circumstances of a majority of suburban households. The concept of casual living was not a hard one to comprehend, yet it had profound effects on domestic life and domestic environments.

Within the household, the primary interest in casual living was based on its stress on family togetherness and the pursuit of group and individual activities within shared space. This widespread societal focus on nuclear family life responded to a range of factors, from Cold War apprehension, to memories of the difficult years of the Great Depression and World War II, to the specific demands of living in a detached house in a subdivision.[3] Removed from

extended families and the tight-knit small towns and ethnic urban neighborhoods of their youth, newly suburbanized Americans turned much of their attention inward, upholding the virtues of a highly gendered nuclear family. Time and money were overwhelmingly spent on the house and home, its purchase, outfitting, maintenance, and enjoyment. Togetherness became a model concept for healthy family life, and it was broadly adopted nationwide (fig. 29).[4] The idea that families would aspire to spending a great deal of time together, and find satisfaction in it, became so ingrained in American life that, in 1951, the National Council on Family Relations sponsored a panel addressing the problem of a "lack of busy families," in part defined as families who "don't know what they are missing by not growing in family togetherness."[5]

FIGURE 29. Family togetherness was a central element of postwar casual living. 1957. (U.S. News & World Report Magazine Photograph Collection, Prints and Photographs Division, Library of Congress; photograph by and courtesy of Warren K. Leffler)

A high degree of informal interaction with other households was also touted by trade and popular periodicals as a benchmark of casual living in the suburbs. The well-known journalist Harry Henderson investigated "mass-produced suburbs" in a two-part series in *Harper's Magazine* that ran in 1953. Written at a point when the suburbs were well into their explosive postwar growth, the article focused on how the character of life unfolding in these new neighborhoods was without precedent. Henderson explained: "Gone also are most rituals and ceremonies. If you want to know someone, you introduce yourself: there is no waiting for the 'right people.' You 'drop in' without phoning."[6] A 1960 study of fifty housewives who had been living for a year in Inglewood Manor, a new subdivision in metropolitan Philadelphia, found that nearly 60 percent had visited with another household on their block in the evening at least once a month, and just shy of one-third did so weekly.[7] The new suburban social order rested on casual living.

A writer for *Better Homes & Gardens* in 1950 contended that an easygoing living environment, lacking all forms of "pretense," made life more enjoyable. This article and others like it in middle-class shelter magazines encouraged their readers to welcome a casual lifestyle as a way to reduce the stress of social distinctions by offering neutral ground for interacting with middle-income neighbors regardless of their personal histories and previous lives.[8] The topic of reducing formality in day-to-day life in the suburbs was a decidedly middle-class conversation. Still, the interests and needs of the newly suburbanized middle-income working class also influenced this trend. A 1959 study of working-class women found that they believed that "the charm and advantages of an inexpensive and unostentatious house [meant] that a family can relax more easily and feel more genuinely at home."[9] Whether middle class or middle-income working class, households locating to new dwellings in the suburbs began to revolutionize their family and social lives through a belief in the value of a more casual lifestyle.

The unprepossessing, seemingly effortless act of living casually among family members, and friends and neighbors, was a complicated response to an array of cultural factors. Transplants from urban neighborhoods or entirely different metropolitan areas turned to the easy social expectations and interaction of casual living as a means of bridging and lessening differences in background with friends and neighbors. Nuclear families distanced from their extended kin trusted the advice that casual living would facilitate togetherness among the members of a household. These beliefs even went so far as to challenge the absolute separation of women's domestic work and household leisure. Casual living revolutionized how individuals and families pursued their daily lives and is one of the most consequential legacies of postwar America.

The concept of casual living became closely linked to a house form even before builders made a strong attempt to accommodate it. The small dimensions and few rooms of the minimum house made it inherently casual. As the minimum house transitioned into the basic six-room ranch house, the allure and desirability of a relaxed Californian or more broadly western sensibility became fixed to the form.[10] The ranch house projected a modern life of ease and also become a potent symbol of personal independence and hopeful promise.[11] As confidence in the postwar economy grew, the ranch house seemed a perfect

FIGURE 30. One-story ranch houses of the 1950s emphasized horizontality. (Photograph by the author)

fit for the new subdivisions spilling out from cities, winning fans for both its aesthetic and, increasingly, its functional properties.

In the 1950s, the postwar ranch house distinguished itself from the one-story minimum house in two principal ways. Its exterior strongly emphasized horizontality—a simplified roofline and low-pitched roofs with broad, over-hanging eaves; window openings that were wider than tall and window walls or sliding glass doors; and innovative use of cladding materials (fig. 30).[12] In many places, the ranch house had the appearance of a long, low rectangular box hugging the ground. It was not necessarily larger than comparable minimum houses; however, its character-defining aesthetic features made it appear larger from the street.

The ranch house was not just stimulating in its appearance; some compara-tively minor adjustments to its floor plan also foreshadowed how casual living would come to revolutionize house design. Rudolph Matern, an architect who worked closely with the building industry and the shelter press, explained in 1952: "The ranch house is more than a style; it's the culmination of good living features, made possible by our new way of life."[13] Key "good living features" centered on the relationships between a house's public/daytime use rooms and circulation. A common example of the ubiquitous six-room ranch house placed the living room and two bedrooms at the front and the dining room/area, kitch-en, and a third bedroom at the rear.

In a much-reported trend, the kitchen now relocated to the front of the house. Some well-known examples were heavily covered in the press, but this development was far from universal and varied considerably from region to region.[14] The arrangement with the kitchen at the front fostered better indoor-outdoor connections between the main living area and the rear terrace or patio and was a draw in places where a terrace could be used most of the year. In regions where homeowners tended to prefer a more traditional room arrangement, kitchens remained at the back of the house. Browsing the graphic-laden advertisements of the weekend real estate sections in newspapers throughout the country or strolling through 1950s subdivisions, which inevitably contain ranch houses, the most straightforward evidence that a majority of living rooms remained at the front of houses is their large and highly visible picture windows.

Wherever the kitchen was located, builders lessened its seclusion in two principal ways. The more drastic one involved either opening up the wall between the kitchen and dining room/area with a pass-through or breakfast bar or removing it altogether. The Levittowner model in Levittown, Pennsylvania, traded a wall between the kitchen and the open-plan living and dining area for a bamboo screen.[15] This solution was problematic. When the screen was open, the workspace was unacceptably in full view of the front door and only partially screened from the living room, and when it was closed, the woman working in the kitchen was again visually, if not audibly, marginalized. The removal of the wall did not necessarily translate into the full merger of kitchen and dining area, as builders often screened the workspace with cabinets or shelving (fig. 31). The second approach for creating connections

FIGURE 31. The ubiquitous six-room ranch house of the 1950s lessened isolation in the kitchen with such things as a pass-through and a second entrance and increased indoor-outdoor connections. 1952. (Drawing by Paul Davidson, after a plan in The Celotex Corporation, "The Celotex Book of Home Plans," 1952, 6)

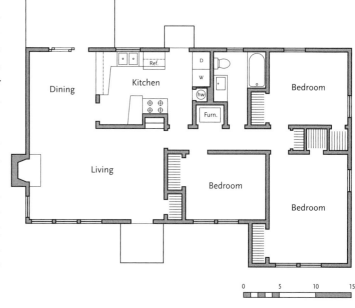

Dining

Ref.

Kitchen

D

W

hw

Furn.

Bedroom

Living

Bedroom

Bedroom

0   5   10   15

with the kitchen was more subtle—a second interior entrance in addition to the existing one between the kitchen and the dining room. In the six-room ranch house, the new doorway was usually positioned near the hallway leading to the bathroom and bedrooms and also furnished a more convenient route between the kitchen and the front door. It also allowed for a pattern of circulation that did not require crossing the living room and dining room to get to the kitchen.

The opening up of the kitchen in the six-room ranch house was the first step builders made toward accommodating casual living in the postwar house. The second interior doorway for the kitchen made a floor plan more permeable and flexible, and along with its aesthetic appeal, it helped to establish the ranch house as the first important new housing form of the postwar period. The adaptability of the six-room ranch as new features appeared—such as kitchens with eating areas, separate entryways, and master bathrooms—kept it as a mainstay of subdivision design and marketing into the 1960s and beyond. The ranch house is more associated with suburbanization and a suburban lifestyle than any other form, even though its limitations hastened its demise as the best form for casual living

THE LIVING-KITCHEN

In the 1950s, American households' interest in casual living transformed the kitchen into a living-kitchen. It moved from a workroom to one of the main centers of household activity, merely with the addition of space for a table and chairs. That a kitchen would be designed without seating is inconceivable at the beginning of the twenty-first century, yet this was expected in many minimum houses. When *House Beautiful* queried in 1946 "What makes a plan bad?," the lack of table space in the kitchen was not mentioned.[16] Similarly, one year later, when *Ladies' Home Journal* asked "will it be a dream house?," space for eating in the kitchen was seemingly not part of the dream.[17] A writer for the *Washington Post* noted in 1954 that, through the late 1940s, the average kitchen in a house was "still a meal factory" and "wasn't yet a place to be lived in."[18] By the mid-1950s few builders would have ventured to design a house without a physically and functionally enlarged kitchen.

At all income levels, postwar families began to blend the domestic work in the kitchen with internal and external socializing along what Elizabeth Collins Cromley calls the "food axis," a concept that takes into account where food storage, food preparation, and meals take place.[19] The food axis of postwar houses eventually settled primarily in an enlarged kitchen. The period press made much of the "opening up" of the kitchen to the rest of the house. In reality, the link between the kitchen and living resulted more from a functional "invitation into" the kitchen, rather than the room's less prevalent physical "opening up" to other rooms.[20] In 1950, "Marian Manners," the pseudonymous writer of domestic advice in the *Los Angeles Times,* proposed that open planning in new houses as a spatial phenomenon had also figuratively "opened up [the kitchen] to include other family activities than cooking and eating."[21] The deceptively simple inclusion of table space in the kitchen, and the lessening of the room's seclusion with a second interior entrance, prompted its conceptual transformation into a living-kitchen. The elemental qualities of this transformation to daily life made the change one of the few postwar housing trends that was truly universal.

The formation of the living-kitchen was a welcome event to the great swath of middle-income women living in new suburban houses. In 1953, *House & Garden* clearly articulated the correspondence between women in servantless households and the kitchen's redesign, further elaborating that women "transformed the clinical-looking kitchen of the '30s and '40s into such varied 'living-kitchens' as you see in this issue."[22] Printed concern for women's isolation and increased time spent in the kitchen was directed to middle-class households coming to terms with changes in domestic work that were not physically reflected in their houses. That said, demand for the living-kitchen did not originate solely in the middle class, as increasing numbers of houses were purchased by prosperous members of the newly middle-income working class. As articulated in the Wrights' *Guide to Easier Living* (1950), "the majority of American families have *never* been able to afford domestic help" and would not have noticed, let alone lamented, its disappearance.[23] As the center of domestic work, the kitchen had always been the center of daily life for urban working-class women, and the idea of what Shelly Nickles has termed the "social kitchen" moved with them when they relocated to the suburbs.[24] The small, closed-off kitchens found in most minimum houses did not provide the right type of space to replicate urban social kitchens.

FIGURE 32. Space for a second table and chairs vastly expanded the functional possibilities in the living-kitchen. 1959. (Photograph by the author)

The limitations of the efficiency kitchen—"just a place where meals were cooked and dishes washed"—concerned all suburban housewives.[25] A middle-class woman from the Washington, DC, area, interviewed in a 1964 survey and described as having a "lower" economic standing among respondents, reminisced about the "home" of her past: "I like a kitchen where you can sit around and have your breakfast and even congregate after dinner and before dinner. We did that at home all the time and this is what I miss."[26] Already modernized in terms of its workspace, kitchen design in housing markets across the country centered on ways to expand the room's functional possibilities beyond domestic work. The *Woman's Home Companion* commented favorably and insightfully on the trend, posing the question, "When is a kitchen not a kitchen?," and the answer, "We think it's when you don't realize where it leaves off and the other side of living begins."[27]

Kitchens set apart from the rest of the house jeopardized the homemaker's ability to manage the varied facets of her "jack-of-all-trades" domestic role.[28] No matter a household's income level or class association, women's work within the home was largely the same. A 1948 publication titled *The American Woman in Modern Marriage* identified five broad categories of household work: organization and management, orderliness and cleanliness, feeding and clothing, personal services, and "sundry work."[29] A 1964 study of house design and families offered four roles viewed as central to the lives of postwar women in the home: housekeeper, hostess, mother, and wife-mistress.[30] The addition of table space in the kitchen allowed women to more easily juggle these varied domestic tasks and roles. In addition to being used for meals, a table could be used for planning grocery shopping, writing out bills or letters, and folding laundry at a time when those facilities were frequently located in or near the kitchen.

Taking cues from the working-class social kitchen, a living-kitchen attained this status by accepting and even inviting the occurrence of activities unrelated to domestic work into the kitchen. Writing for *Parents' Magazine* in 1953, Gladysruth Hanmer described the many ways her family used its living-kitchen:

> It is a commons room; just as in the days when the large friendly kitchen was the most lived-in part of a home. . . . Family and friends just naturally gather around the table for an evening of cards or a spot of conversation. If Bill, my husband, has some office homework to do over the weekend, the dining-living area of the kitchen is the most natural place for him to work on his papers, especially since there is a telephone close at hand. The table also makes a wonderful work place for my two sons, who are avid model airplane builders. . . . Having the family within earshot makes my work seem easier. . . . We are proud of the warm ties of unity in our family and feel certain that these have been stimulated by having this place in which we can all do things together.[31]

Hanmer's reflections indicate how indispensable a living-kitchen was to the operation of her household and for fostering family togetherness (fig. 32).

A 1956 advertisement for Hotpoint appliances illustrated the advantages of the living-kitchen. While the advertisement is obviously a pitch for a brand of appliances, its salient points are revealing: "Hotpoint 'Living-Room' Kitchens are what the 1956 home buyer wants! It's a fact that this year's prospects are looking for kitchens that are as warm and friendly and beautiful as the other 'living' areas in the home—kitchens for living in and entertaining in."[32] Two accompanying illustrations depict how women might simultaneously live and work in their fashionable living-kitchen.

Both images show well-dressed, undoubtedly middle-class women situated in large and colorful kitchens, each bearing a distinct seating area. In one scene, a woman prepares a meal while a female guest, accessorized with hat, gloves, and handbag, sits at the table (fig. 33). This image suggests that well-designed living-kitchens would be proper enough for entertaining visitors and that this social-izing would not impede completion of household tasks. In the second image, a woman, also preparing a meal, watches her daughter, seated at the built-in breakfast bar as she paints. The message forwarded here is that living-kitchens can afford mothers enough space to spend time with children, or supervise their potentially messy endeavors, all while engaged in their own domestic work.

FIGURE 33. A well-appointed living-kitchen was appro-priate enough for entertaining visitors. 1956. ("Hotpoint 'Living-Room' Kitch-ens," *Architectural Record*, mid-May 1956; courtesy of GE)

The living-kitchens in these views (of course replete with Hotpoint appliances) provided expansive, attractive, and versatile space for both work and other activities. They increased visibility for women by encouraging visitation and the nonwork activities of other family members and friends and allowed more freedom in how women managed their own work processes, child rearing, and social activities. All of this accomplished with enough room for a table and chairs.

KITCHEN–FAMILY ROOMS

The transformation of the kitchen into a living-kitchen occurred more or less simultaneously in all forms of houses. This expansion began to be pushed even further to include a seating or lounge area, a trend understood by some as a contemporary update of rooms existing in past American houses. Shelter magazines and the industry presses positioned the living-kitchen on a continuum that included the colonial "keeping room" or rural "farm kitchen," a place where general living could occur simultaneously in a space whose primary function was domestic work.[33] The addition of a lounge area contiguous to or within the kitchen was the next logical step after the inclusion of a second, casual eating area (fig. 34). The change was most prevalent in houses lacking a lower level or basement, places where casual living might otherwise be accommodated in a dedicated room of its own. Houses containing a living-kitchen now expanded to include a lounge area that was often marked on plans and discussed in literature with a new name: the "family room."

Family room has become the near-universal term applied to a second living area in American houses. This only occurred after its role, function, and physical state became codified in the 1960s. When the term came into frequent usage in the 1950s, it might refer to any one of a range of casual living spaces where varied day-to-day activities

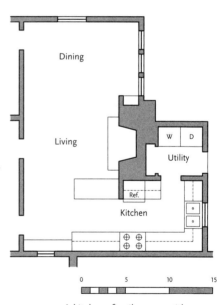

FIGURE 34. A kitchen–family room with a large fireplace as its focus. 1953. (Drawing by Paul Davidson, after a plan in *Better Homes & Gardens*, December 1953, 14)

might occur.[34] This secondary area for living was more multifunctional than the later family room and was variable when considering size, finish, location, and relationship to other rooms. In the end, some of the manifestations had more influence on the evolution of space in typical houses, and as an early type of family room, the expanded living-kitchen, or "kitchen–family room," was one of the two more consequential design arcs for the eventual development of the now-legendary family room.

California and Texas, and more broadly the West, were the areas most associated with casual living, as well as one-story houses without basements. The trend for kitchen–family rooms was very strong in the regions' cities. *Sunset* reported on the phenomenon in 1956, explaining that in family rooms from Seattle to San Diego space for activities as varied as children's play and crafts, household mending and ironing, and the pouring of drinks "was [n]ever too far from the kitchen range and a pot of coffee, or from the refrigerator and ingredients for an after-school snack."[35] The plans and photographs accompanying the article all depicted spaces where the lounge and casual dining areas were contiguous within the bounds of the kitchen or in an adjacent area fully open to or only lightly screened from the kitchen.

The examples with separate spaces can be considered part of the move toward the later and more familiar family room, but these spaces were smaller, and the working, dining, and lounging areas had more physical and functional overlap than what came later. They also occupied less space within the house than the increasingly quiet and formal living and dining room, despite a high level of use. The design and construction of the "Companion House for Family Living," sponsored by the *Woman's Home Companion* in 1955, anchored the house with a kitchen–family room at its center (fig. 35).[36] While recognizing this room's growing importance and desirability, the total amount of square footage allotted to the kitchen–family room was considerably less than the nearby living and dining rooms combined.

Ever with an eye on the pace and direction of consumer desire, famed Levitt and Sons moved toward the incorporation of kitchen–family rooms into all its production models in Levittown, New Jersey. One of the company's cost-saving strategies was constructing houses on concrete pads. This decision forced Levitt and Sons to consider casual living in ways that were distinct from usual trends

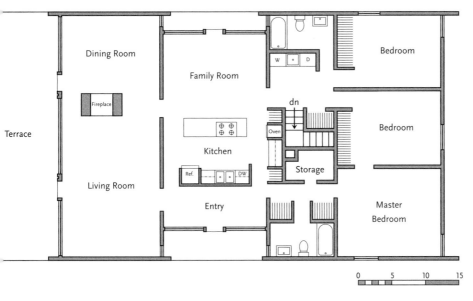

Dining Room

Family Room

Bedroom

Fireplace

dn

Terrace

Oven

Kitchen

Bedroom

Ref.

DW

Living Room

Storage

Entry

Master
Bedroom

0   5   10   15

FIGURE 35. The Companion House for Family Living included a kitchen–family room at the center of the plan. 1955. (Drawing by Paul Davidson, after a plan by architect George Nemeny; original in *Woman's Home Companion*, September 1955, 67)

in the Northeast and Mid-Atlantic. In the 1950s, the region accommodated casual living in basement recreation rooms or lower-level recreation rooms in split-levels, a form that Levitt and Sons did not embrace. The company began experimenting with kitchen–family room spaces in the early to mid-1950s with versions of the top-of-the-line Country Clubber model at Levittown, Pennsylvania, but it was at Levitt and Sons' third mega-development, in New Jersey, that the company began to codify its approach to the space.

The two-story, the largest of the three models created for the 1958 launch of Levittown, New Jersey, offered buyers a kitchen–family room.[37] The space, smaller in total square footage than the living room, was positioned at the back of the house and accessed via louvered doors in the dining room. Not only did the kitchen–family room have to accommodate casual living and dining and domestic work, but it also provided the only access to the powder room, the laundry room, the garage, and the door to the backyard. In time, the company was able to introduce some sort of kitchen–family room in most of its models.

The kitchen–family rooms found in Levitt and Sons houses of the late 1950s are very much in line with the strategy to serve casual living through an expansion of the kitchen. This pathway was atypical for the region in which this company was operating, but it was very common in houses available nationwide that were constructed without basements or lower levels. Still, the tucked-away location of the Levitt and Sons kitchen–family rooms and their ability to be closed off entirely by doors offer evidence of the piecemeal way casual living evolved in postwar suburbia and how it affected house design. Domestic work was much more welcome in spaces for casual living in the 1950s than it would be in the 1960s. By isolating the kitchen–family room, Levitt and Sons maintained a traditional division of domestic space, while simultaneously acknowledging the growing importance of casual living to the American family and the prospective home buyer.

Levitt and Sons' treatment of the kitchen–family room in its houses also speaks to regional architectural trends and expectations. The Northeast, the Mid-Atlantic, and parts of the Midwest were more inclined to retain conventional relationships between living and dining rooms or areas and the kitchen, which, as everywhere, increasingly included space for a table. Facilities for casual lounging in these regions tended to be found in a dedicated room, made possible because they never fully rejected multistory living and more quickly reembraced it as the decade passed. A room for casual living might sometimes be found in a first-floor den or the study of a two-story house, but more often it appeared as a basement recreation room or as a lower-level recreation room in a trio of new multistory house forms.

THE RECREATION ROOM

At the same time the kitchen was undergoing its own transformation, a stand-alone room as a location for casual living was also gaining in popularity. George Nelson and Henry Wright, both outspoken advocates of modern design, wrote about what they called a "room without a name" in their 1945 book. The authors explained the desirability of a room of this type: "It marks the first time a room *for the whole family* has appeared in the home since the days of the farmhouse kitchen. . . . The 'big room' is *intentionally* set up to cover the family's social and recreational needs, and . . . the usual adult-versus-children distinction has been abandoned."[38] That Nelson and Wright called the space the "room without a name" underscores the newness of the idea of casual living as a character-defining feature of suburban life.

Over the course of the 1950s, a number of conceptual and naming alternatives appeared for the "room without a name," sometimes merely referred to as the "extra" room. Newspapers and periodicals interchangeably used "recreation room," "family room," "den," "study," "second living room," "game room," and "rumpus room," among others. To a certain extent, the named spaces had specific characters. A den or study most often appeared as a small room on the first floor of a house, frequently paneled and variously located near the front entrance, as an appendage to the living room or near it, but separate from the kitchen. A recreation room, game room, or rumpus room tended to be located in a basement or on a lower level.

No longer lacking a name, and perhaps suffering under too many, the extra room was a multifunctional swing-space established for casual living that varied in size and location during the architectural experimentation prevalent in the 1950s. Joining the kitchen–family room as one of the more influential solutions for accommodating casual living was the lower-level recreation room.[39] The recreation room was a place where the division between work and leisure was fluid, and this was reflected in the multifunctional nature of the recreation room. Virtually any activity could occur there, sometimes simultaneously—from children's play to domestic work to adult parties; the room could be, according to *American Builder* in 1955, "a catch-all for the entire range of family activities."[40] In 1953, *House & Home* described the second living area as a place "where children can play and eat and be under their mother's eye while she works . . . where the mother can sew or sort laundry without having to clean up everything when company comes."[41] "The 'extra' room can be anything you want to make it," according to a 1955 book on home decoration, including a home office, a party room, a place for television watching, a guest room, "Dad's workshop," or "Mother's sewing center."[42] It might even offer a place to strengthen family ties through shared domestic work.[43]

As with the living-kitchen's actual precedents in the working-class social kitchen and somewhat more fanciful precedents in the colonial keeping room or the farm kitchen, the lower-level recreation room also had actual as well as somewhat tenuous antecedents. Articles in popular periodicals suggested that a separate second living area shared affinities with the back parlor of Victorian houses, yet one did not need to look that far back in time for a workable

FIGURE 36. With cleaner heating and laundry equipment and better water-proofing, a basement could provide additional space for daily activities and social events. 1953. (Courtesy of Judi Siani O'Connell)

FIGURE 37. Beginning in the 1930s, basement recreation rooms having a higher level of finish to compensate for reduced light and ceiling heights became more and more common. 1936. (*American Builder*, February 1936, 58; courtesy of Simmons-Boardman Publishing)

prototype.[44] Basements that were not prone to dampness became ideal places for additional living space with the modernization of laundry and heating equipment.[45] In providing middle-class families "a place to let our hair down," a basement recreation room augmented the livability of a typical house as a place for play, domestic work, and informal parties (figs. 36 and 37).[46]

The room presented households not just with more space, but with space that introduced them to a different style of living. Still, located near the furnace, the laundry, and occasionally the garage, the basement recreation room remained a socially and functionally peripheral space where most living and entertaining did not occur. Nelson and Wright described its physical character in 1945 as "makeshift or [an] afterthought," an opinion echoed by the building design editor of *Better Homes & Gardens* in the same year: "Yesterday's fun rooms were usually areas partitioned in the basement as after thoughts to handle parties or wash-hangings. In them, either was often a damp affair."[47] Whatever merits it possessed, the basement recreation room was frequently finished on an as-needed basis, and its often-dank appearance and remote location were not ideal as casual living more and more colored daily life in the new suburbs.

THE RECREATION ROOM IN MULTISTORY RANCH HOUSES

Postwar Americans remained committed to the ranch house as the ideal type for modern, casual family life, yet the rising cost of land constrained the ability of builders to provide more space while still keeping new houses affordable. Ranch houses statistically accounted for well over half of all houses constructed annually through the 1960s, but the perception that they were the best or only incubators for contemporary life weakened over the course of the 1950s. Rising salaries and equity in existing houses enabled middle-class families to consider larger dwellings with more features and amenities. Favorable economic standing and expanding wish lists were kept in check by rising construction costs and the ballooning value of improved land. Builders knew that two-story houses were the most cost-effective way to increase space. Up until then having fed the obsession with ranch houses, they were also keenly aware that most preferred one-story houses and probably would not immediately accept two-story models. How, then, to design and market a house with more than one story that retained the modern appeal of a ranch house and its associated casual lifestyle?

The building industry answered this question by introducing exciting new products in the form of the split-level, the most memorable of the new multistory forms; the split-foyer; and the bi-level.[48] These three new forms were enlarged versions of the ranch house that all included some sort of recreation room, in almost all cases positioned at grade level or partially below it. The initial market success of the new multistory forms and their subsequent and rapid eclipse were dependent on the way they incorporated space for casual living without disturbing the layout of the conventional six-room ranch house.

The split-level is a visual icon of postwar America (fig. 38). While the split-level was not even included in a 1952 survey by the NAHB and *Living for Young Homemakers* magazine, by 1957 it could be declared "as typically American as baseball. . . . From its handsome exterior to its neat and smartly designed

SPLIT LEVELS ON PARADE

FIGURE 38. The split-level became a national obsession and is the iconic postwar form. 1953. (*American Builder*, October 1953, 68; courtesy of Simmons-Boardman Publishing)

interior, [this] is the house all America wants . . . for living in the American way."[49] The split-level was a splashy headliner and even briefly dominated new construction in a handful of markets. Yet the form never came close to overtaking the ranch house nationally, and many builders correctly forecast that consumer excitement with split-levels was "just a step toward [a] return to the two story plan."[50] In the early 1960s, split-levels quietly disappeared from new annual model lines, not coincidentally at the same time that the revival of two-story houses was getting under way. Famed merchant-builder William Levitt, who largely ignored split-levels, provided a blunt eulogy for them in 1963: "The split level is an abomination. . . . No one has come up with a better design than the two-story."[51]

Cities in California and elsewhere in the Sunbelt are awash with ranch houses and held as the great incubators of postwar domestic design. Yet the suburbs of Mid-Atlantic cities such as New York, Philadelphia, and even conservative Washington, DC, and Chicago and Detroit in the Midwest set the pace when considering multistory housing in the decades following World War II. The split-level form had debuted more than a generation earlier and had been constructed in various places prior to and immediately following World

War II. These predecessors had a cottagelike appearance, distinct from the postwar versions that emerged in ranch-obsessed postwar America. Described, respectively, as "uniquely designed" and "different, unusual, spectacular," a "5 room tri-level" house offered in Williamsburg Village outside Chicago in 1949 and a "3 Level French Provincial" model available in Rolling Hills north of Pittsburgh in 1948 emphasized verticality more than horizontality, promoted traditional curb appeal, and contained an average amount of space for new houses of the period.[52]

Builders transformed the snug tri-level into the more expansive split-level at a time when most Americans desired to live in a one-story ranch house. In 1954, *House & Home* acknowledged some of the postwar split-level forerunners and set them apart from their later 1950s cousins: "The split [level] is not new. It is the 'trilevel,' built in the Midwest for years. Its eastern revival began in New Jersey several years ago, but when Long Island builders picked it up in 1952 they gave it some new twists and pushed it hard."[53] Unlike their predecessors, the split-levels of the 1950s retained the horizontal emphasis of the ranch house even while unselfconsciously celebrating the presence of three or more levels. Indeed, the offset levels made any version of the form appear modern. A split-level constructed in 1960 in the Pictwood subdivision in Glenshaw featured traditional architectural details: brick veneer on the lower levels, a "colonial garrison" overhang on the upper level, gable roofs, a front porch with arched openings, and window shutters. The owner still described his house as "contemporary."[54] The marketing of the split-level centered on its novelty and celebrated its potential for a high degree of livability for households wanting more space and a dedicated room for casual living.

The split-level featured nearly all of the enhancements families wanted within a footprint that took up no more area of an increasingly expensive lot than the ranch house. Builders typically attained this outcome essentially by "splitting" the ranch house down the middle, having a private zone raised a half story up from the public zone and a third, functionally flexible level tucked under the private zone a half story down (fig. 39).[55] An equivalent one-story house necessitated a considerably larger footprint. *House & Home* championed the split-level's many laudable attributes in order to counter the well-established preference for one-story houses:

Revolt against the ranch? The surprising willingness of housewives to climb stairs is clearly a reversal of a national trend. After the war anything but a one-story house was a dead pigeon in a good many towns. . . . Buyers like the split-level because it is a change. It is higher, so it looks bigger than a one-story house. In fact, it has three floors—all clearly in sight so neighbors can count them and be impressed. For many housewives the split-level is obviously a return to their idea of what a house should be: a kitchen, dining and living room on one floor with bedrooms separate from the living quarters and upstairs where no one can peek in the windows.[56]

More than any other element, the bonus level of mostly at-grade or partially below-grade finished space was the split-level's strongest draw. It usually contained a garage, a utility room, and the much sought-after recreation room. The revamped room lessened or eliminated such discomforts found in a basement recreation room as "dampness, cold floors or dim lighting."[57] Builders were "taking the 'wreck' out of 'rec' room" with durable and attractive finish materials in a room "geared to serve many purposes."[58] More attractive spaces meant a broadened spectrum of possibilities for the all-purpose lower-level recreation room, including "TV, study, guest bedroom, sewing room, workshop, children's play area" (fig. 40).[59]

Rooms for casual living in the split-level went beyond the lower-level recreation room, as more and more the middle level included a living-kitchen. Together, the lower-level recreation room and the living-kitchen gave households

FIGURE 39. The most common split-level plan had three living levels. (Drawing by Paul Davidson, after a plan in *House & Home*, December 1952, 119)

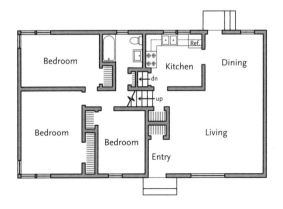

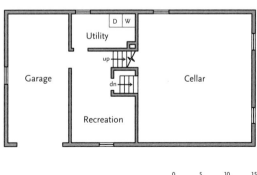

FIGURE 40. A well-finished lower-level recreation room was a center of casual living. Ca. 1960. (Ryan Homes Collection; courtesy of Carnegie Mellon University Architecture Archives)

even more control over how and where casual living would be pursued in the house. Their relative proximity also meant that the two spaces could, to a certain extent, also work in concert with each other. The stairs to the lower level and its recreation room usually descended from the kitchen or just beyond, in an entrance area, a physical link between the casual living spaces that would attain even greater importance in the later development of the zoned house.

The desirability of split-levels as a new domestic form, as a viable product, with a significantly increased amount of livability over most ranch houses, enticed builders to consider them despite the fact their design and construction posed numerous difficulties. *House & Home* noted in 1954 that construction of a split-level required "two separate operations . . . you frame half as a two-story house, half as a ranch."[60] This seemingly simple explanation obscured a reality where the two halves were part of a single house design. The connection between them needed to make spatial and aesthetic sense, and careless design might result in "two entirely separate houses 'locked . . . in mortal combat.'"[61]

Design and construction literature was of the unanimous opinion that split-levels were best constructed on undulating or hilly terrain, while also acknowledging that the potential profit of split-levels for builders was high regardless of the topography.[62] One Long Island builder astutely remarked as early as 1952: "If, as many architects say, the split-level does not make sense on level ground, the builders can always retort: they may not make sense, but they make us money."[63] Bruce Blietz, a major Chicago-area builder, justified the massive amount of grading necessary to construct split-levels on flat land in 1956: "Our aim in this project was to design a house that would offer the maximum in livability and the greatest amount of product appeal without resorting to gimmicks."[64] It could be argued that Blietz's interest in split-levels in a metropolitan area defined mostly by flat ground might itself be categorized as a "gimmick," but his commitment also demonstrated the degree to which the split-level held builder and consumer interest in the 1950s.

The split-level was the opening salvo against the hegemony of the ranch house as the most appropriate form for pursuing a casual lifestyle. It was soon joined by two other multistory forms—the split-foyer and the bi-level, both sometimes referred to as a "raised ranch." In 1961, the NAHB described the raised ranch in a way that could be applied to either the split-foyer or the bi-level: "The raised ranch is simply a ranch type in which the basement has been lifted a few feet above ground and transformed into a finished living area."[65] Cautiously optimistic, the article did question the form's long-term viability, noting: "Some people object to stairs in a ranch house."[66] Split-foyers and bi-levels were less expensive to build than the complicated split-level and required less excavation and foundation wall than most ranch houses with full basements. Like the split-level, both the split-foyer and the bi-level accommodated, and concentrated, casual living in a lower-level recreation room. Despite some similarities, though, they did not architecturally evolve from the split-level, but rather were distinct, multistory variations of the ranch house (fig. 41).

The building industry identified the split-foyer, or, sometimes, split-entry, as the lowest-cost way of enlarging the ranch house while keeping it more or less intact. A pair of builder-writers for *House & Home* effused in 1961: "The split-entry has a head start on becoming to the market of the 60s what the split-level was to the market of the 50s."[67] The upper level of the split-foyer was in most cases a self-contained, six-room ranch house with living and dining areas, a kitchen, and three bedrooms (fig. 42). The lower level was frequently finished with a garage, utility room, and recreation room.

The Chicago-area builder Joshua Muss explained the competitive edge of what he called the "mid-level ranch" over ranch and split-level forms in 1961: "Before the advent of this type of design . . . homeseekers had to chose [*sic*] between the

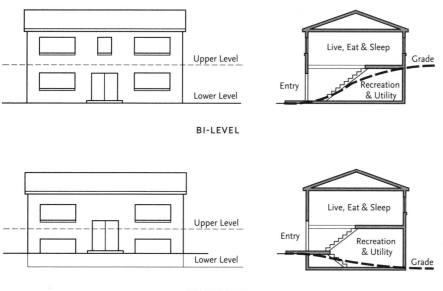

BI-LEVEL

SPLIT-FOYER

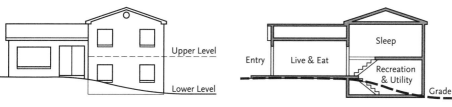

SPLIT-LEVEL

advantages of one-floor ranch living and the more spacious split-level."[68] The split-foyer model offered at his Winston Park Northwest development provided an upper level "complete in itself as a single floor living unit," as well as "a versatile lower level." The "versatile lower level" could be finished a number of ways—all with some sort of recreation room—or it could be left unfinished at the time of construction, providing an even lower-cost alternative to buyers desiring more space on a limited budget. The concentrated visual massing of the split-foyer could also be marketed more directly than the split-level as "an impressive new design that heralds the return of the classic 2 story home!"[69]

FIGURE 42. The split-foyer gained its name from an entry area located midway between the six-room ranch house on the upper level and a lower level with a recreation room. 1961. (Drawing by Paul Davidson, after a plan in the *NAHB Journal of Homebuilding*, February 1961, 63)

The split-foyer's name originated in the inventive entrance area that in all but the most expansive versions was merely a stair landing containing the front door located midway between the upper and lower levels. Ever with an eye on economy in square footage, most builders designed split-foyers with an entry landing that was only as wide as the two adjacent flights of stairs and deep enough to open the front door without tripping up or down the stairs. Not everyone was enthralled with the namesake element of the form: "Split-entry houses take their name from the front entrance which opens directly on a platform (often overbilled as a 'foyer')."[70]

The easily framed stairs and "platform" were riddled with potential design pitfalls. "The entrance is more critical in a split-entry than in any other house," explained *House & Home*. "If badly handled, it seems cramped and forbidding, rather than attractive and inviting. . . . [On the exterior] the very nature of the 'split entry' puts the front door in the wrong place, and it is difficult to make it look right."[71] Regardless, a well-designed split-foyer was thought to be attractive and functional. *Better Homes & Gardens* praised a featured model in 1963: "What makes this split-entry so good . . . [is] it gives you a big, dramatic entry that leads you easily upstairs or down."[72] The split-foyer did not just help in the reintroduction of multistory living; it became a long-lived form in many regions because of its spaciousness and cost-effectiveness.

The split-foyer was an ideal product for builders in the 1950s and early 1960s, but over time it fell short as a solution for how to accommodate casual living. While the entry or foyer was usually situated exactly midway between the levels, design features naturally drew a person upward. The ceiling in the entry or foyer was almost always at the same height as the upper-level rooms, and perceptive builders eliminated the potentially shaftlike quality of the entry by encircling it and the stairs with an open balustrade, half wall, or planter, which facilitated a visual connection with the living room (see fig. 6) In contrast, the stair down usually seemed constricted and dark. The unequal importance of the two levels was sometimes even more overtly expressed in a design. In 1958, Leon Weiner, a builder in Wilmington, Delaware, began early marketing of a split-foyer, describing it as "the cheapest way you can get a lot more living space for a little more money." In his models, the "recreation room is [a] huge expanse with plenty of light from windows at grade"; however, it was eight steps down from the landing, while the living room was just four steps up.[73]

The midlevel entrance of the split-foyer merely made the front door convenient to both levels, but the switchback form of the stair actually lessened connectivity between them. The split-foyer's lower-level recreation room was better lighted and more inviting than the basement recreation room. Still, the physical isolation of the former meant it functioned more like the latter than the lower-level recreation room of the split-level. As time passed, the location of a room for casual living so removed from the rest of the house became problematic, especially as the concept continued to evolve. In the mid-1950s, Charles and Helen Lodge purchased a split-foyer model outside Pittsburgh. One of its principal attractions was the lower-level recreation room, but in the ten years they lived in the house, they did not use it as much as imagined, in part because of its out-of-the-way location.[74]

The aesthetic and functional limitations of the idiosyncratic entry/stair landing of the split-foyer were somewhat reduced in another form of multistory ranch house, the bi-level. The bi-level was never as widespread as the split-foyer, in part because it lacked an identifiable "look." From the street, bi-levels appeared to be one- or two-story models, and they were marketed as a bridge between the two (fig. 43). A sales brochure from 1960 for Sleepy Hollow Woods outside Washington, DC, highlighted the hybrid character of the Wakefield model: "a colonial bi-level that gives you 2-story space and privacy plus the convenience of a rambler," the moniker used for the ranch house in the Washington area.[75] Most economical and prevalent in areas with a rolling or hilly landscape, the bi-level was structurally a ranch house built into sloping ground, with one of the long, lower-level walls entirely above grade and the other built into the hillside as a standard foundation wall. For lots sloping uphill, the two-story façade became one story at the rear; for lots sloping downhill, the one-story façade dropped to two stories at the rear. Builders could even capitalize on having uphill and downhill versions of the same house, as highlighted in a 1965 article: "Except for variations in trim and a minor change in plan, [the two options are] exactly the same two-level model . . . retaining the economy of repeating one basic model" (fig. 44).[76]

The upper level of both the uphill and the downhill types was usually a self-contained ranch house, with a garage, utility room, and recreation room on the lower level. With a fully above-grade wall at the front or back and partially

FIGURE 43. An uphill bi-level reconditioned prospective buyers to view a house with two stories as aesthetically appealing. Late 1950s. (Photograph by the author)

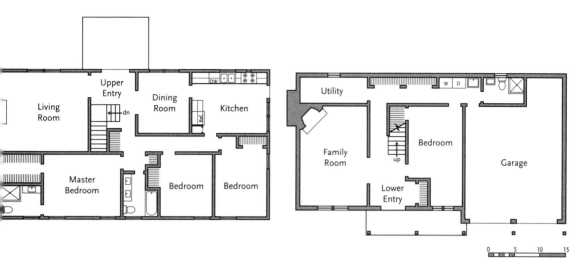

above-grade ones at the sides, the recreation room might contain one or more full-size windows and be as well lighted as the other principal rooms. In downhill versions, the recreation room might also contain doors out to a terrace or patio.

The treatment of the stair in the bi-level also created a clear and inviting connection between the levels. The front door of the uphill variation opened into a spacious entry giving access to the lower-level rooms, with a central stair rising to the level above. The downhill variation did not enclose the stair and shut it off with a door, as with the basement of a ranch house, but opened it to the entry or living room with a balustrade or half wall, encouraging movement up and down.

In 1961, Mr. and Mrs. Wayne Steinbeck had a new house built for them in the Lyndhurst Estates subdivision in Glenshaw. The contemporary bi-level house featured a living room, dining area, and kitchen, all with sloped ceilings, and four bedrooms and two bathrooms on the first floor. The house dropped to a full two stories at the rear. A two-car garage occupied one half of the lower level, and the other side was divided into a laundry/utility room and a recreation room ("gameroom" on the floor plan) that was fully finished with a fireplace and sliding glass doors out to a rear terrace.[77] A stair descended from the entry directly into the recreation room and, surrounded only by a decorative iron balustrade, was entirely open to the living room. The improved quality of space in

FIGURE 44. The downhill version of this bi-level might omit the entry in exchange for a larger family room; in the uphill version the upper entry provided access to the rear patio. (Drawing by Paul Davidson, after a plan in *House & Home*, March 1965, 107)

the lower-level recreation room of the Steinbeck bi-level and stronger visual and functional links between the room and the rest of the house demonstrated a desire to have the casual living space better incorporated into the house and the day-to-day lives of the household.

The lower-level recreation room was essential to the appeal of the split-level, split-foyer, and bi-level. The room's character and its relationship with the rest of the house varied from type to type, but in all these forms it was a self-contained space for casual living. Generally on the same level as the laundry, the lower-level recreation room functioned in a variety of ways that often included domestic tasks and unstructured play. The appearance and finish of such a room improved on its predecessor, the basement recreation room, but when compared with the concurrent expansion of the living-kitchen and the development of the kitchen–family room, its out-of-the-way location became unappealing, and the solution was only temporary. Casual living became an indivisible part of postwar suburban life, and its concentration in a room isolated from the rest of the house became less ideal as middle-class families embraced a still home-based but more complicated lifestyle that could not be as easily pursued with existing forms.

OUTDOOR LIVING

Few discussions of casual living by the building industry and, more particularly, the shelter press lacked at least a reference to outdoor living, and many made it a central feature. Scenes of backyard barbeques and block parties, patios and terraces, aluminum lawn furniture and grills, and games of croquet, badminton, and the ever risky lawn darts run rampant in the collective memory of suburban life (fig. 45). By necessity and, for many, enjoyment, Americans took up gardening and approached lawn care with an unprecedented fervor. At a time when a minority of houses featured year-round air-conditioning, warm and humid summer months meant that outdoor living was, if not essential, often preferable.

Despite these conditions, the inclusion of outdoor living facilities as a finished element of a new house at the time of purchase was by no means standard, even in regions with warmer climates. The ability of outdoor living areas to enhance livability for a household and favorably affect the marketability and salability of a house was evident enough, but they lay literally and figuratively outside the fundamental calculus of basic house design. While the FHA acknowledged the aesthetic and functional appeal of porches, terraces, and patios for residential projects, and encouraged the placement of a house on a lot in a manner that could later accommodate outdoor living, it did not explicitly require such features for insuring residential projects. Without this strong impetus, builders approached outdoor living facilities

FIGURE 45. Outdoor living was an integral part of casual living in the 1950s and 1960s. (Courtesy of Judi Siani O'Connell)

for new houses in two ways. They could be eliminated to reduce the cost of a new house, or they could be a comparatively inexpensive way to set a model apart as a strategy for increasing sales.

It is difficult to draw satisfying conclusions about how many houses included an outdoor living area at the time of completion. The trade and shelter press suggest both that the feature was important to consumers and that it should be addressed by builders, but surveys about newly constructed houses only rarely itemized its presence or absence. The industry journals *American Builder* and *House & Home* are, in general, an excellent resource for understanding changes to plans and interior spaces, but this is less the case outside a house's actual walls. Published plans sometimes depicted patios, terraces, and balconies but often omitted them even for models where accompanying text suggest they were standard. Photographs of a featured builder's new models often showed display houses used for marketing and sales at a subdivision or ones constructed for a "Parade of Homes" or another type of housing festival (fig. 46). As baseline marketing tools, these types of houses usually incorporated all of the optional amenities, rooms, and features available (for a price) to upgrade a builder's standard models, whether a large-scale merchant builder or a small-scale custom builder. In a 1959 article about indoor-outdoor living, *House & Home* reported

that nationwide builders "are enthusiastic about indoor-outdoor living because it is one of the easiest and cheapest ways to offer a better and more salable house."[78] The article went on to note that "a well planned and well proportioned outdoor area can: make your rooms seem larger . . . make your rooms more pleasant, by offering an orderly, well landscaped private view . . . [and] add a lot of extra living space to your house."

Prescriptive literature conditioned Americans to desire an outdoor living area, but this conditioning did not result in a strong correlating expectation that it would be an integral part of a new house. Popular periodicals taught prospective buyers to believe that a private terrace or back garden shielded by the house would be, as reported in the *Los Angeles Times Home Magazine* in 1952, "a bulwark against the noise and confusion of the busy street," an ideal "rendezvous for your friends," and "an irresistible attraction for your children and their companions."[79] The development of a landscaped garden was a way to establish a degree of originality within an often-homogenous suburban landscape, but in an intensely private manner that underscored personal autonomy in a way that was believed to strengthen democracy.[80] With such ideas widely promoted, outdoor living became a feature of casual living as it became ingrained in the suburbs during the 1950s.

Prospective home buyers were understandably more concerned with whether a house offered a living-kitchen, recreation room, or additional bedroom or bathroom than a patio or terrace. A consumer survey conducted at a "Parade of Homes" held in September 1954 in Wichita, Kansas, asked respondents to rate eight features on a level of importance from 1 to 10. An "outdoor living area" scored only 5.1, second to the bottom after such features as more than one bathroom, year-round air-conditioning, general location, a two-car garage, an entrance hall, and a separate dining room; only a wood-burning fireplace had a lower score.[81] In a survey of homeowners sponsored by the *Pittsburgh Press* in 1956, only one-third of respondents said they "would like a porch."[82] At the end of the decade, a chart of eleven "best-seller features" that were thought be "a significant help in selling new houses today," in twenty-five cities, appeared in *House & Home.* "Private outdoor areas" made the list but lagged in popularity behind most of the other rooms, features, and plan characteristics.[83]

Print newspaper advertisements for new subdivisions and building businesses indicate the same level of noncommitment to outdoor living space as part of standard new house construction. If buyers had possessed a strong preference for such an amenity at the time of purchase, then it would have been heavily marketed by builders in their literature, and this was not the case. Advertisements often included laundry lists of features found in new houses that touted things ranging from location, to room number and type, to building and finish materials and name-brand appliances. When they mentioned elements beyond a house's walls, more often than not they referred to the qualities of the neighborhood. A 1954 *Chicago Tribune* advertisement for "luxury, 3-bedroom, tri-level homes" in Pottawatomie Hills is representative of this type of print marketing. Such details as "weather stripping," "full insulation," and the dimensions of the living room and master bedroom establish the level of detail covered in the ad. A house in "beautiful, park-like" Pottawatomie Hills was described as situated "in a setting of country club charm, with that look of permanence" created by "mature shade trees—rolling terrain—[and] winding landscaped roads."[84] Any hint of the outdoor living potential of the house was not talked about. The builder did not think it mattered as much to buyers as construction details and the overall qualities and attributes of the location.

As was the case earlier with the minimum house, a simple rule applied: the more expensive the house, the greater the likelihood that outdoor living space would be included in the purchase price. In 1955, new houses for sale in Maplewood Estates, located in Washington, DC's, affluent suburb of Bethesda, Maryland, were priced between $25,250 and $27,000, considerably above the regional median of $14,400 for that year.[85] All three models unsurprisingly offered "inviting outdoor terraces that bring home activities into the sun." These are in contrast with the houses built two years later by L. R. Broyhill, a prolific builder in the Virginia suburbs of Washington in the then less established area of McLean. Broyhill's houses, priced between $20,450 and $23,600, seem to have provided nothing more than a stoop outside the kitchen door, which was the only access to the backyard.[86]

Even accepting a general correspondence between purchase price and the inclusion of outdoor living, there were still significant exceptions. A 1957 ad for a spacious, custom-built ranch house in the Chicago suburbs called attention to its number of rooms, its amenities, the types of appliances, and its convenient location. As for the lot and the surrounding landscape, the ad mentions only the "1/2 acre estate site set in the rolling beauty of this suburban Chicago countryside" and the fact that the road and driveway were paved. The accompanying plan shows only what appears to be a concrete stoop positioned at the rear door, located in a small vestibule placed between the kitchen, the den, and the stairs down to the basement. The apparent lack of outdoor space, or even an inviting connection to the backyard, is particularly surprising given that the house cost "only $35,400," more than double the median price for new houses in the region in 1956.[87] Similarly, the most expensive model being built by Ryan Homes in 1960 in the Pittsburgh area, priced at $39,900 to $42,900, "depending on lot size and location," does not appear to have included outdoor living space as part of the standard model.[88]

Builders focusing on the upper tier of middle-class housing understood that most of their prospective buyers expected some type of outdoor living space. Those building for the much larger swathe of middle-income families followed no set pattern. Some builders omitted the feature altogether, while suggesting they designed their houses with outdoor living in mind even if it was only a sliding glass door opening onto nothing but dirt in the backyard. Other builders offered outdoor living space as a buyable option above the standard purchase price. *House & Home* observed in 1955: "Some builders offer the patio as an optional extra, which buyers usually take advantage of. . . . A flagstone terrace or a concrete slab need not cost much, [and] can give a house a distinct advantage over one not having either."[89]

Buyers not offered the option of outdoor space or wanting to save money could opt to build it themselves. A patio or terrace was a perfect "do it yourself" project. The culture of DIY was as much a part of suburban life as casual living, and home-based DIY projects, frequently involving various family members, friends, and neighbors, could very well be considered part of the casual living ethos. The strong postwar appeal of DIY resulted from both its viability as a short- and long-term strategy for saving money and its comfortable relationship with the 1950s emphasis on the house and home.[90] Newspapers and periodicals were jammed with ideas about how to create outdoor living space. The *Washington Post* counseled its readers in 1952 to "plan for outdoor living before the heat wave" by building or upgrading a porch or terrace.[91] Similarly, Mary Davis Gillies, the architectural editor of *McCall's,* and Douglas Baylis, a prominent California landscape architect, proposed in 1955: "The new tradition of landscaping puts the emphasis on outdoor living—not just gardening. . . . Ambitious homeowners can do much of the work themselves."[92] Gillies and Baylis observed that for a family living in a "smallish house," outdoor living space could "relieve pressure on the house and provide extra room for playing, eating and entertaining, as well as for gardening."[93]

In the 1950s, outdoor living became an integral component of the casual living ideal, but it did not become a strong component of consumer desire for new housing. Prospective home buyers' wish lists at the time were crowded with many other needed and wanted rooms and features. Outdoor living space remained attractive, but not essential at the time of purchase. Cost certainly had an impact on this outcome, but so too did the relative ease of adding a patio or terrace as compared to, say, another bathroom. As a DIY project, the creation of outdoor living space was undoubtedly among the first and most popular ones for new suburban home buyers who were learning to live casually, indoors and out, in midcentury America.

CONCLUSION

Very quickly in the middle of the twentieth century, casual living became the dominant way of life in the postwar suburbs, and a great majority of houses constructed immediately after the war began to seem outmoded for the ideal pursuit of family life. This realization led to a notably creative and inventive period of architecture in America. Builders enlarged and reengineered existing room types and house forms and designed entirely new models, with casual living in mind. Despite their close association with modern life, a great majority of the popular six-room ranch houses ironically could not adequately support casual living because of their limited building envelope. In response, builders were compelled to find a way to make a multistory model with dedicated space for casual living as exciting and reflective of modern life as the ranch house for consumers. The initial results were three architectural hybrids—the split-level, the split-foyer, and the bi-level—all distinct multistory renditions of the esteemed ranch house. These at times outlandish-looking new forms might well have "out ranched" the ranch house in the long run; however, ideas about how best to accommodate contemporary casual living in new suburban houses continued to evolve.

Households initially welcomed any type of space intended for the purposes of casual living, but its frequent location in a room set apart from the rest of the house became less ideal as middle-class families continued to pursue a home-based lifestyle, but one that was more complicated and not ideally supported by existing plans and forms. In the 1960s, maturing families found they wanted an option to be together or apart. Domestic work and messy activities, previously welcome in the catchall bonus space for casual living, were, with the exception of cooking, moved elsewhere. All types of casual living space grew in size, were moved to more prominent locations within the house, contained levels of finish similar to the other public spaces, and contributed to the creation of the zoned house. Two distinct and equal zones for daytime living—one active and casual and one quiet and formal—became the hallmark of a well-designed house in the 1960s in the same way that space for casual living did in the 1950s. The ultimate establishment of a zone for casual living demonstrates the degree to which it revolutionized the suburban house and home in the middle of the twentieth century.

The Zoned House

HOUSE-STARVED CONSUMERS purchasing minimum houses immediately after the war could have hardly imagined the refined domestic environments that would be available to them less than two decades later. New models in the 1950s principally exhibited a turn away from the minimum with the addition of more square footage and new kinds of spaces for casual living. The decade that followed saw the emergence of even larger houses that, while still efficient in their space planning (one positive legacy of the minimum house), were generously zoned for a range of activities and different styles of living within the same dwelling.[1] Zoning is a planning concept that clusters together rooms with similar functions and isolates them from other zones through buffers and circulation systems. This organization allows potentially disruptive activities to occur simultaneously. Zoning was not a new idea in residential design, but it attained a level of importance and visibility in postwar America not seen since the middle class abandoned complex, sometimes unwieldy dwellings earlier in the century.

As in the past, zoning at the end of the postwar period balanced the straightforward needs of day-to-day living with more abstract notions of the house as a representation and extension of its owner. Be that as it may, the contexts underlying its return were distinct to the mid-twentieth century. The establishment of two daytime use zones—one quiet and formal and one active and casual—enshrined a more polished version of casual living as a central component of domestic life, while acknowledging that rooms with a more staid presence and purpose were also attractive to suburban families. These daytime use zones and houses having more bedrooms also highlight a cultural trend in which "apartness" began to be appreciated as much as togetherness.

Every form of house at all pricing levels benefited from innovations in domestic planning—even the basic six-room ranch house could be enhanced with better circulation and such things as a master bathroom. Yet the new spatial ideal favored still-larger houses with larger price tags that remained within reach of many families who possessed steady-to-rising wages and equity in existing houses and enjoyed favorable federal tax incentives. Builders enticed prospective buyers with new and reconceived models, but they also faced consumers knowing far more about the housing industry and its products than earlier in the period. Industry leaders noted that "second-, third- and fourth-time buyers know what good livability involves" and cautioned that they would search until they found "bigger . . . better planned . . . better designed . . . [and] better equipped" houses.[2] As the decade came to a close, spiking values were sharpest among the more expensive houses intended for middle-class buyers. A writer for *U.S. News & World Report* observed in 1969: "The wildest scramble seems to be in higher-priced homes, with smaller houses in the $18,000-to-$23,000 category not under the same kind of buying and selling pressures."[3] The country's stagnating economic picture notwithstanding, many prospective U.S. buyers had the means and the drive to purchase bigger houses, and a significant number of builders kept their energies focused on this group.

Cost inflation for new houses occurred in all areas related to design and construction, but land values were the single most consequential factor in the 1960s. Building industry experts were already calling attention to this issue at the end of the 1950s: "Although raw acreage prices have always climbed faster than any other building material, last year's hikes were the worst ever. And they promise to continue growing."[4] Land costs did continue to grow, in a way that was unprecedented for the period; in the ten years between 1954 and 1964 the cost of land rose from roughly 12.5 percent of the sales price of a new house to between 20 and 30 percent.[5]

This surge in land costs did not diminish interest in larger houses. Prospective buyers speedily considered new two-story designs in part because they had been conditioned to consider the possibilities of living on more than one level through multistory ranch houses. *American Builder* proclaimed to its industry readers in 1962 that "two-story living [had made a] strong nationwide comeback," basing the renewed popularity almost solely on the correlation between increased space and the expense of land.[6] Two-story houses became most widely available in areas where land costs were highest and in regions such as the Northeast, the

Mid-Atlantic, and the upper Midwest, where interest in two-story houses had never fully waned. Acceptance of two-story models—both spatially and aesthetically—eliminated much of the rationale fueling prior interest in multistory versions of the ranch house. Split-levels, split-foyers, and bi-levels did not disappear entirely, but the feverish fascination with them came to an end.

THE VALUE OF APARTNESS AT HOME

Togetherness among family members had attained near cultlike status in the 1950s, as casual living became the dominant lifestyle in suburbia. Families whose members participated in leisure activities together or pursued individual activities side by side within new multiuse spaces were thought to forge stronger family bonds and have a more satisfying home life. The increased inclusion of living-kitchens and dedicated rooms for casual living in new houses was devised to foster togetherness; however, the potential for chaos in rooms and spaces simultaneously hosting both quiet and active recreation, as well as domestic work, is clearly evident. It was not just the annoyances and grievances related to the incompatible functions and disruption that called into question the practice of togetherness, but less tangible aspects of its purpose and its alternatives.

By the late 1950s, togetherness had begun to lose its luster for many families. Although a key component of casual living and thought by many to be a main ingredient of an ideal domestic life, togetherness could, in practice, be exhausting. Writing for the *New York Times* in 1958, Charles Frankel, a social philosopher at Columbia University, explained that it "is a friendly condition, and no one likes to make a principle of unfriendliness," yet noted that at the same time togetherness "is also a strenuous condition, and no one likes to admit he cannot keep up the pace. . . . Togetherness is becoming something of a nuisance."[7] Family members, especially siblings, did not always want to play nicely with each other, and it was difficult to read or concentrate on homework in a room with the distraction of the television or a stereo. Togetherness could also be tiring, as it required coordinated schedules, a near impossibility for most families as children grew older. A writer for the *Los Angeles Times* pragmatically observed in 1957 that "you have to take [togetherness] where you find it," but that between young children's illnesses and the pull of friends and activities outside the house as they grew older, "it's pretty difficult to achieve togetherness among all the members of a family at one time."[8]

The paramount value of togetherness for American families also began to be doubted for more complex reasons related to personal development. Joseph Prendergast, the executive director of the National Recreation Association, cautioned in 1962: "Don't overdo togetherness."[9] He rationalized that "since each family member spends his work or school day doing different things, recreation needs would vary to some extent." Psychologists also recognized the need for a more sophisticated approach to leisure-time activities. A 1961 feature on the YWCA offered: "Experts are advocating plenty of apartness in everyone's life."[10] Helen Southard, a staff psychologist of the national organization of the YWCA, believed that "togetherness has been oversold and overdone," not just for the functioning of healthy families but as a "solution for all manner of family problems, as well as juvenile delinquency."[11] She cautioned that a family has to "determine when and what kind of togetherness is needed at different times," as well as accept that individual development and activities are just as important. Personal development benefited not only individuals within families but the entire family, if for no other reason, in the opinion of Frankel, than preventing "the members of a family from boring one another silly when they get together."[12]

The desire for greater privacy within the house also fueled the trend toward apartness. Privacy had been a top concern of prospective home buyers in the first decade or so after the war, as they departed teeming urban neighborhoods and overcrowded living situations. The detached, single-family house set in the middle of its own lawn and garden increased privacy between neighboring households through such built-in design features as the varied orientation of adjacent dwellings, limited window openings on the sides of houses, the abandonment of front or side porches in favor of back patios and terraces, and the strategic use of fencing and exterior walls.[13] External privacy became a major preoccupation at the same time that internal privacy began to be sacrificed through smaller houses with fewer rooms, in a culture that placed a high value on togetherness.

Toward the end of the 1950s, a desire for greater privacy within the house began to take hold. In 1957, the Congress on Better Living, a meeting of women in Washington, DC, sponsored by *McCall's* magazine, concluded that privacy was the number-one thing lacking inside typical houses. The *Washington Post* headlined its coverage of the event with the observation that "privacy at home is a crying need" and remarked: "EVERYBODY—from baby to daddy—needs a 'corner of his own.'"[14] The conclusions drawn at this meeting were a bellwether of a consequential shift in how Americans comprehended healthy family life. Four years later, the participants at a market for home-furnishings manufacturers held annually in Los Angeles believed that a new trend had been firmly established, valuing the "preciousness of privacy" over the "tedium of togetherness." Togetherness was still thought to be helpful to maintaining family unity, but opinion also held that "each member should have the time and the place in which to meditate, in which to think, in which to relax and in which to learn the rare art of being alone."[15]

SECLUSION IN THE BEDROOMS

Providing each child of a household with his or her own bedroom, and the parents with their own master bedroom "suite," was the most obvious way to foster privacy and apartness within the house. Issued in 1964, the findings of a nationwide survey titled "Housing Design and the American Family," sponsored by the National Association of Home Builders, *House & Garden* magazine, and a spectrum of building-materials manufacturers, presented both raw and analyzed data on nearly every facet of the house and home. Based on the observations and opinions expressed by a panel of women described as "multi-time home owner[s]," living in six major, geographically diverse cities, the survey facilitators concluded that children's bedrooms were essential to the smooth running of a household because "privacy was as important for a child as for an adult."[16] Elaborating on the topic, one panelist from Cincinnati said that having "separate rooms for each child . . . would be wonderful"; another, from Los Angeles, was of the opinion "that their bedroom [is] their own, just as the master bedroom is ours."[17] Interviewed about the houses available in Hoffman Estates Village outside Chicago, representatives of the F & S Construction company noted that multiple bedrooms in its models not only provided more privacy but also taught children "early" lessons about "respect for the privacy of others" and created a "sense of responsibility and security."[18]

With three bedrooms the standard minimum for the vast majority of new houses by the mid-1950s, industry experts queried builders as early as 1960: "Are you thinking about the four-bedroom market?" They encouraged a fourth bedroom because the upgrade was relatively inexpensive and could be flexibly marketed for a variety of reasons: "You can sell four-bedroom houses to a surprisingly wide variety of buyers . . . families with three or more children . . . families who can afford a bigger house—whether they need it or not . . . families who want an extra room for quiet activities . . . [and] families who want an office at home."[19] Still, the major impetus for purchasing a house with four or more bedrooms was because of the number of children, and not necessarily so that each would have his or her own room. When one couple with eight children relocated to the Pittsburgh area in 1963, they had only a single criterion for a new house: five bedrooms.[20] Although trade literature predicted that the "larger families of the 1960s will need three, four and even five bedroom houses" and stated in 1965 that "houses are getting bigger. The minimum: two baths, and four or five bedrooms," the number of new single-family houses with four or more bedrooms hovered around 25 percent of all units constructed during the 1960s.[21]

The housing industry also focused on a larger and better-appointed master bedroom. Over the course of the 1950s and 1960s, the master bedroom, usually the largest, anticipated to be used by the owners, received more closet space and, increasingly, a small en suite bathroom.[22] The master bathroom was a relatively cost-effective way to increase the livability of a typical house. The single full bathroom found in a majority of new postwar houses was in very high demand, as it was used by both family members and their guests. The shortcomings of this arrangement, particularly for larger families, soon became evident.

When included at the outset, a second full bathroom did not add much to the cost of a house beyond additional fixtures and framing, since the main and master bathrooms usually were immediately adjacent and shared the water and sewer lines.[23] The *Pittsburgh Press* reported on the topic in 1959: "Builders and home loan agencies agree that there is good sense in investing a little more to get a great deal more. Take bathrooms. Building two, back-to-back, in a new house costs less than adding a bathroom in an older house. Tile for walls and floors can be installed by the same contractor at the same time, and the same plumbing and heating unit can be used for both facilities."[24] Interestingly, the arrangement did not usually result in two identical bathrooms; rather, the en suite bathroom serving the master bedroom was a more compact affair.

The tight dimensions of the master bathroom mainly resulted from substituting a stall shower for the bathtub-shower combination of the main bathroom (fig. 47). Its diminutive size also reflected its principal intended user: a household's male head. Although showering had become more or less standard for both sexes by the later decades of the twentieth century, many postwar women still preferred bathing over showering, an action that was historically associated with maleness, rejuvenation, and "athleticism" rather than basic hygiene or "female grooming rituals."[25] A 1955 study of new housing built around 1950 noted: "Generally speaking, women like tubs, both for themselves and for the children.

FIGURE 47. The stall shower distinguished the master bathroom from the main bathroom. (Photograph by and courtesy of Amy Niedzalkoski Brown)

Men like showers."[26] Although one 1966 popular news article on the future of bathroom design remarked that "the only sound reason for taking a bath instead of a shower is greater relaxation," another study released by the building industry around the same time found that 50 percent of women and 20 percent of men still bathed.[27]

While in transition, the midcentury habits of women indicate that they were still bathing in a significant number of households.[28] With most master bathrooms containing only a stall shower, a woman would have been expected to share the bathtub in the principal bathroom with a family's children while her husband enjoyed his own facility. A 1956 survey of homeowners in the Pittsburgh area explained: "One harried father, apparently with teen-age daughters, voted desperately for 'a quiet bathroom,'" hinting that the second full bathroom would be his alone.[29] This sentiment was echoed by *Popular Science* in 1955, when it suggested that its mostly male readers would be able to "kiss those morning traffic jams in your bathroom good-by" with a stall shower.[30]

By the 1960s, the master bathroom had become another part of the housing ideal not entirely reflected in reality. Slightly less than half of all new houses built in 1970 incorporated at least two full bathrooms, which generally indicated the presence of an en suite in the master bedroom.[31] Still, the trend was firmly set in place. In only two decades the number of houses with more than one bathroom had almost doubled, and the master bathroom began its move from a luxury item to an expectation. In addition to the en suite bathroom, the master bedroom's more generous dimensions, often allowing for an easy chair, a desk, or a television, helped recast the space as a private "suite." An additional bedroom or two and a second full bath emphasized the essential value of the private zone of the house for families desiring ways to spend time apart.

APARTNESS IN THE AGE OF CASUAL LIVING

The living and dining rooms became locations where family members, adults especially, could find quiet when they did not want full seclusion. As spaces for casual living proliferated—in kitchens, kitchen–family rooms, and recreation rooms—the living and dining rooms changed. Rooms and spaces for casual living removed many of the more boisterous daytime activities, and the living room became quieter and more sedate. *House & Garden* mentioned the transformation early on in 1955: "With the family room to take the wear and tear of traffic and knockabout daily use, the living room is now a gratifying sanctuary for leisure."[32] Spaces for casual living could be used by the entire family, but their location—in a lower-level recreation room or a lounge area open to the kitchen—meant that children were often the primary users. The recreation room allowed children's play and activities to be separated from the rest of the house, while a living-kitchen or kitchen–family room provided for their easy monitoring. With children initially thought to be the most frequent users of

FIGURE 48. The Fairmont model by Ryan Homes with the master bedroom and living room isolated on their own level. 1959. (Drawing by Paul Davidson, after a plan in *Practical Builder*, November 1959, 70)

casual living areas, builders made attempts to recast the living room as an adult retreat in addition to the master bedroom.

These adults' retreats had a conceptual affinity that translated into elements of some domestic plans. In one-story houses, the master bedroom could be positioned near the living room, on the opposite side of the house from the other bedrooms (see fig. 59). Large split-levels having more than the standard three levels presented an opportunity to dedicate one of them to adults. In 1960, Ryan Homes marketed the Fairmont model in the Pittsburgh area, a four-level split that dispensed with the conventional arrangement of rooms (fig. 48). Instead, the Fairmont grouped the entry, family room, dining room, and kitchen together on the principal floor and placed a large living room and master bedroom with an en suite bathroom one level up. The description cheerily noted aspects of the plan: "The family room on the same level as the kitchen and separate dining room is perfect for the younger set when adults are entertaining in the 20 foot third level living room."[33] This description underscores how the living room was at first reimagined as a room for adults and more directly turned the casual living space over to children and their leisure activities. The division of living spaces by age affected their broad classification, but it never fully took hold as households needed and sought a more flexible outlook on room use.

At the same time that casual living spaces permitted rethinking how the living room would be used in postwar houses, casual table space in the kitchen allowed the dining room to again function in a way that had only recently been discarded as old-fashioned and irrelevant. As kitchens grew even larger in size, they could be used for most of the day's meals, leaving dining rooms for dinner or reserved for special occasions. A survey conducted in 1960 for Kentile, a major maker of resilient flooring used in kitchens and bathrooms, found that among the roughly three thousand middle-income housewives interviewed, 81 percent of their families ate breakfast in the kitchen, and 74 percent ate lunch there. A majority (59 percent) also ate dinner in the kitchen, yet over a quarter still used the dining room regularly for dinner, signifying that more structured meals in the dining room remained appealing or had become so again.[34] Regardless of how often it was used, the dining room was no longer viewed as a nonessential component in the house. In 1958, *Good Housekeeping* issued "a warm welcome back to the most-missed, most-mannerly room in the house." The articled mused: "Your evening mealtime may very well be the only hour of the day when the whole family is gathered together without the distraction of work to be done or of mechanical entertainment. And we believe this is the most important hour of the day for teaching children the fundamentals of gracious behavior and living."[35]

The frequent emphasis on instructing children at the dining table suggests that at the same time casual living was embedded in the postwar household, families were still recognizing the value of traditional rituals. A 1960 *McCall's* article described how one economizing family "ate out" once a month "at home" to teach their four children about manners and sociability: "Long after the most memorable meal is forgotten, the pleasant ritual of the dining room will be remembered: gleaming cloth under gleaming china . . . the friendly talk . . . listening and being listened to . . . the awareness, even in the very young, that manners in the dining room may be easy but never careless. . . . Here it is that children acquire the graceful social behavior that will smooth their lives."[36] This function of dining and the dining room was also an act of togetherness, although meeting different expectations than casual living. Most entertaining and socializing still occurred in the home, and children had to be acquainted with how to behave at a "sit-down" dinner, a staple of middle-class life. The spatial and social division between casual meals in the kitchen and formal meals in the dining room also fashioned another layer of separation in the expanding postwar house.

Interest in dining rooms began increasing even in Southern California, a hotbed of casual living. Dorothy Roe, the women's editor for the Associated Press, led off a brief piece about casual living in 1958 with a summary of a successful female restaurateur's thoughts on the topic: "If American living gets any more casual, we all might as well move back to the cave."[37] The interviewee went on to make a dubious claim: "There would be fewer divorces if women would take the trouble to set a decent table." It is doubtful that many people saw a dining room as a strategy for strengthening a marriage. Nevertheless, its value to homeowners was real enough and not just something devised by journalists looking for the next trend in housing.

Three years later, the *Sunday Home Magazine* of the same newspaper asked five "housewives and mothers" to comment on new house designs, using the "best tract houses" among recently constructed dwellings in the area, which had been selected by the HBA of Los Angeles, Orange, and Ventura Counties specifically for this purpose. The two-page report published both general and specific comments along with the plans. Casual living and togetherness comprised one main area of focus. On this topic, the reporter summarized the respondents' opinions: "California's vaunted casual living can be carried too far. All members of the Home magazine panel would like to return to a more formal kind of house and living pattern. For example, they much prefer separate dining rooms" as a means of teaching children "to eat properly."[38] The Eichler house that Joan and Frank Clarkson purchased in Marin County, California, in 1961 lacked a dedicated area for dining. The house's living room was not designed as a combined formal living-dining space. The couple ultimately used the merged kitchen and "multi-purpose room" (kitchen–family room) for all types of dining, with casual meals and snacks served at the built-in table and breakfast bar, along one side of the kitchen's work area, and more structured meals at the nearby table and chairs.[39]

What had only a decade earlier been discarded by the shelter press and building industry leaders, and many prospective home buyers, as an expendable room in new houses quickly returned to a position of prominence in the ideal house. In 1960, a "study of home planning preferences" revealed that approximately 68 percent of survey respondents wanted a "separate dining room" in their next house, and about 29 percent wanted an open-plan "dining ell" off the living room.[40] With just shy of 100 percent of respondents indicating a desire for a formal, or at least defined, dining space, the feature was most assuredly important to American households. *House & Home* explained the appeal of dining rooms in new houses in 1960: "The dining room sells houses because, to most families, it is the symbol of gracious living."[41] Albert E. Riley, the president of a Chicago-area building company, echoed this idea a year later, explaining that a plan having "one room flowing into another," common to the ranch houses and split-levels of the 1950s, was no longer desirable, for both practical and symbolic reasons.[42] He interpreted the return of the "formal dining room" above all as "a symbol of the good life 30 years ago, which is what so many people yearn for." This idea of gracious living as a foil to casual living grew even stronger in the 1960s, as casual living was embedded more prominently in the house with the codification of family room design.

THE ACTIVE AND CASUAL FAMILY ROOM, THE QUIET AND FORMAL LIVING ROOM

In the 1960s, the family room and the living room became related in a more symbiotic manner than had previously been the case. The living-kitchen, the kitchen–family room, and the recreation room had lessened demands on the living room; however, the living room remained the most prominent space and one with an adult-oriented emphasis. This outlook was not viable in the long term as it oversimplified the needs of maturing families and limited the full use of the house. Distinctions between work and leisure also refined the concept of casual living, altering how the major casual living space—the family room— would be used. These conditions gave rise to two rooms for living with equal status: a quiet and formal living room and an active and casual family room.

The family room had its immediate roots in the casual living spaces increasingly found in houses built over the course of the 1950s. It came of age in the 1960s as an essential part of the domestic ideal. Cynthia Kellogg, a design columnist for the *New York Times,* straightforwardly reported in 1958: "The family room, a mid-century innovation, grows increasingly popular."[43] By 1965, a writer for the *Chicago Tribune* could more confidently state: "The family room, once considered a 'nice to have' feature in a home, now has achieved near-must status with today's new home buyers."[44] Features in newspapers and popular periodicals were matched by and informed widely held beliefs by consumers and builders. Charles and Helen Lodge recalled that during the selection and customization of a model in the mid-1960s, their builder "talked about how it [the family room] was frequently being included in new homes." The couple was already familiar with the space, as "most of our friends (with new homes) had family rooms," and also understood the limitations of a lower-level recreation room in the house they had lived in for the past decade. The Lodges sought a room that was more conveniently located and better finished, a "second" rather than a secondary room for living.[45] Their penchant for this type of space mirrored that of millions of prospective buyers across the country, as the idea of casual living was refined and attained an even more central place in the house.

The utility and character of dedicated rooms and spaces for casual living began to be questioned not long after they first became widely available in the 1950s. The delegates to the 1958 Congress on Better Women, convened by *McCall's* magazine in Washington, DC, concluded: "Family rooms have 'become too many things to too many people.'"[46] On the other side of the country, a panel of Los Angeles housewives gathered in 1961 to review building-industry plans found the variation in family room design problematic. While all the models being considered offered a family room, they ranged "from vague extensions of the living room to fully enclosed, separate areas."[47] As a result, the panelists believed that the family room had become "too nebulous to be of much value. It tended to become a catch-all without doing any one thing well."

Although the two spaces were often viewed solely as either "formal" or "informal," the living room and the family room had a relationship that went deeper than a superficial comparison of their appearance or a narrow focus on one aspect of their character. A panelist from Boston who participated in the "Housing Design and the American Family" study in 1964 offered different terms to describe her living room and family room, terms that give a near-perfect structure to how these rooms evolved in the 1960s. In discussing her family room and living room, she stated:

> I don't like the use of the words formal and informal. I would prefer to use the words quiet and active. I like an active [family] room, and that's where the TV is.

> I like a quiet room, which is our living room, and my husband and I use it all the time. . . . [It is a place where we] have a drink, a cocktail or some coffee. And I'll knit or mend and he'll read. . . . The children are [also] welcome there for quiet activity, for playing solitaire if they like or reading their books or being read aloud to for the younger ones. Sometimes I just sit there in the afternoons and look out at the changing colors of the leaves. . . . I feel it should be a restful and a welcome place.[48]

In this emerging planning trend, the living room became a comfortable place for quiet and formal activities regardless of the age of the family member. In 1960, a market research firm hired by Milton Kettler, a major Washington-area builder, released its findings from a poll of recent purchasers of Kettler houses. One of the conclusions was that "owners endorse 'gracious living' but want to be casual about it."[49] Along these lines, the *Evening Star* informed its Washington-area readers one year later "that more and more families are asking for an 'informal formal' living room, inviting to all members of the family from tots to grandparents."[50]

Surveys and interviews with the original homeowners in the Lyndhurst Estates, Pictwood, and New Glen Manor subdivisions explained the varied uses of living rooms in new houses that also had family rooms at the time of construction. All of the owners in some way indicated that their family rooms allowed the living room to be nicely furnished and remain neat at all times. They also revealed that the living room was hardly a static place. Families used them for a variety of quieter pursuits taking place in the room, such as cards, dinner parties, instrument playing, meetings, resting, reading, doing homework, writing out bills and letters, and "conversation time for family members."[51] Vera Hahn, the decorating editor for *American Home* magazine, explained that in the houses featured in a 1967 article on living room use and décor, "all evidence of every-day use and personal involvement has not been relegated to the family room" and that while they should be attractive and well kept, "living rooms need to be livable first and foremost."[52]

In 1959, a writer for *Business Week* primarily adhered to the adults-versus-children functional split for the family and living rooms yet still acknowledged that, while the living room would be "your status symbol" and was "the 20th Century version of the old-time parlor," the room "works harder for the family than the parlor did."[53] The living room never fully shed its association with adult activities, and it continued to be a "status symbol" of sorts and a location of formal entertainment. Still, the appeal of apartness and the divergent activities of all family members furthered broader use of the room.

The family room became an active and casual foil to the quiet and formal living room, for use by all family members. The family room maintained its function as a setting for children's play during the day. A convenient family room was important to Albert and Dolores Sybo in the house completed for them in 1971 because "our children were small, so they could be on the same floor with me [Dolores], but not underfoot."[54] The family room was also thought to be a place where teenagers might entertain guests in a separate location, but one that could still be monitored. A Los Angeles mother indicated in 1964 that she wanted "a place [for my daughter] to go with her company."[55]

These observations demonstrate that age divisions were still in place to a certain degree, and no one recommended that the children of a household entertain their friends in the living room. Still, the family room of the 1960s was also in common use by parents for their own active and casual pursuits. It became the preferred location for the television and often the hi-fi, the common location of the fireplace and related activities, and the place for less structured social gatherings and playing games.[56] The family room became a place associated with a certain type of domestic leisure rather than specific members of a family; it ceased being a functional catchall and instead was the place for active and casual living.

The emphasis on leisure in the family room meant that there was a marked reduction of daily domestic work activities there. This change meant that a more refined version of casual living occupied an increasingly established and prominent place in the house. The distinction between domestic work and domestic leisure had socioeconomic foundations. Consumer rejection of the minimum house by the emerging postwar middle class meant that multipurpose rooms of any type began to fall out of favor, and differentiated space became a tangible marker of middle-class membership. The division between work and leisure at home also reflected its gendered realities. Middle-class housewives, who spent most of their days at a place that was both their place of work and their place of leisure, found that the latter could not be easily achieved if both occurred in the

Then   Now

FIGURE 49. Casual
living areas in the
1960s were less
multifunctional
than in the 1950s.
1959. (Drawing by
Paul Davidson, after
a plan in *House &
Home*, January 1959,
138)

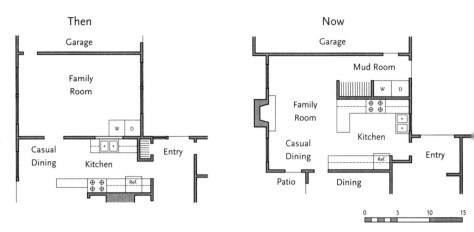

same rooms and spaces.[57] The separation of work and leisure in the midcentury house helped to facilitate the smooth running of a household.[58] The boundaries between these environments were rarely absolute and forced certain family members (housewives) to constantly grapple with the line between them, a situation further complicated by a societal inability to view domestic work as "work."[59]

Against the backdrop of these cultural currents, builders began rethinking the family room. As part of the improvements made to an existing model in 1959, Scholz Homes relocated the laundry facilities to a utility area adjacent to, but removed from, the family room (fig. 49). Their justification for this change referenced a goal to make the family room more explicitly a place for living, explaining that before this alteration, the room was "neither fish nor fowl, not wholly a living area [n]or wholly a work area."[60] This redesign stood at the leading edge of a trend that resulted in two equal rooms for living—both ideally devoid of domestic work.

There are many precedents in the history of American domestic architecture where prosperous families had two rooms loosely corresponding to the postwar living room and family room—the hall-parlor plan in colonial dwellings, the farm kitchen and the sitting room of rural homesteads, and the front and back parlors of Victorian houses. Then only recently understood by postwar Americans as obsolete for modern family life, Victorian-era houses became convenient as a marketing angle as more formal patterns of living were again being emphasized. The headline for a 1963 advertisement in the *Chicago Tribune* proclaimed: "Grandmother had 2 parlors . . . and so does your 1963 Hoffman Home!" In the ad, the builder carefully balances the favorable associations of differentiated space and status with the expectations of contemporary home life: "The finest homes in Grandmother's day had both a formal parlor and family sitting room. Today, every family can enjoy a better, 1963 version of this practical arrangement, in a new Hoffman Home."[61] In the same way a casual living area had been trumpeted in the 1950s as both a comforting return to the real and imagined domestic spaces of the past and "a new idea, a new room," so too was the presence of two equal living areas simultaneously tied to the past and present in the 1960s.[62]

One of the linchpins in the creation of two equal areas for living was the movement of the family room to a more central position in the plan and an increase in its overall size. A 1966 article in *House & Home* highlighted a decade of change in the residential building industry by featuring the most popular design by Herman H. York for each year, beginning in 1956. York was a well-known and influential architect within the building industry who "specialized in the design of merchant built houses" and by 1966 was also the "director of the NAHB's Research Foundation."[63] In general, houses designed by York were larger than average, and his inclusion of certain rooms and features were bellwethers of what would become widespread later, rather than representations of what was broadly available in any given year. In contrast to earlier models, York's top 1959 model positioned the second living area "nearer the front door and . . . now as important as the living room," indicating the correlation between a convenient location and status.[64]

The higher-profile location of the family room demanded that more thought be given to its appearance. In 1963, *American Builder* explained that the family room was not only increasing in size but also "has gained importance as a design element" in the house.[65] With domestic work functions removed, the family room could become better and more stylishly finished. As a place for active and casual living that variously hosted informal gatherings and entertainment, children's play and roughhousing, games, and television watching, the family room needed furniture and finishes that were durable but also stylishly

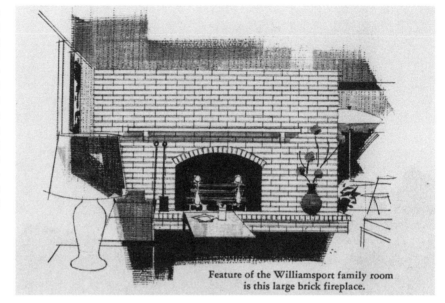

Feature of the Williamsport family room
is this large brick fireplace.

coordinated. In attaining this balance of function and fashion, whether contemporary or more traditional in expression, family rooms frequently were fitted with built-in bookshelves or cabinets; featured vaulted or beamed ceilings;
and had one or more walls sheathed in wood paneling and, more and more,
a house's only fireplace (fig. 50). These visual enhancements helped builders
maintain a marketing edge at a time when the mere presence of a second living
area, even a large and conveniently located one, was no longer enough.

DAYTIME LIVING IN TWO ZONES

The quiet and formal living room and active and casual family room helped
households negotiate the age-old tension between the house as an outward
social symbol and the practicalities of day-to-day life. As a representation of the
needs of the midcentury suburban family, these rooms also anchored the organization of the house's public spaces into two well-defined zones for daytime
living. Articulated and discernible zones for active and casual and quiet and formal living became the widespread ideal for a high degree of livability in houses

during the 1960s and were the most consequential and far-reaching rethinking of domestic planning since before World War II.

Well into the 1950s, most of the houses built in the United States during the twentieth century were arranged in two principal zones, a public one used mainly in the daytime—living room, dining room, and kitchen—and one used mainly in the nighttime or for private needs—bedrooms and bathroom(s) (fig. 51). Some commentators and critics divided the daytime zone into an area for living and an area for domestic work, but the latter was rarely a zone so much as a single room, the kitchen, or two frequently disjointed work areas, the kitchen and the laundry or utility room.[66] In 1956, *House & Home* disdainfully concluded that such simple approaches to zoning were characteristic of "yesterday's house" and no longer ideal.[67] The Chicago builder Bruce S. Blietz echoed this sentiment in a 1961 interview by linking the desire for privacy with greater interest in better domestic zoning; based on Blietz's answers, the interviewer predicted that "the future home will see more of this stratification."[68]

Daytime / Public

Nighttime / Private

FIGURE 51. Conventional divisions of daytime and nighttime space in houses before the mid-twentieth century. (Drawing by Paul Davidson)

FIGURE 52. Two zones for daytime living became the domestic ideal in the 1960s. (Drawing by Paul Davidson)

The refinements that remade the family room and raised its status relative to the living room did not by themselves consolidate the daytime use rooms into two zones. The dining room and the casual dining space of the living-kitchen shared a parallel relationship to the living and family rooms and further underscored the division of the house into active and casual and quiet and formal spaces (fig. 52). The delineation of zones and their high degree of livability were as much dependent on well-planned circulation and effective buffering as they were on their component rooms. The domestic zoning that became commonplace in the 1960s offered the still predominantly home-oriented suburban family an environment that promoted togetherness as well as apartness, elevated casual living through the removal or screening of domestic work from most areas dedicated to it, and acknowledged the complex and varying needs of families through the presence of spaces for both active and casual and quiet and formal leisure.

The affiliation between the living room and the dining room grew even stronger in the zoned house of the 1960s. This connection had been reforged in the 1950s as a defined dining area returned as a design feature, and spaces for casual living relieved these rooms of their active pursuits. The two quiet and formal rooms could be used independently for day-to-day activities, but their full potential as a suite for major social events was a draw in houses that also had convenient casual living spaces. In explaining why he and his wife had selected a two-story neocolonial model when they had their new house built outside Pittsburgh in 1962, Robert Anderson noted one of the reasons: "My wife likes to entertain . . . [and because of this] we wanted a family room, formal living room & dining room."[69] Four years later, an advertisement for Pittsburgh's "Ladies Choice Home," a design reflecting the suggestions of three thousand women who had attended the previous year's Pittsburgh Home Show, touted: "The formal dining room, sunny breakfast area and guest sized living room create the perfect atmosphere for carefree family life and gracious entertaining."[70]

In the refined zoned plans that became the domestic ideal in the 1960s, the dining room also maintained a parallel relationship with the casual dining area, which was located either within the kitchen or, more preferably, in its own separate, adjacent area screened in some way from the kitchen's workspace. By the early 1960s, living-kitchens that by definition had some sort of casual eating area had become standard in all but the most modest new houses. In 1964, *House & Home* reported that 94 percent of "leading builders" offered kitchens with "dining space (tables and chairs)."[71]

The most cost-effective and pervasive way to include table space in the kitchen remained the design of a roughly square room with cabinets and appliances in an L-shaped arrangement along two walls and the opposing corner left free for a table and chairs. The footprint for this type of kitchen was a favorite planning element, as it could be paired with the dining room and the living room in a regularized unit. While adequate, the L-shaped arrangement was not ideal within the new system of zoning, seeking to remove as many as possible of the nonleisure activities from the active and casual living areas. Domestic work could never be fully removed from the kitchen as it was with the family room, but some types of work were no longer welcome in the kitchen, for example, the laundry. The facilitators of the study "Housing Design and the American Family" found that the common location of laundry in or near the kitchen had become problematic—even "sharing an informal cup of coffee with a friend [was] not possible in a room which doubles as a laundry."[72]

The desired distinction between work and leisure within the kitchen could be better accomplished by screening the casual dining area from the work area. A Cincinnati housewife expressed her opinion about this arrangement in 1964: "If you are eating any meals at all in the kitchen, I would like to have the eating area divided in some way away from the food preparation, so that as you sit at the table and eat you don't see all the dirty pots and pans, the cooking preparation staring you in the face."[73] Women wanted the kitchen to be easily accessible, yet one survey of Baltimore housewives in 1960 also reinforced the idea that kitchen work and leisure were mutually exclusive: "She does want the kitchen activities to be away from the front door used by visitors and away from the areas devoted to entertainment and relaxation."[74]

The zoned house located the living-kitchen and the family room near one another. A building industry survey of ten thousand homeowners concluded that the "1967 home buyer" wanted "a separated family room near or adjacent to the kitchen."[75] All nine houses showcased as "fast movers" in an issue of *American Builder* from that year had a family room positioned next to the kitchen.[76] Many of the panelists for "Housing Design and the American Family" remarked that the family room should be close to the kitchen, but not integrated with it.[77] The living-kitchen also had to be positioned next to the dining room, but its daily use for casual living made it visually and functionally related to the family room, whereas it played only a supporting role for formal meals in the dining room.

The close relationship of the kitchen and its casual dining area and the family room could be underscored through shared décor. This had already occurred in the quiet and formal rooms, which could be filled with "good" furniture and heirlooms since active living—always a threat to "nice things"—was occurring elsewhere in the house. In contrast to the living and dining rooms, which tended to be physically austere independent of their movable contents, builders or homeowners often united the living-kitchen and the family room through fixed materials and finishes installed at the time of construction. Builders and consumers frequently indulged in more adventurous decorating concepts for these rooms, whether inspired by historical or contemporary themes. *American Builder* reported in 1964: "Modern kitchens tend to blend with other rooms—dining areas and family rooms where color schemes, lighting and textures are in harmony. The architectural style must complement that of neighboring rooms."[78] Three years later, the same journal reiterated that, in the kitchen, women "won't settle for an atmosphere that is less attractive than that in any other part of the house."[79] During the design and construction of their neocolonial house in 1966–67, Charles and Helen Lodge specified a group of targeted upgrades to the materials and finishes of their kitchen, casual eating area, and family room that not only strongly related to the house's overall architecture but also set the spaces apart from the quiet and formal rooms elsewhere on the first floor.[80]

More consequential than the size, adjacency, and décor of the daytime use rooms in defining the two living-dining zones and assuring their livability was a system of logical and efficient circulation and proper buffering. "Zones should be separated by something more than an ordinary partition. Otherwise their separation will be theoretical rather than real," said a writer for Kiplinger's *Changing Times.* And to the question "Is the plan distinctly zoned, with buffers between the zones?" the writer responded: "You should be able to get from here to there— wherever you are and wherever you are bound—without taking devious routes or traversing congested areas."[81] Builders began grouping such things as closets and bathrooms into a bank of interstitial spaces between rooms. These buffered rooms and zones from potential disruptions and also made logical contributions to efficient space planning within the building envelope. Existing homeowners were particularly attuned to the necessity of buffers through personal experience. When Albert and Shirley Robick hired Frank T. Bozzo late in 1970 to construct their second new house, they selected a two-story model that had a large, conveniently located family room buffered by the entry hall and staircase and further isolated in its own one-story wing (fig. 53). Shirley Robick commented: "I liked it separate from the rest of the house."[82]

Circulation pathways demarcated zones in a less subtle manner than buffers. Builders and buyers no longer viewed these interstitial spaces as wasted square footage that might otherwise be given over to a house's rooms. They were essential for eliminating "devious routes" and were an indication of a well-designed house no matter its size. A *House & Home* feature on "traffic flow" explained in

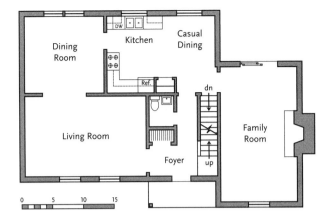
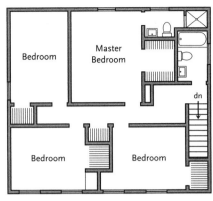

FIGURE 53. The Ro-
bick house placed
the family room in
its own one-story
wing and further
buffered it from the
living room with the
entry and the stair-
case. 1971. (Drawing
by Paul Davidson,
after plans in the
author's collection)

1965: "No single feature of a house plan is more important than its traffic pattern. Comfort, convenience and privacy all depend on good traffic flow, and the
second- and third-time buyer who has lived with poor traffic will seldom settle
for it again, no matter how good the house is in other respects."[83]

The core of the system of domestic circulation was the entrance foyer. This
was one of the many elements eliminated in the earlier design of minimum
houses. The reintroduction of some sort of entry area was part of the initial turn
away from minimum houses. Whether in its own alcove or merely in a corner
of the living room screened by a closet or shelving, the space functioned independently from the rest of the house. With a social purpose that extended back
to Victorian houses—and even earlier, to the lobby entries and central passages
of colonial houses—the postwar entry area buffered the house from uninvited
visitors and provided a defined place for the household to greet invited visitors.

In the 1960s, the entrance area was enlarged into a fully separate entrance
foyer or entry not only for social buffering or conspicuous show but also as the
organizational focus of a house's circulation and zoning. *American Builder* summarized expectations for the space in 1965: "The foyer should provide an attractive place to greet guests, be well lighted, have adequate closet space, screen
main rooms and be an effective traffic control center."[84] The separate entry
became an indispensable part of good design, and prospective buyers knew to
look for it. A 1968 survey of recent buyers in the Chicago suburb of Park Forest
South listed the "entrance foyer" as third out of ten elements "deemed essential
in a new home."[85]

The role of the entrance foyer for circulation was apparent in the design revisions made as Charles and Helen Lodge worked with their builder in the 1960s. In one early sketch of the first floor, the spacious entry area at the front door contained the stair to the second floor, a guest closet, and a powder room. The similarly dimensioned family and living rooms could both be entered from the foyer, establishing their equal roles as anchors for the active and casual and quiet and formal zones. The shortcoming in this version related to circulation—one needed to pass through the living and dining rooms or the family room to get to the kitchen from the foyer. In a second sketch, a hallway connected the entrance foyer with the back of the house without the need to pass through the main living spaces. This hallway provided access to the family room as its door into the foyer was closed, establishing more of a buffer between the living and family rooms. To create the hallway, however, the powder room was moved to the back of the house, requiring the casual dining area and the kitchen work area to share a single, undifferentiated space. In the final, as-built version, the stair was moved forward against the front wall and the powder room located behind the guest closet in the foyer, accessible from the hallway connecting to the back of the house. These changes created enough space at the back for a casual eating area next to the family room that was also screened from the work area of the kitchen (see fig. 53 for a similar plan). This process of change demonstrates the important role of the entry foyer in establishing movement through a house, as well as defining and providing adequate buffers for the daytime use zones.

Individuals and building companies whose businesses had a speculative component also revised their plans to incorporate new planning features for unknown buyers. In 1965, the St. Louis builder Fred M. Kemp marketed a spacious one-story model that was an improved and enhanced version of one from 1963.[86] Both houses had similar plans, and their rooms were about the same size (the one from 1965 included a fifth bedroom); however, modifications to the later version resulted in a more prominent family room and a better-zoned house. An implied circulation route across the house linked all zones and also joined with the entry (fig. 54). The house's sole fireplace moved from the living room to the family room, where it became a visual feature and also more fully separated the room from the kitchen and its casual dining area. With the kitchen better screened, the opening from the entry into the back of the house

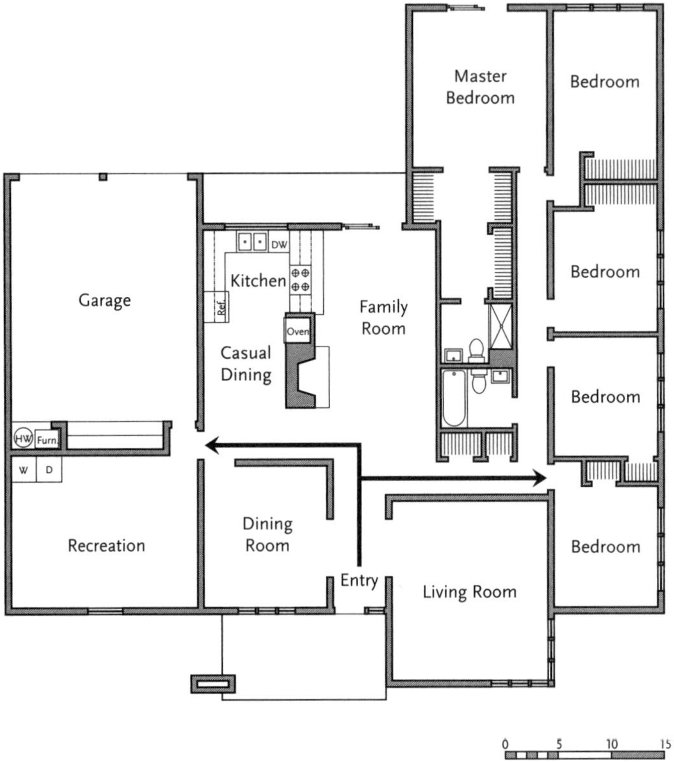

FIGURE 54. Large one-story houses could be easily zoned. (Drawing by Paul Davidson, after a plan in *House & Home*, March 1965, 89)

was widened, with the family room on full view upon entering the house. Finally, the rebranding of the large "storage-utility" space adjacent to the garage into a "recreation room" further corralled aspects of casual living to a place away from the quiet and formal zone.

Relatively few home buyers ended up living in models as large and well zoned as Kemp's; however, many builders incorporated the same thoughtful space planning into one-story models more typical of what was available on the market. The Spacemaker III model, built by United Homes in Tacoma, Washington, in 1965, had three zones defined by meaningful circulation and buffers within a more constricted building envelope (fig. 55).[87] This model shared many features with the one-story floor plan embellishing the cover of a government report about new houses constructed between 1963 and 1967, which graphically depicted the statistical averages for size, rooms, and features in the mid-1960s.[88]

Even the conventional six-room ranch could be improved with circulation. In 1966, an ad for Ryan Homes' one-story Hancock model commanded readers: "Please step to the rear of the home," parenthetically noting that "(you can, without going through the living room)."[89] The advertisement went on to say: "It's quieter in the living room . . . and the floor plan is the reason." Ryan Homes simply inserted a hallway between the daytime and nighttime zones of a conventional bifurcated six-room plan. The hallway bypassed the living room and connected the front door with the kitchen, the stairs down to the garage and laundry, and the bedrooms and bathroom. A modest increase in overall dimensions could considerably improve the function of smaller houses.

New one-story models and improvements to existing ones kept them relevant to buyers attuned to the latest space trends. The form's limitations became most apparent in areas with prospective buyers searching for large houses and in those markets with the most expensive land. The relationship between space and land had become apparent in the 1950s as the prospect of adding even just a single room for casual living helped spur the creation of multistory versions of the ranch house. One-story houses remained popular for aesthetic and ease-of-living reasons in many parts of the United States, particularly in regions with warmer climates and in metropolitan areas with lower population densities. That said, their share of the national percentage of all new houses dropped off noticeably during the 1960s as Americans reacquainted themselves with two-story models.

FIGURE 55. Houses aligned more with national averages could still boast two discernible daytime use zones. 1965. (Drawing by Paul Davidson, after a plan in *American Builder*, December 1965, 91)

THE REEMBRACE OF THE TWO-STORY HOUSE

During the 1960s, the ambivalence about, and even outright distaste for, two-story houses held by many Americans began to lessen. As the decade began, the building industry acknowledged that the increasing cost of land in suburban areas had become a "critical problem" and that "more and more single-family houses are being built split-level or two-story in order to get more living space on less land."[90] In 1956, one-story models represented 87 percent and two-story houses only 4 percent of the new houses constructed in the United States; by 1971, the percentages had shifted to 65 percent and 23 percent, respectively.[91] The availability of two-story houses varied from region to region, but they could be appreciated anywhere. Among the five houses considered outstanding by a panel of five Los Angeles housewives in 1961, the sole two-story model "generated by far the most individual magnetism. Its appeal was instant."[92] The submission's "magnetism" and "appeal" may have been based on the form's relative rarity in Southern California, although the writer of the article did concede: "There may be more buyers for such a house than builders have suspected."[93]

With each new subdivision, the value of nearby undeveloped land rose, and such increases were passed on to the consumer. In a manner not unlike the impetus for tall buildings in urban commercial districts of the late nineteenth and early twentieth centuries, builders and prospective buyers now found a two-story house a reasonable, even desirable compromise. In answer to its 1962 question, "What's the most important factor in home design today?," *American Builder* responded: "It's a race for the *maximum usable [square] footage* for the money. Buyers want space, and the successful builder has to deliver it. It calls for exacting and exhaustive study: comparison of lineal footage of partitions, counting doors, eliminating waste corners, making every inch usable—and attractive."[94] More than any other form, the two-story house gave builders an envelope that was conducive to efficient interior planning. Beyond addressing the issue of land values, the form's boxiness contributed to lower framing costs, as compared to other house forms with similar amounts of space, as well as such other savings as reduced roof areas and shorter runs of utility lines and chases. The popular and trade presses hailed the two-story house for its economy, dignified street presence, and easily zoned interior spaces (fig. 56).

The success of two-story models that began in the 1960s occurred because the layout of the form was reconsidered to integrate various planning lessons learned over the course of the postwar period. While split-levels, split-foyers, and bi-levels had launched a dialogue about the possibilities of living on more than one floor, these multistory versions of the ranch house did not easily incorporate two equal daytime use zones. Existing two-story plans often sacrificed effective circulation, and livability, in exchange for formality and zoning that marginalized the kitchen. The architect Rudolph Matern cautioned builders in 1959:

> Building vertically does not mean going back into the files and pulling out a two-story house of prewar or even postwar vintage. People's wants in houses have changed considerably in the past few years. The basic two-story house . . . contained a living room, dining room, kitchen and perhaps a lavatory on the first floor . . . with three bedrooms and bath on the second floor. Nowadays, however, buyers have begun to demand family rooms, mud rooms, utility rooms, laundries, impressive foyers, added storage space and one to one-and-a-half more baths. . . . The whole concept of building houses vertically thus requires a long, critical, analytical look.[95]

FIGURE 56. Two-story models with new types of plans returned to popularity in many parts of the United States in the 1960s. (Drawing by Paul Davidson, after plans in the author's collection)

Year by year, builders began introducing and refining two-story models in ways that showcased their good zoning and potential for livability and increased consumer affection.[96] *American Builder* highlighted the trend in 1962: "Like old soldiers, the two-story house never dies. Other styles obscure its conservative appeal from time to time but never put it out of the running. There has always been a segment of home-owners who prefer two-story living, who find it the most economical means for gaining space. Today this group is growing by leaps and bounds."[97] The shelter press joined building industry leaders in heralding the form. Writing for *Better Homes & Gardens* in 1964, the architect John D. Bloodgood explained the benefits of a featured two-story model: "Like most two-story houses, this one combines unusual space and economy. It has 1,893 square feet of enclosed space, with minimum roof and foundation costs. It has the complete privacy of a separate floor of bedrooms, and the flexibility of large, well-planned rooms."[98]

Many consumers preferred two-story houses, especially those making a second or third home purchase. The "1967 home buyer" included in one study had previously "bought a one-story house but leans toward another . . . next time. His preference in higher-priced homes: a two-story structure."[99] The study noted that, generally, the average buyer's overarching concern was space and the desire for a family room, a separate dining room, a "foyer entrance," and a powder room. These features were all part of the domestic ideal that had emerged over the course of two decades, rendering obsolete the once-common two-story house of six rooms. In the 1960s, many prospective house buyers made wish lists for two-story models having rooms and spaces such as these.[100]

All types of builder were eager to respond, sometimes with what was essentially the same model. In mid-1965, Ryan Homes, by then one of the nation's largest building companies, hired an advertising agency in an effort to better integrate the information in its print marketing and the knowledge of on-site sales staff. The process relied on the input and expertise of the Ryan salesmen in identifying the features they knew would most resonate with prospective buyers in the Pittsburgh area. The outcomes were integrated into new ads that dispensed with "tricky or cute headlines and themes" in favor of an approach

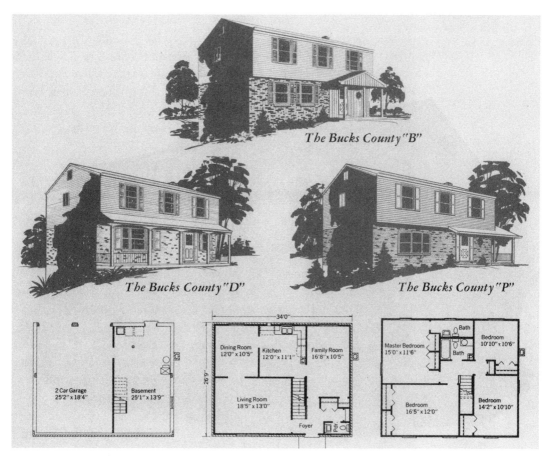

The Bucks County "B"

The Bucks County "D"

The Bucks County "P"

showcasing "those features of the new models that make them superior in total value to other homes in the area," including the new two-story Stratton C model.[101]

The first ad for the Stratton C included a perspective rendering, floor plans, and more than the usual amount of text, all of which was intended to "help to pre-sell the new models and bring more prospective *qualified* buyers to the Ryan Home Openings."[102] The 1,862-square-foot neocolonial house featured eight rooms total, with four bedrooms and two and a half bathrooms (fig. 57). The

FIGURE 57. Plans and elevations of the Bucks County (Stratton C) model. 1966. (Ryan Homes Collection; courtesy of Carnegie Mellon University Architecture Archives)

front entry anchored the circulation system and was showcased in the ad. It contained the stair up to the second-floor bedrooms and bathrooms; in addition, buyers were asked to "note that the entrance gives immediate access to the powder-room, family room, kitchen or living room and that it is not necessary to pass through one room to enter another."[103] The description fudged a little, as the plans show that a person needed to pass through a corner of the family room to enter the kitchen, yet the larger point remained clear: the entry area would be a draw for an "experienced home owner."

The Stratton C, renamed the Bucks County within a year, was a widely utilized model in Ryan's Pittsburgh-area developments in the late 1960s.[104] Even without the marketing study and associated advertising campaign, this large merchant builder would have been confident of its sales potential, as it had been a mainstay of local custom builders for a number of years. When Ryan began offering the model in the Farmingdale Estates development in Glenshaw in 1965, custom variations of it already dotted the nearby Lyndhurst Estates and Pictwood subdivisions. The custom builder Warren G. Goss had even chosen one as a showcase of his work for the North Suburban Builders Association's "Home-O-Rama" in 1960.[105]

The new two-story models that became widely available in the 1960s included additional enhancements making them attractive to better-informed buyers and to those purchasing a new house for the second or third time. A first-floor "half bath" or powder room had always been a welcome feature for two-story houses, but it became indispensable for livability in new two-story designs. The family bathroom in one-story houses was usually close enough to the front door to double as a guest bathroom, but requiring guests and family members to traipse upstairs was antithetical to good zoning and livability in the 1960s. The first-floor half bath was also useful in reducing demand on the full bathroom(s) on the second floor as they served an increasing number of bedrooms. The family room, larger kitchens, entry foyers, and powder rooms required a larger building envelope that, likewise, created a larger second floor. The popular design convention in all types of multistory houses—overhanging the second floor by a couple of feet at the front, the back, or in both directions—substantially augmented square footage on the upper level. In two-story houses, the additional space generally meant a fourth or fifth bedroom could be added.

CONCLUSION

The zoned houses available to prospective buyers in metropolitan suburbs at the end of the 1960s were appreciably distinct from typical ones available at the end of the 1950s and bore little to no resemblance to those found in subdivisions at the end of the 1940s. The zoned house emerged from a variety of factors—ease in managing the varied activities of growing families still intensively using their houses, a desire for apartness in addition to togetherness, and the ability to purchase larger houses because of amassed equity or comfortable incomes. Most of all, the zoned house responded to the full ascendancy of casual living in postwar domestic planning and the daily life of the middle class.

By the 1960s, the establishment of a family room equal in status to the living room spurred the development of a system of zoning for daytime use rooms, one quiet and formal and the other active and casual. This planning trend both fostered and responded to a level of complexity in middle-class domesticity that fully reversed decades of spatial simplification in the American house. Elements of this type of zoning appeared in all house forms, but new types of two-story plans most fully implemented it, returning the two-story form to a level of popularity not seen since before World War II.

A quarter century of favorable social and economic conditions had permitted builders to unabashedly experiment with residential design and construction. The building industry—from the small-volume custom builder to the large-volume merchant builder—gave shape and structure to prevailing and in-flux notions of the domestic ideal that many believed could incubate a rewarding family life among similar neighbors in suburban subdivisions. The decades-long discourse involved builder-producers, buyer-consumers, and a national government that directly and indirectly lubricated the engine of the postwar domestic economy.

The outcome was sharply raised consumer expectations and dramatically redefined notions of livability in new detached, single-family houses. The differences between the minimum house and the zoned house are evident enough. Yet it is important not to lose focus on the underlying context for all postwar houses. No matter when or where they were constructed, what they looked like, and which design features and amenities they included, these houses all incorporated ideas and components that either had not existed formerly or had been out of reach for most households.

Epilogue

IN SEPTEMBER 1951, Milton J. Brock, the president of the Los Angeles Home Builders Institute, opened National Home Week in that city with these hyperbolic words: "Nowhere in the universe do families have the freedom of selecting and acquiring their own homes as they do in this country. . . . The best part of housing under the American system is good-quality construction, craftsmanship and design, containing an abundance of modern features of livability that older countries have never dared undertake."[1] For the next two decades, newspapers, popular news, shelter and lifestyle magazines, trade and professional journals, newspapers, and television and movies steadily fed Americans a diet of ideas that conflated notions of freedom, superiority, consumerism, and happy home ownership and livability in a redefined suburban house. They nurtured the belief that mere home ownership alone had not vaulted the United States to the apex of democracy; rather, what distinguished the United States was the whole consumer process, in which buyers were presented with a spectrum of options when purchasing a house or other goods.

With the federal government absorbing a significant portion of the financial risk involved with the construction and sale of new houses, the confidence of the building industry rose in tandem with a broad consensus that the quality of life in the United States was unsurpassed anywhere in the world. The evidence for the elevation of the "American way of life" above all others can be found in the millions of suburban houses whose livable design was inseparable from a new way of casual living, adopted and enjoyed by middle-class families.

The postwar housing boom in the United States stood out from earlier periods of residential expansion in its scale, its rapid turnover in design, and its level of marketing. In only twenty-five years, the country became perceptively, and to a great extent actually, a suburbanized nation composed mainly of single-family houses. This period saw typical new houses nearly double in size and offer many standard features previously considered luxuries. Ownership of a comfortable, well-designed house became, if not an attainable reality for all, a pervasive domestic goal for middle-class American families and the most basic evidence of their class identity.

Extending from the entrenched high value placed on home ownership and a suburban residence, this transformation was also deeply integrated into the postwar period's ever more sophisticated and pervasive culture of consumerism. The house did not lose its long-held status as a place of refuge and object of security, but tastemaker advice, building-industry marketing, and consumer participation elevated the house to the apex of consumer goods. The remaking and immense expansion of the middle class in the suburbs was a sustained consumer-based process facilitated by the pursuit of a new casual lifestyle and reflected in the design of domestic space. The accommodation of casual living within the detached, single-family house steered its postwar reinvention, as the constricting minimum house gave way to commodious zoned houses, with a number of interesting stops along the way.

This study presents the themes and trends having the greatest effect on the spatial organization of new house plans over the course of the postwar period. There are aspects of domestic design worth noting that, although only playing supporting roles as agents of change, perennially informed wish lists and deliberations about specific houses—storage, garages, and air-conditioning.

The total amount of square footage was always a top concern for people looking for a new house, in terms of the number of rooms and their dimensions, as well as storage. From the outset, the FHA advised that a house should have at least one closet in each of the bedrooms, a linen closet usually located adjacent to the bathroom, and a guest closet ideally positioned near the front door. These basic closet types were found in all houses during the entire period, although they grew in size and became more user friendly. For example, bedroom closets became wider, with access provided by sliding or bifold doors that made the closet more like a built-in wardrobe.

Different types of closet, no matter how enlarged and improved, were not enough for postwar families as they amassed more and more consumer goods.[2] Directed to its upper-middle-class readership, an observation expressed in

House Beautiful in 1954 was broadly applicable to suburban families: "We need plenty of storage space for the plenty around us."[3] Pantries and broom closets joined longer expanses of cabinets in kitchens. Built-in shelves and storage cupboards appeared in family rooms for games and record albums. The master bedroom closet increased in size or number to better accommodate the room's two occupants. Bulk and out-of-season storage in houses lacking basements or attics could be found in utility rooms, large storage rooms, and walk-in closets. For garden tools, lawn furniture, and bikes, sleds, and other large toys, many households had no choice other than the garage.

The garage, or carport, in postwar houses moved from being, in most cases, a shedlike dependency separate from the house to its single largest interior space and a major element of its street façade. In 1940, an average of 80 percent of new, FHA-insured, single-family houses included a garage or carport, over half of which were physically independent of the house.[4] This number plummeted to an estimated 47 percent of all new houses constructed during the first half of 1950, as the minimum house was stripped of most spaces beyond those elemental for living. Yet, importantly, the portion of garages and carports fully detached from the house had also dropped, to 17 percent, which indicates that enclosed or covered parking facilities were well on their way to being integrated into residential design.[5] Unsurprisingly, the fast-growing, car-oriented cities of Texas, the Southwest, California, and the Pacific Northwest included garages or carports at a rate double or triple the rest of the country.[6]

Builders seemed at first uncertain about how to incorporate garages into designs. A writer for *American Builder* fretted in 1950: "The garage, an essential component of modern living in the United States today, is being neglected in the current record production of new homes."[7] The suburban lifestyle demanded at least one car, and it did not take long for builders to figure out how garages and carports might best relate to the form, appearance, and layout of houses. In areas where basements were standard or where multistory houses with lower levels, such as split-levels, split-foyers, and bi-levels, were popular, a garage occupied a portion of the basement or the lower level. Garages became significant components of the house in terms of volume but were on the very fringe of the house's living areas.

Builders initially appended garages to one end of one-story houses built on a slab or over a crawl space. They were frequently entered from an exterior door and only later connected directly to the kitchen, utility room, or casual living area (fig. 58). The size of the garage and carport meant that it had an unquestionable bearing on the way a house looked, and its importance to consumers was clear—58 percent of new houses in 1970 had a garage, and 17 percent had a carport.[8] Relative to the layout and function of the rest of the house, the garage was a distinct space that is best comprehended as a large area for storage. Certain rooms or zones were usually located near it, but its day-to-day role was mostly static, and it supported activities occurring elsewhere (fig. 59).

FIGURE 58. Builders initially appended garages to one end of the house and entered them from an exterior door. 1948. (Drawing by Paul Davidson, after a plan in *American Builder*, April 1948, 95)

The idea that a house might include a room—and a large one at that—whose primary purpose was to store an automobile speaks directly to the theme of modernity and consumerism in the postwar house. Houses built during this period glittered with the latest technologies, and their many forms were favored topics for marketing. Basic features like telephone lines with multiple jacks became part of the standard design package, while more gimmicky technologies such as intercom systems were installed sporadically. Air-conditioning, which first became widely available during the postwar period, was neither standard nor gimmicky. It stood apart as an accessible but expensive luxury item even in the regions with the hottest climates. The term *air-conditioning* initially indicated any forced air-circulation system, warming or cooling, but soon came to be associated specifically with cooling. Only 29 percent of new houses in 1967 included whole-house air-conditioning; even in the South the number of houses with air-conditioning was less than half of the total constructed.[9] In a world far less climate controlled than today, air-conditioning remained something that few postwar buyers expected to have in a new house. As houses have grown since the end of the postwar period, fully enclosed garages—more and more with

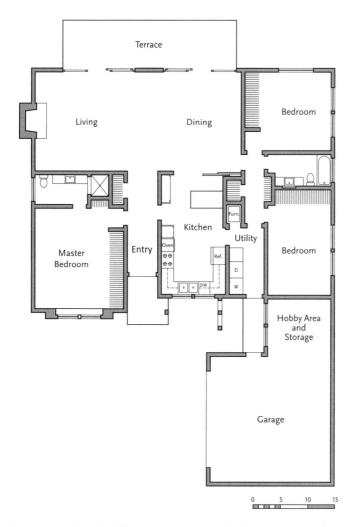

Terrace

Living

Dining

Bedroom

Master
Bedroom

Entry

Oven

Ref.

Kitchen

Furn.

Utility

Bedroom

D

W

DW

Hobby Area
and
Storage

Garage

0   5   10   15

FIGURE 59. During the postwar period, garages grew larger, became more visually prominent, and included more storage space. 1961. (Drawing by Paul Davidson, after a plan in the *Los Angeles Times Sunday Home Magazine*, 17 September 1961, 22)

three bays and often doubling or used entirely for nonautomobile storage—and air-conditioning have become ubiquitous parts of the domestic ideal. In 2012, 87 percent of new single-family houses featured garages, and 89 percent included air-conditioning.[10]

The almost universal incorporation of once nonstandard features and amenities contribute to a suburban landscape at the beginning of the twenty-first century that is considerably different than at the close of the postwar period. Since 1970, subdivisions and developments have sprawled even further from metropolitan centers in places known generally as "exurbs." Interestingly, these newer neighborhoods distant from downtown are decidedly denser than the older, closer-in suburbs of the 1940s, 1950s, and 1960s. Larger houses occupy smaller lots, chains of attached townhouses are draped over hills and inserted as infill in already built-up areas, and apartment and condominium buildings of varying heights sometimes uncomfortably occupy the same suburban locales.

An infinite amount of knowledge of design trends is now available 24/7 through high-definition television and cable channels fully dedicated to domestic design, as well as through ever-present multimedia offerings on the Internet. These sources have in large part replaced printed periodicals in the transfer of information about new houses. They encourage a level of remote experience to the point of information saturation and overload that make the most eye-catching and kicky full-page newspaper advertisements of the postwar era seem like period pieces that are severely limited in their content.

Despite these glaring distinctions, the ownership of a detached, single-family house remains constant as a broadly popular goal for American families, and the motivations for making this purchase are frequently the same: a safe and friendly place to raise children and to realize the full potential of comfortable middle-class family life. This remained true even as the nation once again became reacquainted with the perils of home ownership and credit-driven consumerism.

The housing boom during the first decade of the twenty-first century came to a spectacular collapse in 2007 for reasons both varied and complex. Some of the bust was attributable to cyclical changes in value, but the principal cause was the widespread availability of credit to financially marginal borrowers. Legitimate debate continues about who holds greater responsibility for the housing crisis. Did predatory lenders hawk mortgages with dodgy terms to uninformed consumers before cleverly repackaging them as mortgage-backed securities for other types of investor? Or did greedy consumers, caught up in the whirl of a boom and wanting to realize a quick profit, turn a blind eye to the limits of their household budgets?

Whoever can be saddled with more responsibility, the tremendous housing collapse precipitated the "Great Recession" in 2007–9, the severe effects of which are still reverberating. Between their peak in mid-2006 and their trough in early 2012, average housing values in the United States dropped by about 35 percent.[11] Focusing specifically on new single-family houses, construction during this boom peaked in 2006 at 1,654,000 and plummeted to below 500,000 for three consecutive years in 2010, 2011, and 2012, lows not experienced since the end of World War II.[12] Home ownership fell from an all-time high of 69 percent in 2004 to about 65 percent in 2013, a figure only a couple of percentage points higher than at the end of the postwar period.[13]

The bursting of the housing bubble, the subsequent recession, and lingering weaknesses in the domestic economy occasioned a spate of articles proposing that Americans might, at last, be ready to turn toward smaller houses. In a 2010 article in the *New York Times Magazine,* the journalist Andrew Rice asked: "Will Americans re-evaluate cultural assumptions that equate ever-larger houses with success and stability? Or will they invest more in their lived environments, figuring that with the demise of the quick flip, they are now in for the long term?"[14] If Americans did seriously question the linking of "ever larger houses with success and stability," this seems to have only been temporary. The average size of a new single-family house did shrink from a record high of 2,521 square feet to 2,392 between 2007 and 2010, but it has since climbed, reaching a new record of 2,598 in 2013.[15]

American households are still entranced with the dreams and available realities of a detached, single-family house in the suburbs and still view it as the foundation of middle-class family life. Interestingly, they do so even as the average size of households continues to diminish and as individuals and families spend more of their days outside the house. The largest of the houses constructed at the end of the 1960s still meet the minimum level of housing expectations for many American families; however, they no longer represent the domestic ideal for contemporary home life in the early twenty-first century. An entry foyer that pragmatically buffers and organizes circulation, but lacks the visual and emotive drama of volumetric space and an impressive stair, falls short of the mark. A tiny master bathroom with its stall shower feels like a constricted afterthought rather than a welcome luxury and could even be a sales liability. Multiple bedrooms are not considered fully functional without their own en suite

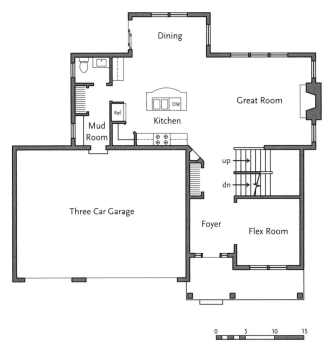

or jack-and-jill bathrooms. A two-bay garage is hardly enough space if there is any intention to actually park the car there.

The most intriguing departure from the postwar house as it stood in 1970 is the complete ascendancy of casual living within the house and in the structure of family and social interaction. The rooms making up the active and casual zone from the end of the postwar period have morphed into a vast multifunctional space that combines living, dining, and opulently finished kitchen work areas (fig. 60). Such "great rooms" dominate the spatial organization of new suburban houses and have become the unilateral locus of American domestic life in the early twenty-first century. Where vestigial quiet and formal zones are still discernible, they are much reduced and increasingly jettisoned in total in exchange for a home office, a media room, or even, tellingly, a "flex" room with no assigned function. These shifts have even altered perceptions of postwar houses by their original owners. Field surveys confirmed the continued high desirability and heavy use of living rooms in new houses of the 1960s also containing family rooms. Yet these same surveys also found original owners now characterizing their living rooms as an infrequently used and always presentable "nice to have extra space," which more reflects the living room's present and falling status in the house than how the room was viewed and used historically.[16]

These differences and distinctions notwithstanding, the detached, single-family houses built in the American suburbs between 1945 and 1970 remain the starting point and incubators for nearly every standard room and amenity available in most new houses being constructed today. They are the grandparents

and parents of today's much-maligned "McMansions," whose size and ameni-ties are easy and, in many ways, justifiable targets for harsh criticism in an age of economic uncertainty and greater social and environmental awareness of the downsides of detached America's low-density sprawl. Critics should keep in mind, however, that the consumption of domestic space in the form of houses is neither new nor radical in the United States. The entangled housing interests of government and business, and producers and consumers, as well as the hope for a better life that millions of Americans see in the form of a new, single-family house in the suburbs, became deeply engrained parts of national cul-ture and identity during the postwar period (fig. 61). The long-range future of detached America cannot be predicted, but the strength of its popular ideologies and its level of integration in the domestic economy suggest that it will continue to define America for many years to come.

FIGURE 61. The skewed promise of detached America still holds allure for many today. (U.S. News & World Report Magazine Photograph Collec-tion, Prints and Pho-tographs Division, Library of Congress; photograph by and courtesy of Warren K. Leffler)

Notes

INTRODUCTION

1. Key works and collections on suburbaniza-
tion include: Jackson, *Crabgrass Frontier;* Fish-
man, *Bourgeois Utopias;* Stilgoe, *Borderland;*
Hise, *Magnetic Los Angeles;* Baxandall and Ewen,
Picture Windows; Hayden, *Building Suburbia;*
Wiese, *Places of Their Own;* Fogelson, *Bourgeois
Nightmares;* Beauregard, *When America Became
Suburban;* Kruse and Sugrue, *New Suburban
History;* Wiese, *Suburb Reader;* and D. Harris,
Little White Houses. See also specific case stud-
ies: Kelly, *Expanding the American Dream;* Wil-
son, *Hamilton Park;* Randall, *America's Original
GI Town;* and D. Harris, *Second Suburb.*

2. Anna Vemer Andrzejewski and Barbara
Miller Lane have in-process manuscripts that
investigate individual builders and various
dimensions of the domestic building industry
in postwar America. With "One Builder: Marshall Erdman and Postwar Building and Real
Estate Development in Madison, Wisconsin,"
Andrzejewski will provide a deep study of a
single builder, demonstrating how his business
was shaped by period economics, government
policy and zoning, architectural trends, and
the building and design professions. Lane's
"Houses for a New World: Builders and Buyers
in American Suburbs, 1945–1965" contains ten
case-study developments built throughout the
United States as a means of drawing conclusions about the building industry, its practices,
and the purchasers of its houses.

3. Key works on the postwar domestic
economy and consumerism include: Matthaei,
Economic History of Women in America; E. T.
May, *Homeward Bound,* particularly chapter 7;
Hine, *Populuxe;* Cross, *All-Consuming Century;*
Hurley, *Diners, Bowling Alleys, and Trailer Parks;*
and Cohen, *Consumers' Republic.*

4. For more on the intersections of race,
class, and the suburban home, see D. Harris,
Little White Houses.

5. For postwar houses as part of broader studies, see G. Wright, *Building the Dream;* C. E.
Clark, *American Family Home;* Archer, *Architecture and Suburbia;* Isenstadt, *Modern American
House;* and Hubka, *Houses without Names.*

6. Jeffrey Hornstein argues that the tendency
for many Americans to consider themselves
"middle class" was well in place at the outset of
World War II. See Hornstein, *Nation of Realtors,*
201–6.

7. Key texts on women and families in the post-
war period include: Matthaei, *Economic History of
Women in America;* Cowan, *More Work for Mother;*
E. T. May, *Homeward Bound;* Coontz, *Way We
Never Were;* and Spigel, *Make Room for TV.*

8. "Today's Woman Selects Colors of Roof
Shingles," *Washington Post,* 18 Feb. 1961, sec. B:
15.

9. "Why Buyers Buy," 54.

10. "22 Ways to Get More Sales from a Model
House," 148.

11. For more on mid-twentieth-century suburban development and domestic design in these countries, see Stretton, *Ideas for Australian Cities;* Irving, *History and Design of the Australian House;* Ferguson, *Building the New Zealand Dream;* R. Harris, *Unplanned Suburbs;* Pickett, *Fibro Frontier;* R. Harris, *Creeping Conformity;* Jenkins, *At Home;* Schrader, *We Call It Home;* and O'Callaghan and Pickett, *Designer Suburbs.*

12. For 1945 to 1964, see U.S. Department of Commerce, Bureau of the Census (Census Bureau), *Housing Construction Statistics, 1889 to 1964,* 18; for 1965 to 1970, see Census Bureau and U.S. Department of Housing and Urban Development (HUD), *Characteristics of New One-Family Homes: 1974,* 4.

13. There is no single source that provides percentages for the total number of dwelling units built each year that were privately constructed, detached, single-family houses. Government and other reports about housing starts and housing units constructed do not always differentiate between attached and detached "one-family" or "one-unit" structures. Still, a rough conservative estimate puts the total number that were fully detached between 60 and 80 percent of all new units constructed each year between 1945 and 1970, with a much higher total in some years. For raw figures, see Housing and Home Finance Agency (HHFA), *Housing Statistics Handbook,* table 2; Newman and Stucke, *Structure of the Residential Building Industry in 1949,* 15, note 48; Census Bureau, *Housing Construction Statistics, 1889 to 1964,* 18; Census Bureau and HUD, *Characteristics of New One-Family Homes: 1974,* 4.

14. For essential studies of government housing programs in the 1930s, see Weiss, *Rise of the Community Builders;* Radford, *Modern Housing for America;* and Freund, *Colored Property.*

15. Doan, *American Housing Production 1880–2000,* 62–63; Hyman, *Debtor Nation,* 49, 53–54;

Jackson, *Crabgrass Frontier,* 196, 204–5; Weiss, *Rise of the Community Builders,* 145.

16. "FHA: Revolution by Accident," 103.

17. Lizabeth Cohen refers to this stage of American consumer history as "segmenting the mass." See her *Consumers' Republic,* part 4, "The Political Culture of Mass Consumption."

18. For more information on co-owned multifamily housing, see Lasner, *High Life.*

19. Key works include G. Wright, *Moralism and the Model Home;* McMurry, *Families and Farmhouses in Nineteenth-Century America;* Cromley, *Alone Together;* Cromley, "History of American Beds and Bedrooms"; Robertson, "Male and Female Agendas for Domestic Reform"; the essays collected in Foy and Schlereth, *American Home Life, 1880–1930;* A. Adams, "Eichler Home"; Jacobs, "Social and Spatial Change"; the essays collected in D. Harris, *Second Suburb;* Cromley, *Food Axis;* and the essays collected in Carson and Lounsbury, *Chesapeake House.*

20. Paxton, *What People Want,* v.

21. "What House Buyers Are Looking For," 107.

22. Paxton, *What People Want,* 16. Table 17-01 (117), titled "features buyers liked in houses bought in 1949–50," indicates that the two characteristics checked by the most respondents were "floor plan, room arrangement" (39 percent) and "location" (38 percent).

23. Robert Anderson and Frances Anderson, survey form, 21 Aug. 2002; Grace H. Crane, survey form, 23 Aug. 2002 (incorrectly dated 2003); James Greenen, survey form, 22 July 2002; Albert Jacobs and Barbara Jacobs, interview with the author, 15 Feb. 2002; George Kisak and Judith Kisak, survey form, 4 Aug. 2002, and interview with the author, 13 Aug. 2002; Robert Ponter, survey form, 21 July 2002; Shirley Robick, interview with the author, 16 Feb. 2002; Leo Schmitt and Carmen Schmitt, survey form, 20 July 2002;

Leo Schmitt, interview with the author, 12 Aug. 2002; George Thompson and Marjorie Thompson, survey form, 22 July 2002; Albert Sybo and Dolores Sybo, interview with the author, 16 Feb. 2002; James Werth and Shirley Werth, survey form, n.d. [July–Aug. 2002]. All interviews were conducted in the interviewees' houses in Glenshaw, Pennsylvania.

24. For more information on the formation of middle-class culture and popular publishing, see Ohmann, *Selling Culture;* Walker, *Shaping Our Mothers' World;* and D. Harris, *Little White Houses,* chapter 2, "Magazine Lessons: Publishing the Lexicon of White Domesticity."

25. Endres, *"Better Homes and Gardens,"* 25–26.

26. "Better Keep Your Eye on the Newsstands," 168–69; see also "Better Homes and Gardens Shows."

27. Bloodgood, "If You're Looking for a Good Two-Story."

28. The roots between an idealized house as embodying and having an effect on home life extend, in the United States, back at least to Andrew Jackson Downing's *Cottage Residences* (1842). For more on how specific cultural values were reinforced in the postwar period through certain types of graphic representation, see D. Harris, *Little White Houses,* chapter 3, "Rendered Whiteness: Architectural Drawings and Graphics."

29. Portions of this research have appeared in Historic American Buildings Survey (HABS) documentation (see HABS MD-1253 for an overview) and were used to produce Jacobs, "Beyond Levittown."

1. THE HOUSING INDUSTRY REINVENTED

1. "Houses Best Buy for Today's Dollar," 84.

2. "Man of the Year," 46; C. E. Clark, *American Family Home,* 221.

3. "Americans Called Best Housed People in World," *Los Angeles Times,* 9 Sept. 1951, sec. V: 1.

4. J. Lippincott, *Design for Business,* 19.

5. Harding and Lissner, "Huge Potential Market for Housing," 536.

6. G. Wright, *Building the Dream,* 242.

7. See Radford, *Modern Housing for America,* in particular chapter 7, "The Struggle to Shape Permanent Policy."

8. Cortright, "Address," 4.

9. "Home Ownership—Our Nation's Strength," 69.

10. Franklin D. Roosevelt to the NAHB, 8 Nov. 1943, as transcribed in a press release of Frank W. Cortright's statement before the House Committee on Public Buildings and Grounds, 26 Jan. 1944, 1–2, RG 162, General Records of the Federal Works Agency, Entry 23, Records Concerning Plans for Postwar Public Works, 1941–1944, box 1, National Archives and Records Administration (NARA). For more about the links between construction and World War II, see Albrecht, *World War II and the American Dream.*

11. Cortright, statement, 26 Jan. 1944, 5, 8.

12. Senate Report No. 1131 from the Committee on Banking and Currency to accompany S. 1592 (General Housing Act of 1946), 79th Cong., 2nd sess., 8 Apr. 1946, 8.

13. For the 1947–48 McCarthy hearings, see Baxandall and Ewen, *Picture Windows,* chapter 8. For a period editorial, see Dunn, "Publisher's Page."

14. House Report No. 590 from the Committee on Banking and Currency to accompany H.R. 4009 (National Housing Act of 1949), 81st Cong., 1st sess., 16 May 1948, 12.

15. Shanken, *194X,* 12.

16. "Housing: Up from the Potato Fields," 68. For the entanglement of public-private housing interests, see Hayden, "Building the American Way."

17. "Place of Real Estate," 27.

18. See Freund, *Colored Property*, in particular chapter 4.

19. For FHA racism before and during World War II, see Cohen, *Consumers' Republic*, 166–73; G. Wright, *Building the Dream*, 247–48; and Jackson, *Crabgrass Frontier*, 208–15.

20. "'Equal Rights' Order," 5.

21. Freund, *Colored Property*, 178–79.

22. Hyman, *Debtor Nation*, 67.

23. Cohen, *Consumers' Republic*, 138–46.

24. "WHO Are the Postwar Builders?" 126.

25. For an in-depth study of restrictions and suburbia, see Fogelson, *Bourgeois Nightmares*.

26. Ibid., 202–3.

27. Weiss, *Rise of the Community Builders*, 147

28. In most cases, small-volume builders constructed houses for specific clients already in possession of their lots, and their business was thus less dependent on FHA approval. The clients might desire to obtain their own FHA or VA loan, but their initial deposit constituted the funds that builders used to start a house. See Dietz, Day, and Kelly, "Current Patterns of Fabrication."

29. "Mr. Average Builder," 68.

30. For 75,000, see "WHO Are the Postwar Builders?" 126; for 100,000, see "Ryan Second Biggest in the U.S.," *Pittsburgh Press*, 22 Sept. 1968, sec. 7: 1.

31. James Funk and Margaret Funk, interview with the author, Glenshaw, PA, 13 Aug. 2002. All information related to Dreier is drawn from this conversation with his daughter and son-in-law.

32. Johnstone and Joern, *Business of Home Building*, v.

33. For example, see Cobb, *Your Dream Home*.

34. "Home Builder—Who Is He?" 15.

35. Newman and Stucke, *Structure of the Residential Building Industry in 1949*, appendix B. In 1949, professional or commercial builders

constructed 71 percent of nonfarm dwellings houses overall and 84 percent of those in metropolitan areas.

36. NAHB, *Housing Almanac*, 15–16; Haeger, "Four Kinds of Builders," 201.

37. Haeger, "Four Kinds of Builders," 200.

38. "Mr. Average Builder," 68.

39. "Here's How One Custom Builder Operates," 127.

40. Jones, "Operative Building—One Way Out."

41. William K. Trosene, "More People Show Desire for Custom-Built Houses," *Pittsburgh Press*, 5 Sept. 1948, 35.

42. "Shelter Magazines Know," 155.

43. Tom Cameron, "Today's Buyers 'Customize' Their New Homes," *Los Angeles Times*, 5 Sept. 1965, sec. G: 1.

44. Advertisement, "Capitol Hill in Beautiful Prospect Heights," *Chicago Tribune*, 11 Sept. 1965, sec. 1B: 5.

45. Advertisement, "Your Family Need a Special Kind of House?" *Chicago Tribune*, 11 Sept. 1965, sec. 1B: 4.

46. "Why a Buyer's Market Is Forcing Builders," 44.

47. Ibid.

48. Frank T. Bozzo, interview with the author, Glenshaw, PA, 17 Feb. 2002.

49. For ranking, see "Ryan Second Biggest in the U.S."; Huntoon, "'Could Houses Cost Less?" 131.

50. Huntoon, "'Could Houses Cost Less?'" 127; "Could Houses Cost Less?" 29.

51. "Builder Today Must Be Expert in Many Fields," *Pittsburgh Press*, 5 June 1960, sec. 6: 4.

52. King, "Publicity," 112.

53. "How to Merchandise Your House," 151.

54. "How to Sell Houses," 146.

55. Advertisement, "Benz Realty Company . . . Advance Viewing," *Pittsburgh Press*, 22 May 1960, sec. 3: 18; advertisement, "We Bend Over

Backwards to Make Sure Your Home Is Right in Lyndhurst Estates," *Pittsburgh Press,* 5 June 1960, sec. 6: 12; advertisement, "Lyndhurst Estates," *Pittsburgh Press,* 12 June 1960, sec. 6: 3.

56. Advertisement, "Lyndhurst Estates," *Pittsburgh Press,* 30 Sept. 1962, sec. 5: 10.

57. Kisak and Kisak, interview, 13 Aug. 2002; Kisak and Kisak, survey form, 4 Aug. 2002.

58. "Business of Home Building," 132.

59. "Mr. Average Builder," 69.

60. Advertisement, "Nearly Ready—for Families Able to Enjoy Fine Living!" *Pittsburgh Press,* 17 Aug. 1947, 40; advertisement, "Palisades View Homes," *Los Angeles Times,* 15 Sept. 1957, pt. 6: 8; advertisement, "Preview Showing, Elegant Living," *Chicago Tribune,* 11 Sept. 1965, sec. 1B: 14.

61. "Report from Washington," 172–73.

62. "22 Ways to Get More Sales from a Model House," 144.

63. Advertisement, "New 6 Room Homes Ideally Located in Beautiful Linden Manor," *Chicago Tribune,* 13 Sept. 1949, 5.

64. "Home Builder—Who Is He?" 32.

65. "Why and How the Furnished Model Helps Sell," 135.

66. "How to Sell," 137.

67. Campbell, "Consuming Goods," 24–26.

68. George Katona, "American Prosperity Is Freedom's Best Hope!" *Los Angeles Times,* 30 June 1963, sec. C: 7.

69. For a full discussion of the development of Belair, see Jacobs, "Beyond Levittown."

70. Levitt and Sons, Inc., "Belair at Bowie, Maryland," 1962 (in author's collection).

71. "Belair Homes Open: Levittown Moves to Maryland," *Washington Post,* 13 Oct. 1960, sec. C: 3.

72. Jacqueline Federici, interview with the author, Bowie, MD, 21 Feb. 2006.

73. Ben H. Chastaine to Jim Williams, 13 Nov. 1964, Model Homes, Furnishings, Papers, 1961–64, Ryan Homes Collection (RHC), Architecture Archives, Carnegie Mellon University, Pittsburgh, PA.

74. Sales Bulletin, no. 6, 16 May 1956, Sales Bulletins, 1955–57, 1960, RHC.

75. Gerald S. Snyder, "'House Shopping' on Sundays Gives Baseball Run for Money: Great Diversion for the Family," *Pittsburgh Press,* 9 June 1963, sec. 7: 1.

76. "Levitt's Biggest Opening," *Washington Post,* 15 Oct. 1960, sec. C: 1.

77. Ellis Yochelson, interview with the author, Bowie, MD, 17 Feb. 2006.

78. "Origin and History of National Home Week," *Washington Post,* 18 Sept. 1955, sec. G: 2.

79. Onslow, "Impressing the Public," 39.

80. "National Home Week," 102.

81. "New National Pastime: House-Hunting Gaining Popularity," *Pittsburgh Press,* 22 Sept. 1957, sec. 8: 9.

82. For planning the early NHWs, see "National Home Week," 101–7.

83. William K. Trosene, "Builders to Open Houses for Inspection Next Week: Public Can Visit 35 Homes Being Built During First National Home Week," *Pittsburgh Press,* 29 Aug. 1948, 58.

84. "Origin and History of National Home Week."

85. Hugh L. Morris, "Resistance Tested: Home Week to Provide Clues to 1958 Market," *Washington Post,* 14 Sept. 1957, sec. C: 6.

86. National Home Week, 1955–57, Memorandums (folder), Record Group 8: Products and Services, box 08-037, National Association of Home Builders (NAHB) Archives, Washington, DC. For more information about the role of television programming in disseminating postwar ideas about house and home, see D. Harris, *Little White Houses,* chapter 7, "The Home Show: Televising the Postwar House."

87. Memorandums related to NHW participation of the Westinghouse Appliance Division, Youngstown Kitchens, and Bell Telephone, in National Home Week, 1955–57, Memorandums (folder), NAHB Archives.

88. "Parade of Homes," National Home Week Program, 1954 (folder), Record Group 8, box 08-037, NAHB Archives.

89. "National Home Week Roundup," 59.

90. Advertisement, "Twin Home-O-Rama," *Pittsburgh Press,* 7 July 1963, sec. 6: 5.

91. "Parade of Homes," 68.

92. "Challenge of Right Now," 122.

93. "Merchandising from the Ground Up," 90.

94. "Newest Marketing Trends," 112.

95. "Merchandising from the Ground Up," 90.

96. Eichler, *Merchant Builders,* 79.

97. Funk and Funk, interview, 13 Aug. 2002.

98. "Design: Builders Hear What Architects Think," 58.

99. Ames and McClelland, *National Register Bulletin, Historic Residential Suburbs,* 61.

100. Federal Housing Administration (FHA), *Technical Bulletin No. 4* (1937), 2.

101. York, "Young Architect's Role in Mass Housing," 16.

102. "Architects, Builders, Lenders and Suppliers Agree," 121.

103. Sternlieb and Hughes, "Post-Shelter Society," 40–41.

104. "Designing for Today's Reluctant Buyers," 45.

105. "Why Buyers Buy," 52.

106. For a period essay on housing industry research, see Dietz, "Housing Industry Research"; for the Small Homes Council, see D. Harris, *Little White Houses.*

107. For examples of important studies, see Bodek, *House and Why People Buy Houses;* Fuller & Smith & Ross, "National Consumer Survey of the Housing Market."

108. "Home Builder—Who Is He?" 30.

109. For the design of Eichler houses, see Adamson and Arbunich, *Eichler,* and Adams, "Eichler Home," 164–78.

110. For the term, see Martin, "Tract-House Modern."

111. Jacobs, "Belair at Bowie, Maryland," 8–11.

112. "Here's How One Custom Builder Operates," 127–28.

113. "Design: Builders Hear What Architects Think," 58.

114. Bozzo, interview, 17 Feb. 2002.

115. Lynes, *Domesticated Americans,* 18.

2. THE IMAGINED CONSUMER

1. Berger, "Preface to the 1968 Printing," xx–xxi.

2. Some of the better-known works of this group include: John R. Seely, R. Alexander Sim, and Elizabeth W. Loosely, *Crestwood Heights* (1956); John Keats, *The Crack in the Picture Window* (1956); William H. Whyte, *The Organization Man* (1956); Russell Lynes, *The Domesticated Americans* (1957); Louis Winnick, *American Housing and Its Use* (1957); William M. Dobriner, *The Suburban Community* (1958); Richard E. Gordon, Katherine K. Gordon, and Max Gunther, *The Split-Level Trap* (1960); Betty Friedan, *The Feminine Mystique* (1963); William M. Dobriner, *Class in Suburbia* (1963); Herbert J. Gans, *The Levittowners* (1967); Scott Donaldson, *The Suburban Myth* (1969); H. Paul Douglass, *The Suburban Trend* (1970); and Thomas A. Clark, *Blacks in Suburbs* (1979).

3. Cohen, *Consumers' Republic,* 200–203. Since nonwhite prospective home buyers, regardless of their class or economic standing, could not easily purchase a new house, many members of ethnic, or historically "racial," groups, such as Italian Americans and Jewish Americans, saw benefit in being considered "white" and increasingly positioned themselves

as such. They were able to do this in part because national racial politics from the 1930s onward focused on black-white relationships and ending segregation. For more on this complex process, see Jacobson, *Whiteness of a Different Color;* Guglielmo, *White on Arrival;* Roediger, *Working toward Whiteness;* and D. Harris, *Little White Houses.*

4. Seligman, "New Masses," 153.

5. Riesman, "Suburban Sadness," 401.

6. "How to Sell New Houses," 136.

7. The movement toward this association had begun a generation earlier. See Hornstein, *Nation of Realtors,* 202–3.

8. For 1940, see NAHB, *Housing Almanac,* 9; "Home Ownership Now 63 Per Cent," *Pittsburgh Press,* 23 May 1965, sec. 6: 1.

9. For working-class home ownership early in the twentieth century, see Marsh, "From Separation to Togetherness," 520.

10. Colean, "After All . . . ," 60.

11. Lynd, "Foreword," viii, ix.

12. William K. Trosene, "Many Ex-GIs Wading Too Deep into Home-Buying Market," *Pittsburgh Press,* 23 June 1946, sec. 3: 11; Lynes, *Domesticated Americans,* 20.

13. Kaufman, *Homeseekers' Handbook,* 18–19, 42–43; "Buy a House—or Rent?"

14. "Place of Real Estate," 27.

15. Colean, "You Can't Dream Yourself a House," 46–47 (for illustrations), 89 (for quote).

16. Janet Levritz, telephone interview with the author, 2 July 2009.

17. "How Much House You Can Buy," 13.

18. "How to Tell if You Can Afford"; Grief, "Hidden Costs in Building or Buying"; Soule, "How Much House Can You Afford?"; Springer, "What Can You Afford to Pay"; Watkins, "How Much House Can You Afford?"

19. "How Much Besides the Down Payment?" 49–50.

20. Mortgage Bankers Association of America, "Jane and Bill Learn How a Mortgage Works," RHC.

21. Robick, interview, 16 Feb. 2002.

22. Charles Lodge and Helen Lodge, survey form, 9 Aug. 2002.

23. Remsburg and Remsburg, "What Went Wrong in Dreamland," 136.

24. England, "Changing Suburbs, Changing Women," 40.

25. Scheick, "What's Happened to Housing," 63.

26. C. E. Clark, "Ranch-House Suburbia," 171.

27. E. T. May, *Homeward Bound,* 143–44.

28. Bell, "Social Choice, Life Styles," 227.

29. Checkoway, "Large Builders," 38–39.

30. As quoted in "Differences in Tomorrow's Housing Market," 83.

31. Archer, *Architecture and Suburbia,* 259.

32. H. Henderson, "Rugged American Collectivism," 83.

33. Kisak and Kisak, survey form, 4 Aug. 2002.

34. D. Harris, *Little White Houses,* 20–22.

35. "Business and the Urban Crisis," insert: C3. See also Sugrue, *Origins of the Urban Crisis.*

36. Nicolaides and Wiese, *Suburb Reader,* chapter 11; Cohen, *Consumers' Republic,* 212–27; and Pattillo-McCoy, *Black Picket Fences,* 23–25.

37. Wiese, *Places of Their Own,* chapter 7; "Atlanta Housing Council Proposes 'Negro Expansion Areas,'"

38. "Cornerstone for a New Magazine," 107.

39. Jacobs, "Beyond Levittown," 92–93.

40. Alan Lupe, "The Changing Face of Bowie," Baltimore *Evening Sun,* 9 Oct. 1963, sec. D: 11.

41. Eichler, *Merchant Builders,* 91. For the Eichlers' experience with integrated developments, see Center for the Study of Democratic Institutions, *Race and Housing;* "How Eichler Sells Open Occupancy"; and Adamson and Arbunich, *Eichler,* 197–204.

42. Neil MacNeil, "Builders Open Drive to House Minorities," *Washington Post*, 7 Mar. 1954, sec. R: 7.

43. Ibid.

44. "Typical White Suburbanite," 128.

45. Robert E. Baker, "'Income Integration' Is the Real Solution," *Washington Post*, 20 Mar. 1966, sec. E: 3.

46. H. Henderson, "Rugged American Collectivism," 85.

47. Cohen, *Consumers' Republic*, 213.

48. For 1940 and 1960, see Nicolaides and Wiese, *Suburb Reader*, 322; for 1977, see T. A. Clark, *Blacks in Suburbs*, 21.

49. Weise, *Places of Their Own*, 160–62.

50. Sternlieb and Lake, "Aging Suburbs and Black Homeownership," 107.

51. Rapkin, "Heart of the Matter," 22. These vacated neighborhoods tended to be located adjacent to established black areas of cities. See Lacy, *Blue-Chip Black*, 47–50.

52. Baxandall and Ewen, *Picture Windows*, 184.

53. Weise, *Places of Their Own*, 154 55; Pattillo-McCoy, *Black Picket Fences*, 24–25.

54. Donald Ungar, "Minority Housing Sped by Decision," *Washington Post*, 23 May 1954, sec. R: 19.

55. T. A. Clark, *Blacks in Suburbs*, 103; Sternlieb and Lake, "Aging Suburbs and Black Homeownership," 114–15. See also Lipsitz, *Possessive Investment in Whiteness*, in particular chapters 1 and 2.

56. Weise, *Places of Their Own*, 154–55, T. A. Clark, *Blacks in Suburbs*, 97–98; Rapkin, "Heart of the Matter," 25.

57. Cordtz, "Taunted by Black Extremists," 224.

58. Rapkin, "Heart of the Matter," 25.

59. See Hardwick, "Homesteads and Bungalows"; an observation forwarded by Sies, "North American Suburbs," 336–37.

60. Myers, *Sticks 'n Stones*, 3. See also Sugrue, "Jim Crow's Last Stand."

61. Cohen, *Consumers' Republic*, 252.

62. Wiese, *Places of Their Own*, 165.

63. As quoted in Wilson, *Hamilton Park*, 79.

64. See Reese, "Separate but Equal?" For period coverage, see "Lesson in Merchandising"; Earnest, "Selling the Minority Buyer."

65. Little, "Other Side of the Tracks," 278.

66. "How to Increase Sales Volume Today," 116–17.

67. "Editorial: Here Is the Great New Challenge," 124.

68. Ibid., 129.

69. Galbraith, *Affluent Society*, 128.

70. Lynes, *Domesticated Americans*, 85.

71. Anderson and Anderson, survey form, 21 Aug. 2002.

72. Fuller & Smith & Ross, "National Consumer Survey," 2, 9; Census Bureau, *Housing Construction Statistics, 1889 to 1964*, 18.

73. Berger, *Working-Class Suburb*, 4–14, chapter 2.

74. Hurley, *Diners, Bowling Alleys, and Trailer Parks*, 13–14; Cohen, *Consumers' Republic*, chapter 7.

75. Eichler, *Merchant Builders*, 136.

76. Morgan-Ryan, "This Is Oskaloosa," 104.

77. As Levittown's upwardly mobile, white-collar residents moved on in the 1950s, they were largely replaced by middle-income, blue-collar migrants from the city. See Dobriner, *Class in Suburbia*, as analyzed in Cohen, *Consumers' Republic*, 200–202. The second Levittown, in Pennsylvania, was segregated economically because each section was composed of a single type of model. See D. Harris, "'House I Live In,'" 202.

78. Mowrer, "Sequential and Class Variables," 108.

79. Seligman, "New Masses," 155.

80. "A Survey Tells Why You Buy," *Chicago Tribune*, 12 Oct. 1968, sec. W: A16.

81. "Better Houses Abuilding," 106.

82. Kammen, *American Culture, American Tastes*, 167–68.

83. Beauregard, *When America Became Suburban*, 14.

84. Packard, *Waste Makers*, 204.

85. Sears, Roebuck & Co., *Sears, Roebuck Catalog of Houses*, 1.

86. Five survey respondents offered that "security" was still a consideration for some purchasers in the 1960s. See Clifford Deedler and June Deedler, survey form, 25 July 2002; Mary Kay Dillman, survey form, n.d. [July–Aug. 2002]; George Kushner and Teresa Kushner, survey form, 8 Aug. 2002; William Lisac and Lois Lisac, survey form, 13 Aug. 2002; Ponter, survey form, 21 July 2002.

87. Prentice, "Should I Trade in My House," 30. This article was balanced with a "No!" argument written by Fred C. Hecht, chairman of the board of the "Home Improvement Council." See Hecht, "Should I Trade in My House."

88. For one example of how equity and family changes worked to encourage trading up, see "Buying a Home Proves to Be a Growth Investment."

89. "Is This a Good Time," 116.

90. "Buy a House—or Rent?" 9.

91. Jacobs, "Beyond Levittown," 108.

92. Mark Clements Research, "Housing Design and the American Family," 137; C. E. Clark, *American Family Home*, 209–10.

93. Fuller & Smith & Ross, "National Consumer Survey," table 117.

94. Brenneman, "Houses America Needs," 53.

95. Kammen, *American Culture, American Tastes*, 55.

96. "Buying Trends in the U.S.," 12.

97. "Higher Incomes, More Spending," 16. See also "No Drop in Consumer Buying Plans."

98. "U.S. Life Is Different"; "Consumer Spends His Dollar Differently."

99. "U.S. Life Is Different," 69.

100. Campbell, "Consuming Goods," 26.

101. Lippincott, *Design for Business*, 10. Interestingly, Lippincott rethought his stance by 1960, when he penned the article "The Yearly Model Changes Must Go," chronicling how flashy annual changes trumped product quality. See Whitely, "Toward a Throw-Away Culture," 8.

102. For the American family and domestic purchases, see E. T. May, *Homeward Bound*, chapter 7.

103. Lynes, *Domesticated Americans*, 20.

104. For obsolescence, see Packard, *Waste Makers*, 65–66 (quote on 142).

105. Ibid., 142.

106. "1936–1956: 20 Years in Review," 253.

107. Lizabeth Cohen cites George Katona and Eva Mueller's *Consumer Expectations, 1953–1956*, for this explanation of consumer demand. See Cohen, *Consumers' Republic*, 133.

108. Lyon, "Take Your Shopping List with You," 31.

109. "Challenge of Right Now," 121.

110. Klaber, "Where?"; Sturm, "Before You Buy a House"; Nunn, "50 Money-Stretching Tips"; Yarmon, *Getting the Most for Your Money*; "Buying a House," 13–15.

111. Colean, "Should You Build, Buy or Alter?" 62.

112. Springer, "Pitfalls to Avoid in Buying," 179.

113. "What You Can Expect," 20.

114. Sudman, Bradburn, and Gockel, "Extent and Characteristics of Racially Integrated Housing," 78.

115. Robick, interview, 16 Feb. 2002.

116. Springer, "Pitfalls to Avoid in Buying," 181–82.

117. Ingersoll, "What to Look For," 53.

118. "Don't Build Your House on a Handshake."

119. Cobb, "How to Get Along with Your Builder," 37.

120. Ibid., 37, 82.

121. Watkins, "Keep a Cool Head," 18.

122. "Editorial: Here Is the Great New Challenge," 124.

123. Sam Dawson, "U.S. Standard of Living Was Never Higher Than in 1948," *Washington Post*, 3 Jan. 1949, sec. C: 6; "Living Standard Keeps Rising, U.S. Reports," *Los Angeles Times*, 18 Nov. 1962, sec. D: 13.

124. Coffin, "Maryland's Montgomery County," 55.

3. LIVABILITY IN THE MINIMUM HOUSE

1. "Tomorrow's Homes Today," 92.

2. Census Bureau, *Sixteenth Census of the United States, 1940*, 87, table 47.

3. Winnick, "Housing," 90–91.

4. In *Expanding the American Dream*, Barbara Kelly demonstrates how working-class residents in Levittown, New York, who remained in their houses created middle-class environments and forged middle-class identities through additions to their minimum houses. These included dining rooms, family rooms, carports and garages, and additional bedrooms and bathrooms.

5. Marshall Andrews, "Youth's First Hope: Elders Held Unable to Give Advice on Better Family Life," *Washington Post*, 8 May 1948, 3.

6. W. Adams, "What America Wants to Build," 24.

7. "Houses Best Buy for Today's Dollar," 85.

8. "Worst Is Over," 11; Haeger, "Facts You Should Know," 48.

9. Haeger, "Facts You Should Know," 47.

10. "Regulation X Ends," *Wall Street Journal*, 16 Sept. 1952, 3.

11. "How Controls Affect Buyers," *Chicago Tribune*, 11 Oct. 1950, 4.

12. "'52 Building Boom Surprised Experts," *Washington Post*, 4 Jan. 1953, sec. R: 2.

13. Jackson, *Crabgrass Frontier*, 193; Census

Bureau, *Housing Construction Statistics, 1889 to 1964*, 18–19.

14. Jackson, *Crabgrass Frontier*, 232.

15. Wyatt, "When You Will Get Your Home," 48.

16. Curtis Publishing Company, *Urban Housing Survey*, 22.

17. For the interplay between urban decline and suburban growth in the postwar period, see Beauregard, *When America Became Suburban*, in particular chapter 5.

18. The National Register of Historic Places also uses the terms *minimal traditional* and *FHA house* in the documentation of postwar suburbs. The origin of *minimal traditional* is generally cited as McAlester and McAlester, *Field Guide to American Houses*, 478.

19. Although the FHA was a New Deal initiative of the Roosevelt administration, many of its "institutional guidelines governing subdivision development and large-scale [housing] operations" were an outgrowth of Herbert Hoover's "President's Conference on Home Building and Home Ownership," held in Dec. 1931. The ideas "discussed and concluded" at the conference, about raising standards of design and construction, maintaining real estate values, and establishing a new and more robust system of home financing, formed the core of the FHA's mission. See Wallace and Reed, with McClelland, National Historic Landmark nomination for "Radburn," 30–31.

20. Tobey, *Technology as Freedom*, 94, 101.

21. Federal Housing Administration, for the Central Housing Committee, flow chart titled "Federal Agencies in the Field of Urban Housing, 1938," 6 Oct. 1938, box 8, Federal Housing Administration Correspondence, Entry 3, General Records of the Executive Secretary, 1935–42, RG 207, Records of the Central Housing Committee, Records of the Housing and Home Finance Agency, NARA.

22. Memorandum, Sub-Committee on Technical Research to Peter Grimm, 17 Sept. 1935, box 2, Central Housing Committee, Entry 3, RG 207, Records of the Central Housing Committee, Records of the Housing and Home Finance Agency, NARA.

23. Hise, *Magnetic Los Angeles,* 56–65.

24. FHA, *Principles of Planning Small Houses* (1937), 2.

25. G. Wright, *Moralism and the Model Home,* 33–40; G. Wright, *Building the Dream,* 109–13; C. E. Clark, *American Family Home,* chapter 2, "Dreams and Realities," and chapter 4, "The House as Artistic Expression"; Volz, "Modern Look"; Grier, "Decline of the Memory Palace"; Cromley, *Alone Together,* 91–101, 173–85.

26. G. Wright, *Moralism and the Model Home,* 244–46; G. Wright, *Building the Dream,* 171–72; C. E. Clark, *American Family Home,* chapter 6, "The Bungalow Craze"; B. A. May, "Progressivism and the Colonial Revival"; Robertson, "Male and Female Agendas for Domestic Reform"; Volz, "Modern Look"; Grier, "Decline of the Memory Palace," 63–70.

27. G. Wright, *Moralism and the Model Home,* 235–40.

28. For more on these organizations, see Tucker, "Small House Problem"; Hutchison, "Cure for Domestic Neglect"; Reiff, *Houses from Books,* 208–11.

29. Reiff, *Houses from Books,* chapter 7; Stevenson and Jandl, *Houses by Mail.*

30. Tucker, "Small House Problem," 43.

31. *Small Homes of Architectural Distinction.*

32. For German architecture between the world wars, see Lane, *Architecture and Politics in Germany.*

33. For more on May and the *siedlungen,* see S. R. Henderson, *Building Culture.*

34. For more on Bauer, see Radford, *Modern Housing for America.*

35. Ibid., 196–97.

36. G. Wright, *USA,* 123.

37. Mennel, "'Miracle House Hoop-La,'" 340–61.

38. Shanken, *194X,* chapter 3.

39. Mennel, "'Miracle House Hoop-La,'" 349; Shanken, *194X,* 166–73; Archer, *Architecture and Suburbia,* 269–83.

40. Curtis Publishing Company, *Urban Housing Survey,* 68.

41. "House Omnibus," 119.

42. "Home Items Once 'Extras' Now Considered as Integral," *Washington Post,* 3 July 1949, sec. R: 5.

43. Sherman, "Higher Living Standards Encouraged," 78.

44. Hise, *Magnetic Los Angeles,* 67–68.

45. Riemer, "Livability," 149. The concept in the United States extends back to Andrew Jackson Downing's ideas about "convenience" within his discussion of the "Utility of Fitness" in his seminal *Cottage Residences* (1842).

46. FHA, *Principles of Planning Small Houses* (1946), 4.

47. Hise, *Magnetic Los Angeles,* 66–69.

48. "Home Building under Titles II and III," 12.

49. FHA, *Principles of Planning Small Houses* (1946), 37.

50. Ibid.

51. Dean and Breines, *Book of Houses,* vii.

52. "Home Building under Titles II and III," 11.

53. FHA, *Principles of Planning Small Houses* (1946), 1.

54. For one example of this occurrence, see Liccese-Torres, "Arlington Forest Historic District," sec. 7, 6–7.

55. "What Is 'the ECONOMY HOUSE'?" 21.

56. Entry 2, Case Files for Homes, Dec. 1934–Dec. 1938, RG 31, Records of the Federal Housing Administration, NARA. A majority of the submitted projects date from 1937

through 1939, beyond the end year noted for the collection.

57. HHFA, *Materials Use Survey,* 4.

58. Ibid., 5.

59. Greg Hise notes that the average number of rooms in FHA-approved houses was already falling in the late 1930s, from 5.8 rooms in 1936 to 5.1 rooms in 1940 (*Magnetic Los Angeles,* 69).

60. "Planning the Postwar House," 77.

61. "'Economy' Home Matures," *Washington Post,* 25 Dec. 1949, sec. M: 12.

62. "Cape Cod Simplicity Needed for Postwar," 97.

63. William K. Trosene, "Pittsburgh Builders Turning More to Cost-Saving Ideas," *Pittsburgh Press,* 25 Mar. 1951, 63.

64. HHFA, *Materials Use Survey,* 4.

65. Mehlhorn, "What Makes a Plan Good or Bad?" 156.

66. Normile, "Open Planning," 42.

67. "Open Planning"; "Cliffwood."

68. Isenstadt, *Modern American House,* 175.

69. Ibid., 210.

70. "What Can Be Done about It?" 120.

71. Advertisement, "Encino Park Homes," *Los Angeles Times,* 11 Sept. 1949, sec. E: 4 (for quote) and 4 Sept. 1949, sec. E: 5 (for image). The "porch" noted in the text of the 11 Sept. 1949 advertisement refers to the modest sheltered area at the front door.

72. C. E. Clark, *American Family Home,* 228.

73. Reisner, "Trend to Make"; "Rooms Have a New Job Today." See also C. E. Clark, *American Family Home,* 198–200.

74. Dean and Breines, *Book of Houses,* 71.

75. Some of the information in this section previously appeared in an edited version without notes as Jacobs, "Master of the House."

76. Lupton and Miller, *Bathroom, the Kitchen,* 34. See also Schlereth, "Conduits and Conduct."

77. Lupton and Miller, *Bathroom, the Kitchen,* 34; Davidson, "Early Twentieth-Century Hotel Architects," 86–87.

78. Houses constructed in suburban areas would have fallen largely under the "urban" label, of which 71 percent had full private bathrooms, although some would have been included in the "rural non-farm" category, which stood at a much lower 36 percent. Controlling for race, a shocking 83 percent of dwellings occupied by nonwhites lacked a private full bathroom, while for whites the figure was 45 percent. See Census Bureau, *Sixteenth Census of the United States, 1940,* 15, table 6a, and 18, table 6c.

79. In Sept. 1949, the *Washington Post* reported that 90 percent of newly constructed houses included a shower either in a stall or over a bathtub. See "Today's Homes Improved over Decade Ago," *Washington Post,* 4 Sept. 1949, sec. R: 2.

80. "Bathroom Layouts Need Revamping," 73; Brooks, "How Large Should Your Bathroom Be?" 208; and "Will It Be a Dream House?" 207.

81. Mehlhorn, "What Makes a Plan Good or Bad?" 156; Brooks, "How Large Should Your Bathroom Be?" 210; Lupton and Miller, *Bathroom, the Kitchen,* 34.

82. Dean and Breines, *Book of Houses,* 115.

83. Lupton and Miller, *Bathroom, the Kitchen,* 25–26.

84. HHFA, *Materials Use Survey,* 5; Henn, "Second Bathroom Boosts Sales," 146.

85. Haeger, "Facts You Should Know," 50.

86. Paxton, *What People Want,* 46.

87. Ibid.

88. Cromley, *Food Axis,* 190.

89. M. Wright and R. Wright, *Guide to Easier Living,* 5.

90. Faulkner and Faulkner, *Inside Today's Home,* 68; Cromley, *Food Axis,* 199.

91. G. Wright, *Moralism and the Model Home,* 239–40, 271–73; C. E. Clark, *American Family Home,* 136–38, 159, 162; Lupton and Miller, *Bathroom, the Kitchen,* 46–48. For more on home economics and the kitchen in the early twentieth century, see Cromley, *Food Axis,* 137–43; and M. Wright and R. Wright, *Guide to Easier Living,* chapter 7, "The Housewife-Engineer.".

92. G. Wright, *Building the Dream,* 172.

93. Palmer, *Domesticity and Dirt,* 2.

94. S. R. Henderson, "Revolution in the Woman's Sphere," 234–37.

95. S. R. Henderson, "Revolution in the Woman's Sphere," 236–37. See also Kinchin, with O'Connor, *Counter Space,* chapter 2.

96. Lupton and Miller, *Bathroom, the Kitchen,* 50–55; Ierley, *Comforts of Home,* 243–49.

97. Tobey, *Technology as Freedom,* chapter 1, "The Limits of Private Electrical Modernization, 1919–1929"; "How to Plan for Modern Electrical Living."

98. Between 1919 and 1929, for example, 96 percent of the families of Mount Holyoke College students reduced their dependence on household servants in one way or another; during the same period these families also purchased four or five household appliances. See Cowan, *More Work for Mother,* 175. See also Sutherland, "Modernizing Domestic Service," 245. Even Lihotzky's Frankfurt Kitchen was entirely closed off from the rest of the dwelling in order to maintain "coexisting spheres" within the home. See S. R. Henderson, "Revolution in the Woman's Sphere," 236.

99. Rainwater, Coleman, and Handel, *Workingman's Wife,* 177; G. Wright, *Building the Dream,* 169–71; Cowan, *More Work for Mother,* 196–201.

100. Cromley, *Food Axis,* 177.

101. Beveridge, "Trends in Home Equipment," 402.

102. "Kitchen Planning," 96.

103. Nickles, "More Is Better," 601.

104. HHFA, *Materials Use Survey,* 17.

105. Tobey, *Technology as Freedom,* 119.

106. Beauregard, *When America Became Suburban,* 112–13; Cross, *All-Consuming Century,* 88–89; Hyman, *Debtor Nation,* 136–37.

107. "Trends in the Building Field: Residential Building Down," 16.

108. HHFA, *Materials Use Survey,* 4; "Characteristics of Single-Family Homes," 51, table 1.

109. Hess, *Ranch House,* 13.

110. Ibid., 28–29.

111. Faragher, "Bungalow and Ranch House," 165.

112. Hess, *Ranch House,* 56. For plans, see "Project Larger Than Levittown Planned," 144. For the development of Panorama City, see Hise, *Magnetic Los Angeles,* chapter 6.

113. "Functional Planning Assures," 84.

114. "Two Houses by Builder Kinsey," 104; "Western Style Invades," 103; "Large Homes and Big Values Here," 108.

115. Dean and Breines, *Book of Houses,* 83.

116. "Architectural Potpourri," 204.

117. Matern, "Home Buyers Are Voting," 80–81.

118. Gillies, "What Is a Modern House?" 714.

119. "What House Buyers Are Looking For," 109.

120. HHFA, *Materials Use Survey,* 5; "Characteristics of Single-Family Homes," 51.

121. Silpher, "Progress Report," 4–39.

122. Paxton, *What People Want,* 30.

123. "What House Buyers Are Looking For," 107.

124. "Return of the Large House," 108.

125. "Today's Homes Improved over Decade Ago," R2.

126. "Ranch Type Home Still Most Popular," *Chicago Tribune,* 16 Sept. 1951, sec. SW: A1.

127. "Architectural Potpourri," 205.

128. Paxton, *What People Want,* 34.

129. "What House Buyers Are Looking For," 108.

130. "Gew-Gaws Termed Home Buyers' Lure," *New York Times,* 12 July 1950, 25.

131. Carter and Hinchcliff, *Family Housing,* 45–46.

132. Ibid., 46.

133. "Trends in the Building Field: Why People Buy," 16, 188.

134. "No 'Minimums,'" *Washington Post,* 8 Sept. 1956, sec. H: 22.

135. FHA, *Principles of Planning Small Houses* (1937), 2.

136. David L. Bowen, "New FHA Standards Inspire This Ranch Dwelling," *Washington Post,* 28 Mar. 1959, sec. B: 5.

137. "Better Houses Abuilding," 106.

138. As transcribed in Goodman, "Do People Want Traditional? NO," 138.

139. Herman H. York et al., "What People Want in a Home," *New York Times,* 5 May 1957, 401.

4. CASUAL LIVING

1. Allen, "Big Change in Suburbia, 26.

2. M. Wright and R. Wright, *Guide to Easier Living,* 5.

3. E. T. May, *Homeward Bound,* xxi.

4. Mintz and Kellogg, *Domestic Revolutions,* 180.

5. Dorothy Barclay, "'Lack of Busy Families' Worries Experts, Who Suggest Counsel for Household as Unit," *New York Times,* 31 Aug. 1951, special: 17.

6. H. Henderson, "Mass-Produced Suburbs I," 29.

7. "Plan-itorial . . . Home Buying Motivations."

8. Liston, "It's A Good Life." See also M. Wright and R. Wright, *Guide to Easier Living,* 4–5.

9. See Rainwater et al., *Workingman's Wife,* 187 (for quote), chapters 10 and 11.

10. C. E. Clark, "Ranch-House Suburbia," 171, 174, 177; C. E. Clark, *American Family Home,* 211.

11. Hess, *Ranch House,* 14.

12. Ibid., 17; C. E. Clark, "Ranch-House Suburbia," 174.

13. Matern, *52 House Plans for 1952,* n.p. (30).

14. For a discussion of the evolution in the location, character, and equipment in Levitt and Sons kitchens in the 1950s, see Miner, "Pink Kitchens for Little Boxes."

15. D. Harris, "'House I Live In,'" 220–21; D. Harris, *Little White Houses,* 197–98.

16. Mehlhorn, "What Makes a Plan Good or Bad?" 156.

17. "Will It Be a Dream House?" 206–7.

18. "New Kitchens Are the Heart of the Home," *Washington Post,* 12 Sept. 1954, sec. H: 6.

19. Cromley, *Food Axis,* 196. Cromley also describes an architect-designed "living-kitchen" featured in the May 1945 issue of *Architectural Forum* (194). The concept behind this renovation of a house built earlier in the century, which merged space for domestic work, dining, and lounging, foreshadowed multifunctional spaces that would not become prevalent in new middle-class houses until the late 1950s and early 1960s.

20. Clifford Clark explains that at least one period source defined a "living kitchen" as something open to the living room, an arrangement not unlike the kitchens of the one-story Levittowner models at Levittown, Pennsylvania (*American Family Home,* 209).

21. Marian Manners, "Modernized Kitchens Become Living Center," *Los Angeles Times,* 11 June 1950, part IV: 4.

22. "Come into the Kitchen," 39. For additional connections between enlarged kitchens

and the disappearance of servants, see also "Family Room," 139.

23. M. Wright and R. Wright, *Guide to Easier Living,* 3.

24. Nickles, "More Is Better," 601. See also Cromley, *Food Axis,* 193–98. For more about working-class living space and its evolution over time, see Heath, *Patina of Place.*

25. "Today's Kitchen Given Charm of an Earlier Day," *Chicago Tribune,* 16 Sept. 1951, part 6, sec. 3: 11.

26. Mark Clements Research, "Housing Design and the American Family," 72. This study divided the women into two groups based on house value at the time of the data collection. Regardless of the city, the "lower" group lived in houses valued between $14,000 and $24,999 and the "upper" group in houses valued between $25,000 and $50,000 (5). In 1964, the year the findings were released, the median sales price of a new house purchased using all types of financing was $18,900, and the average sales price was $20,500. See Census Bureau and HUD, *New One-Family Homes Sold and for Sale,* 8, 10.

27. "Kitchen to Feel at Home In," 62.

28. C. E. Clark, *American Family Home,* 215; Cromley, *Food Axis,* 187; A. Adams, "Eichler Home," 168–69.

29. Das, *American Woman in Modern Marriage,* 114.

30. Mark Clements Research, "Housing Design and the American Family," 7. This survey also listed a fifth role, less related to the daily function of the house, called the "aesthetic woman." Embodying a somewhat subjective, catchall role, the "aesthetic woman" was concerned with such issues as the location of windows, "to look out on the world," and bathroom lighting, "by which to make-up properly" (8).

31. Hanmer, "Kitchens for Family Living," 61. See also "Kitchens for Family Living"; "When Good Housekeeping Builds Kitchens";

advertisement, "OK, Girls, Here's Your LIVING KITCHEN," *Washington Post,* 8 Apr. 1956, sec. G: 11.

32. Advertisement, "Speed Up Your Home Sales with Hotpoint Kitchens in 1956!" *Architectural Record: Record Houses of 1956* 119 (mid-May 1956): 50.

33. "Keeping Room Comes Back," 49; "Come into the Kitchen," 43; "Family Room," 139; and "New Concepts in Kitchens," 96–97. As with colonial and Victorian spaces, linking the postwar family room to the "farm kitchen" is problematic: in the nineteenth century, kitchens became more or less segregated by gender and were work oriented. A precedent for the mid-century family room can be more appropriately found in the country sitting room. See McMurry, *Families and Farmhouses in Nineteenth-Century America,* 109–12 (for the kitchen) and chapter 5 (for the sitting room).

34. For this term relative to its function, see Jacobs, "Social and Spatial Change," 82, note 21.

35. "There's a New Room," 75.

36. Strawn and Matthews, "Companion Plans a House," 66–67.

37. "Bill Levitt's Third Big Town," 74. The publisher accidentally transposed the plans for the "old" two-story (p. 74) and the "old" one-and-one-half-story (p. 75) models.

38. Nelson and Wright, *Tomorrow's House,* 79.

39. For the lower-level recreation room as a type of "early" family room, see Jacobs, "Social and Spatial Change," 75–76. See also G. Wright, *Building the Dream,* 255 (for a room fostering togetherness); and Spigel, *Make Room for TV,* particularly 37–40 (for linking togetherness, the television, and the family room).

40. "Buyers Tastes Are Changing," 80.

41. "Don't Forget the Children," 149.

42. Gruen, *Modern Home Decorating,* 140–41.

See also "Taking the 'Wreck' Out of 'Rec' Room," *Washington Post,* 6 Sept. 1958, sec. B: 14.

43. Jacobs, "Social and Spatial Change," 72.

44. "Keeping Room Comes Back," 49; Nelson and Wright, *Tomorrow's House,* 78–79; Pepis, "Return of the Two-Parlor Plan"; Forester, "Where *IS* the Living Room?" 33.

45. Jacobs, "Social and Spatial Change," 74–75.

46. See "Keeping Room Comes Back," 49 (for quote).

47. Nelson and Wright, *Tomorrow's House,* 79; "House Omnibus," 96.

48. For the model as product, see Hine, *Populuxe,* 53.

49. "What Do *They* Want in a Home?" 16–18; John Wallace, "'Typical' American Home Has Style," *Washington Post,* 21 Sept. 1957, sec. C: 7.

50. Associated Plan Service, *Architects' 1957 Selection of New Home Plans,* 48.

51. "Bill Levitt Reorganizes," 45.

52. Advertisement, "Ready for Your Inspection," *Chicago Tribune,* 11 Sept. 1949: part 6, sec. 1: 5 (for "uniquely designed"); advertisement, "Fuel-Thrifty Trouble-Free Mueller Climatrol Heating Stars in 30 Official Model Homes!" *Chicago Tribune,* 18 Sept. 1949: part 3: B (for "5 room tri-level"); advertisement, "Today . . . All Roads Lead to the 3 Level French Provincial Display Home," *Pittsburgh Press,* 20 June 1948: 46 (for "different, unusual, unique").

53. "On Long Island," 111. For the prevalence of the split-level in the New York suburbs, see "New Jersey Using Split-Level Home," *New York Times,* 29 Sept. 1951: 26L; "Split-Levels Set the Sales Pace"; "Split Levels on Parade"; "On Long Island."

54. Schmitt, interview, 12 Aug. 2002; and Schmitt and Schmitt, survey form, 20 July 2002.

55. A 1955 *American Builder* article about a Chicago development explained: "Turning a ranch house into a split level required no drastic changes in floor plans. The bedroom

area was simply framed 4 ft. higher than the other half of the house." See "One Plan . . . 11 Houses," 108.

56. "Split-Levels Set the Sales Pace," 117.

57. "Family Rooms," 40.

58. "Taking the 'Wreck' Out of 'Rec' Room," B14.

59. "Split-Levels Set the Sales Pace," 117.

60. "On Long Island," 118.

61. "Do Split Level Houses Have to Be So Ugly?" 139.

62. Ormston, "Split-Level—Pro and Con," 75.

63. "Split-Levels Set the Sales Pace," 119.

64. Blietz, "Split-Level Siting Pays Off," 83.

65. "Raised Ranch Stimulates Sales," 62.

66. Ibid., 63.

67. Huntoon and White, "Split-Entry House," 139.

68. As quoted in "Mid-Level Ranch from East Catches On in N.W. Suburb," *Chicago Tribune,* 9 Sept. 1961, part 2: 4N.

69. Advertisement, "The Oxford," *Washington Post,* 21 Apr. 1962, sec. D: 3.

70. Huntoon and White, "Split-Entry House," 140.

71. Ibid., 144, 145.

72. "Remarkable Split-Entry House," 69.

73. "This House Sells," 133–35.

74. Lodge and Lodge, survey form, 9 Aug. 2002; and Charles Lodge and Helen Lodge, interview with the author, Glenshaw, PA, 12 Aug. 2002.

75. "Sleepy Hollow Woods: An Award-Winning Community of Colonial Homes in Annandale, Va.," 1960, http://www.sleepyhollowwoods.org/the-woods/from-the-archives/brochure/.

76. "20 Outstanding Houses," 106.

77. Plans of the Steinbeck house, 1961, Glenshaw, PA (in possession of John and Dorothy Petrancosta).

78. "Everywhere Today More and More People Want," 97. For more information on indoor-

outdoor design, see D. Harris, *Little White Houses,* 277–94.

79. Borncamp, "What Happened to the Porch?" 10.

80. D. Harris, "Making Your Private World," 193. See also D. Harris, *Little White Houses,* chapter 8, "Designing the Yard: Gardens, Property, and Landscape."

81. "What Home Buyers Want," 78.

82. Dave Bollinger, "Larger Living Space Prime Need of Family, *Press* Survey Shows," *Pittsburgh Press,* 2 Sept. 1956, sec. 1: 11.

83. "This Chart Tells You," 155.

84. Advertisement, "Pottawatomie Hills," *Chicago Tribune,* 24 Apr. 1954, part 1: 12.

85. Advertisement, "Maplewood Estates: Bethesda Originals," *Washington Post,* 10 July 1955, sec. G: 5; Murphy, "Characteristics of New 1-Family Houses," table 1, 573 (for median).

86. "Veteran McLean Area Builder of Homes for 'Gracious Living,'" *Washington Post,* 7 Sept. 1957, sec. E: 46.

87. Advertisement, "Delightfully Smart . . . This 7 Room Ranch Home," *Chicago Tribune,* 22 Sept. 1957, part 6, sec. 1: 2; Murphy, "Characteristics of New 1-Family Houses," table 1, 573.

88. Ryan Homes, "Homes of Distinction," 1960, RHC.

89. "What's So Good About Splits?" 151.

90. Goldstein, *Do It Yourself,* 37. See also Randl, "'Live Better Where You Are.'"

91. John Peter, "Plan for Outdoor Living before the Heat Wave," *Washington Post,* 23 Mar. 1952, sec. R: 4.

92. Gillies and Baylis, "Expand Your Living Outdoors," 46.

93. Ibid., 47.

5. THE ZONED HOUSE

1. The conceptual relationship between functional zoning and spatial efficiency in later postwar suburban houses shares affinities with planning in late-nineteenth- and early-twentieth-century apartments. See Cromley, *Alone Together.*

2. "31 Best-Sellers Reflect Today's New Emphasis," 96.

3. "Undaunted Home Buyers," 50.

4. "Land: The Squeeze Is On," 143.

5. "Land-1," 42.

6. "Two-Story Living," 72–79.

7. Charles Frankel, "The Trouble with 'Togetherness,'" *New York Times,* 27 Apr. 1958, sec. SM: 26.

8. May Osinga, "Togetherness—Yeah?" *Los Angeles Times,* 27 Aug. 1957, sec. III: 5.

9. Joseph Prendergast, "In Family Recreation, Don't Overdo Togetherness," *Washington Post,* 12 Sept. 1962, sec. C: 2.

10. "Psychological Pendulum Swinging from Togetherness to Individualism," *Los Angeles Times,* 16 Nov. 1961, sec. D: 17.

11. Ibid.

12. Frankel, "Trouble with 'Togetherness,'" SM26.

13. D. Harris, *Little White Houses,* chapter 4, "Private Worlds: The Spatial Contours of Exclusion and Privilege."

14. Sarah Booth Conroy, "Privacy at Home Is Crying Need, Say Homemakers in Parley Here," *Washington Post,* 11 Oct. 1957, sec. C: 8.

15. Stella Roach, "Happier Home Balance: Privacy Gaining on Togetherness," *Los Angeles Times,* 13 July 1961, sec. E: 3.

16. Mark Clements Research, "Housing Design and the American Family," 3, 28.

17. Ibid., 102–3.

18. "Designers Strive for Privacy for Each Child," *Chicago Tribune,* 22 June 1963, sec. 1A, W: 6.

19. "Are You Thinking about the Four-Bedroom Market," 134.

20. Ponter, survey form, 21 July 2002.

21. "America's Exploding Population," 110;

"There's a Lot to Learn," 90; Census Bureau and HUD, "New One-Family Homes Sold and for Sale," 15; Census Bureau and HUD, *Characteristics of New One-Family Homes: 1974*, 27.

22. Some of the information in this section previously appeared in an edited version without notes as Jacobs, "Master of the House."

23. "39 Ways to Build a Better Bathroom"; "Extra Bath Convenient, Adds to Resale Value," *Pittsburgh Press*, 20 Sept. 1953, sec. 5: 17; "How to Plan Your 1956 Bathrooms"; "What Price an Extra Bathroom?"

24. "Home Buyers Want Space," *Pittsburgh Press*, 13 Sept. 1959, sec. 5: 3.

25. Lupton and Miller, *Bathroom, the Kitchen*, 31.

26. Paxton, *What People Want*, 47.

27. "Getting Set for Tomorrow's Bath," 104; "Spotlight on Bathrooms," 56.

28. "Truth about Tubbing vs. Showering," 56, 123–24; "What Happened to the Saturday Night Bath?" 57.

29. Bollinger, "Larger Living Space," 11.

30. J. Parker, "Need an Extra Shower?" 176.

31. Census Bureau and HUD, *Characteristics of New One-Family Homes: 1974*, 33.

32. "House & Garden's 1955 House of Ideas," 80.

33. Ryan Homes, "Homes of Distinction," "The Fairmont," RHC.

34. "Center of the Home," 54.

35. "Return of the Dining Room," 56.

36. "Dining Room Is the Familiest Room," 111, 114.

37. Dorothy Roe, "Casual Living: Road Back to the Cave?" *Los Angeles Times*, 28 July 1958, sec. II: 1.

38. MacMasters, "Housewife Talks Tract Housing," 14.

39. A. Adams, "Eichler Home," 173–74. See Adamson and Arbunich, *Eichler*, 79, for a nearly identical 1959 floor plan by Anshen

& Allen that also included a furnishing plan to give some idea of how Eichler thought the spaces should function.

40. "Study of Home Planning Preferences," 17.

41. "When Your Houses Have Enough Exciting Features," 149.

42. "Builder Senses a Trend Back to Tradition and Formality," *Chicago Tribune*, 21 Oct. 1961, part 3, S: 3.

43. Kellogg, "Family Rooms Fancified," 76.

44. "Home Buyers Consider Family Room Vital," *Chicago Tribune*, 23 Oct. 1965, sec. 1C, N: 9.

45. Charles Lodge and Helen Lodge, survey form, 6 June 2004.

46. Maxine Cheshire and Peg Johnson, "Without Futuramic Electronic Marvels 'Dream House of Today' Is Roomy Low Colonial," *Washington Post*, 8 Oct. 1958, sec. D: 2.

47. MacMasters, "Housewife Talks Tract Housing," 15.

48. The use of this quote as the foundation for defining the character of the two daytime zones occurs in Jacobs, "Social and Spatial Change," 73–74, based on original text in Mark Clements Research, "Housing Design and the American Family," 90. *Family* is in brackets because of an apparent transcription error in the document, with *living* used to refer to both the "active" room and the "quiet" room. Elsewhere in the commentary the woman indicates that the television is not located in the living room—"we don't happen to care for television"; rather, it is in the other "active" living area, generically the "family" room.

49. John B. Willmann, "A Vote for Gracious Living: Home Owners Surveyed on What Makes Them Buy," *Washington Post*, 9 July 1960, sec. C: 1.

50. "Living Room Changing," *Washington Evening Star*, 7 Oct. 1961, sec. B: 12.

51. For "conversation," see Lois Lisac, survey form, 28 May 2004.

52. Hahn, "Give Your Living Room a Social Life," 62–64.

53. "Ideas That Sell Houses," 82.

54. Albert Sybo and Dolores Sybo, survey form, 9 June 2004.

55. Mark Clements Research, "Housing Design and the American Family," 123.

56. Ibid., 121–24. Uses are also drawn from the following: Grace H. Crane, survey form, n.d. [May–June 2004]; Mary Kay Dillman, survey form, n.d. [May–June 2004]; James Greenen, survey form, n.d. [May–June 2004]; Albert Jacobs and Barbara Jacobs, survey form, 28 May 2004; George Kisak, survey form, n.d. [May–June 2004]; Lisac, survey form, 28 May 2004; Lodge and Lodge, survey form, 6 June 2004; Robert Ponter, survey form, 9 June 2004; Shirley Robick, survey form, n.d. [May–June 2004]; Leo Schmitt, survey form, n.d. [May–June 2004]; Sybo and Sybo, survey form, 9 June 2004; James Werth and Shirley Werth, survey form, 5 June 2004.

57. S. Parker, *Leisure and Work*, 63; Spigel, *Make Room for TV*, 73.

58. Spigel, *Make Room for TV*, 92.

59. Cowan, *More Work for Mother*, 210.

60. "How to Design for the Market," 139.

61. Advertisement, "Grandmother Had 2 Parlors . . . and So Does Your 1963 Hoffman Home!" *Chicago Tribune*, 30 Mar. 1963, sec. 2, N: 12.

62. "There's a New Room," 74.

63. "Ten Plans by a Top Production-House Architect," 92.

64. Ibid., 94. While the description for this two-story model refers to this room as the "recreation room," its location and size were typical of family rooms in the 1960s, also indicated by the use of *family* for the space in the accompanying published plan.

65. "Kitchen-Family Rooms Are Getting Larger," 90.

66. Carter and Hinchcliff, *Family Housing*, 45; C. Clark, "Ranch-House Suburbia," 179.

67. "Do Split Level Houses Have to Be So Ugly?" 140.

68. "Coming Soon: More Livability," *Chicago Tribune*, 17 June 1961, part 2, W: 9.

69. Anderson and Anderson, survey form, 21 Aug. 2002.

70. Advertisement, "See the Home That 3,000 Women Designed: 1966 Ladies' Choice," *Pittsburgh Press*, 16 Oct. 1966, sec. 7: 3.

71. "Report on Interiors," 80.

72. Mark Clements Research, "Housing Design and the American Family," 34.

73. Ibid., 74.

74. "Making Sure You Know Their Kitchen Likes," 53.

75. Kizzia, "Profile: The 1967 Home Buyer," 102.

76. "Fast Movers and What Makes Them Go."

77. Mark Clements Research, "Housing Design and the American Family," 120–21.

78. "Boost Sales Appeal," 89.

79. "Engineered Kitchen Is High on Liveability," 45. For more on kitchen aesthetics, see "Kitchens"; and "Are Kitchens Old Hat?"

80. Jacobs, "Social and Spatial Change," 79–80.

81. "What Makes a Floor Plan Good?" 35.

82. Robick, interview, 16 Feb. 2002.

83. "Design File: Traffic Flow," 82.

84. "Six 'Building Boners' Customers Talk About," 74.

85. Whipple, "Stay Close to Your Buyers," 46.

86. "Today's Best Marketing and Merchandising," 117; "20 Outstanding Houses," 88–89.

87. "There's a Lot to Learn," 91.

88. Census Bureau and HUD, "New One-Family Homes Sold and for Sale, 1963 to 1967," cover.

89. Advertisement, "Please Step to the Rear

of the Home," *Pittsburgh Press,* 1 May 1966, sec. 8: 3.

90. "Most of the Land Shortage Talk," 107.

91. NAHB, *Housing Almanac,* 75; Census Bureau and HUD, *Characteristics of New One-Family Homes, 1974,* 52 (for 1971).

92. MacMasters, "Housewife Talks Tract Housing," 18.

93. Ibid., 28.

94. "Designing for Today's Reluctant Buyers," 44.

95. Matern, "Trend in Houses," 66.

96. Jacobs, "Social and Spatial Change," 76–79.

97. "Two-Story Living," 72.

98. Bloodgood, "If You're Looking for a Good Two-Story," 62.

99. Kizzia, "Profile: The 1967 Home Buyer," 102.

100. Anderson and Anderson, survey form, 21 Aug. 2002; Mary Conroy, telephone interview with the author, 3 Mar. 2000; Greenen, survey form, 22 July 2002; Jacobs and Jacobs, interview, 15 Feb. 2002; Margo Kyle-Keith, telephone interview with the author, 7 Mar. 2000; Lodge and Lodge, survey form, 9 Aug. 2002; Lodge and Lodge, interview, 12 Aug. 2002; Robick, interview, 16 Feb. 2002; Sybo, interview, 16 Feb. 2002.

101. W. Killmeyer of John R. C. Williams Advertising Agency for Ryan Homes, "A Plan," 26 Aug. 1965, (1), RHC.

102. Ibid.

103. Advertisement, "A Home for Experienced Owners," *Pittsburgh Press,* 12 Sept. 1965, sec. 7: 12.

104. Advertisement, "The Bucks County," *Pittsburgh Press,* 13 Mar. 1966, sec. 7: 3.

105. Advertisement, "1960 Home-O-Rama," *Pittsburgh Press,* 18 Sept. 1960, sec. 7: 8.

EPILOGUE

1. "Americans Called Best Housed People in World," *Los Angeles Times,* 9 Sept. 1951, sec. V: 3.

2. For an in-depth discussion of storage and its meanings in postwar middle-class houses, see D. Harris, *Little White Houses,* chapter 6.

3. "Where to Keep the Good Things," 43.

4. HHFA, *Materials Use Survey,* 5.

5. Ibid. A Bureau of Labor Statistics survey placed the total number of new houses having garages in the last quarter of 1949 at 53.3 percent. See "Garage," 75.

6. HHFA, *Materials Use Survey,* 5.

7. "Garage," 74.

8. Census Bureau and HUD, *Characteristics of New One-Family Homes: 1974,* 57.

9. Census Bureau and HUD, *New One-Family Homes Sold and For Sale, 1963 to 1967,* 147.

10. Census Bureau, "Characteristics of New Single-Family Houses Completed," 2013.

11. S&P/Dow Jones Indices, "S&P Case—Shiller U.S. National Home Price Index," Dec. 2013.

12. These totals include all single-family houses, both attached and detached. See Census Bureau, "Characteristics of New Single-Family Houses Completed," 2013 (figure in "Number of Stories").

13. Callis and Kresin, "Homeownership Rates for the United States: 1995 to 2013," table 4.

14. Rice, "Elusive Small-House Utopia."

15. Census Bureau, "Characteristics of New Single-Family Houses Completed," 2013.

16. Dillman, survey form, n.d. [May–June 2004].

Bibliography

ARCHIVES

Bowie Museum Archives at Belair. Bowie, MD.

National Archives and Records Administration (NARA), College Park, MD.

National Association of Home Builders (NAHB). Archives. Washington, DC.

Ryan Homes Collection (RHC). Architecture Archives. Carnegie Mellon University. Pittsburgh, PA.

Shaler Township Land Records. Township Municipal Offices. Glenshaw, PA.

INTERVIEWS

Alexander, David. Telephone interview with the author. 11 Aug. 2002.

Baumann, Renee. Telephone interview with the author. 3 Mar. 2002.

Bozzo, Frank, Jr. Interview with the author. Glenshaw, PA. 17 Feb. 2002.

Conroy, Mary. Telephone interview with the author. 3 Mar. 2000.

Federici, Jacqueline. Interview with the author. Bowie, MD. 21 Feb. 2006.

Fleming, Pam. Interview with the author. Bowie, MD. 14 Mar. 2000.

Funk, James, Margaret Funk, and Marge Goss. Interview with the author. Glenshaw, PA. 13 Aug. 2002.

Jacobs, Albert, and Barbara Jacobs. Interview with the author. Glenshaw, PA. 15 Feb. 2002.

Kisak, George, and Judith Kisak. Interview with the author. Glenshaw, PA. 13 Aug. 2002.

Kyle-Keith, Margo. Telephone interview with the author. 7 Mar. 2000.

Levritz, Janet. Telephone interview with the author. 2 July 2009.

Lodge, Charles, and Helen Lodge. Interview with the author. Glenshaw, PA. 12 Aug. 2002.

Mills, Barbara. Telephone interview with the author. 11 Mar. 2000.

Petrancosta, John, and Dorothy Petrancosta. Interview with the author. Glenshaw, PA. 8 Aug. 2002.

Resnick, Ira, and Merrill Resnick. Telephone interview with the author. 3 Mar. 2000.

Rize, Martin, and Tanya Rize. Interview with the author. Bowie, MD. 8 Mar. 2000.

Robick, Shirley. Interview with the author. Glenshaw, PA. 16 Feb. 2002.

Schmitt, Leo. Interview with the author. Glenshaw, PA. 12 Aug. 2002.

Sybo, Dolores, and Pamela Sybo. Interview with the author. Glenshaw, PA. 16 Feb. 2002.

Whalen, Michael. Telephone interview with the author. 3 Mar. 2000.

Yochelson, Ellis. Interview with the author. Bowie, MD. 17 Feb. 2006.

SURVEY FORMS

Anderson, Robert, and Frances Anderson. 21 Aug. 2002.

Anderson, Robert, and Frances Anderson. 8 June 2004.

Crane, Grace H. 23 Aug. [2002].

Crane, Grace H. N.d. [May–June 2004].

Deedler, Clifford, and June Deedler. 25 July 2002.

Dillman, Mary Kay. N.d. [July–Aug. 2002].

Dillman, Mary Kay. N.d. [May–June 2004].

Greenen, James. 22 July 2002.

Greenen, James. N.d. [May–June 2004].

Jacobs, Albert, and Barbara Jacobs. 28 May 2004.

Kisak, George. N.d. [May–June 2004].

Kisak, George, and Judith Kisak. 4 Aug. 2002.

Kushner, George, and Teresa Kushner. 8 Aug. 2002.

Lisac, Lois. 28 May 2004.

Lisac, William, and Lois Lisac. 13 Aug. 2002.

Lodge, Charles, and Helen Lodge. Aug. 2002.

Lodge, Charles, and Helen Lodge. 6 June 2004.

Ponter, Robert. 21 July 2002.

Ponter, Robert. 9 June 2004.

Robick, Shirley. N.d. [May–June 2004].

Schmitt, Leo. N.d. [May–June 2004].

Schmitt, Leo, and Carmen Schmitt. 20 July 2002.

Sybo, Albert, and Dolores Sybo. 9 June 2004.

Thompson, George, and Marjorie Thompson. 22 July 2002.

Werth, James, and Shirley Werth. N.d. [July–Aug. 2002].

Werth, James, and Shirley Werth. 5 June 2004.

OTHER SOURCES

Adams, Annemarie. "The Eichler Home: Intention and Experience in Postwar Suburbia." In *Perspectives in Vernacular Architecture, V, Gender, Class, and Shelter,* edited by Elizabeth Collins Cromley and Carter L. Hudgins, 164–78. Knoxville: University of Tennessee Press, 1995.

Adams, Walter. "What America Wants to Build." *Better Homes & Gardens* 24 (June 1946): 23–25, 96.

Adamson, Paul, and Marty Arbunich. *Eichler: Modernism Rebuilds the American Dream.* Salt Lake City, UT: Gibbs Smith, 2002.

Albrecht, Donald, ed. *World War II and the American Dream: How Wartime Building Changed a Nation.* Exhibition catalog. Washington, DC, and Cambridge, MA: National Building Museum and MIT Press, 1995.

Allen, Frederick Lewis. "The Big Change in Suburbia, Part I." *Harper's Magazine* 208 (June 1954): 21–28.

"America's Exploding Population Will Bring On the Big Change of the 1960s." *House & Home* 15 (Jan. 1959): 105–13.

Ames, David L., and Linda Flint McClelland. *National Register Bulletin, Historic Residential Suburbs.* Washington, DC: U.S. Department of the Interior, National Park Service, 2002.

Archer, John. *Architecture and Suburbia: From English Villa to American Dream House, 1690–2000.* Minneapolis: University of Minnesota Press, 2005.

"Architects, Builders, Lenders and Suppliers Agree on Tomorrow's Best-Selling House." *House & Home* 3 (May 1953): 120–27.

"Architectural Potpourri Feature of 'All-American House of 1950.'" *American Builder* 72 (Mar. 1950): 204, 206, 208, 210.

"Are Kitchens Old Hat?" *Better Homes & Gardens* 47 (Sept. 1969): 90–91.

"Are You Thinking about the Four-Bedroom Market." *House & Home* 17 (Feb. 1960): 134–42.

Associated Plan Service, Inc. *Architects' 1957*

Selection of New Home Plans. New York: Universal Publishing and Distributing Corporation, 1956.

"Atlanta Housing Council Proposes 'Negro Expansion Areas.'" 1947. In Nicolaides and Wiese, *Suburb Reader,* 333–35.

"Bathroom Layouts Need Revamping." *American Builder* 70 (Aug. 1948): 72–75.

Baxandall, Rosalyn, and Elizabeth Ewen. *Picture Windows: How Suburbia Happened.* New York: Basic Books, 2000.

Beauregard, Robert A. *When America Became Suburban.* Minneapolis: University of Minnesota Press, 2006.

Bell, Wendell. "Social Choice, Life Styles, and Suburban Residence." In Dobriner, *Suburban Community,* 225–47.

Berger, Bennett M. "Preface to the 1968 Printing." In *Working-Class Suburb: A Study of Auto Workers in Suburbia,* xiv–xxii. 1960. Berkeley: University of California Press, 1969.

———. *Working-Class Suburb: A Study of Auto Workers in Suburbia.* 1960. Berkeley: University of California Press, 1969.

"Better Homes and Gardens Shows Its 4,350,000 Readers 15 Ideas to Look for in a New House." *House & Home* 11 (May 1957): 160–66.

"Better Houses Abuilding because Buyers Demand Them." *Time,* 14 May 1956, 106.

"Better Keep Your Eye on the Newsstands, Because Your Customers Do." *House & Home* 7 (May 1955): 168–75.

Beveridge, Elizabeth. "Trends in Home Equipment." *Journal of Home Economics* 39 (Sept. 1947): 401-2.

"Bill Levitt Reorganizes for the Second Postwar Surge in Home Buying." *American Builder* 85 (July 1963): 42–46.

"Bill Levitt's Third Big Town." *House & Home* 80 (Aug. 1958): 72–85.

Blietz, Bruce S. "Split-Level Siting Pays Off in Sales." *NAHB Correlator* 10 (Apr. 1956): 82–83.

Bloodgood, John D. "If You're Looking for a Good Two-Story, This Is It!" *Better Homes & Gardens* 42 (June 1964): 62–65.

Bodek, Ralph. *How and Why People Buy Houses: A Study of Subconscious Home Buying Motives.* Philadelphia, PA: Municipal Publications, 1958.

"Boost Sales Appeal with the Best-Designed Kitchen in Your Market—the Room Women Rate Tops in Any New Home." *American Builder* 86 (Apr. 1964): 88–89.

Borncamp, Bett. "What Happened to the Porch?" *Los Angeles Times Home Magazine,* 17 Feb. 1952, 10.

Brenneman, John. "The Houses America Needs." *Ladies' Home Journal* 80 (May 1963): 53, 120.

Brooks, William W. "How Large Should Your Bathroom Be?" *Better Homes & Gardens* 26 (Mar. 1948): 208–12.

"Business and the Urban Crisis: A McGraw-Hill Special Report." *House & Home* 33 (Feb. 1968): insert: C1–C13.

"The Business of Home Building." *American Builder* 69 (July 1947): 92–97, 130, 132, 134.

"Buy a House—or Rent? The Answer Lies in Your Heart, As Well As in Your Head." *Changing Times* 7 (Apr. 1953): 7–11.

"Buyers' Tastes Are Changing: Here's How Home Week Forecasts the Big Trends." *American Builder* 77 (Nov. 1955): 80–84.

"Buying a Home Proves to Be a Growth Investment." *NAHB Journal of Homebuilding* 21 (Oct. 1967): 67.

"Buying a House: The 9 Most Common Questions." *Changing Times* 20 (Feb. 1966): 13–15.

"Buying Trends in the U.S.: Search for Durable Goods." *U.S. News & World Report,* 30 Aug. 1946, 11–13.

Callis, Robert R., and Melissa Kresin. "Home-ownership Rates for the United States: 1995 to 2013." *U.S. Census Bureau News,* 5 Nov. 2013, table 4. http://www.census.gov/housing /hvs/files/qtr413/q413press.pdf.

Campbell, Colin. "Consuming Goods and the Good of Consuming." In *Consumer Society in American History: A Reader,* edited by Lawrence B. Glickman, 19–32. Ithaca, NY: Cornell University Press, 1999.

"Cape Cod Simplicity Needed for Postwar." *American Builder* 67 (Nov. 1945): 96–-97.

Carson, Cary, and Carl R. Lounsbury, eds. *The Chesapeake House: Architectural Investigation by Colonial Williamsburg.* Chapel Hill: Colonial Williamsburg Foundation by the University of North Carolina Press, 2013.

Carter, Deane G., and Keith H. Hinchcliff. *Family Housing.* New York: John Wiley & Sons, 1949.

Center for the Study of Democratic Institutions. *Race and Housing: An Interview with Edward P. Eichler, president, Eichler Homes, Inc.* Santa Barbara, CA: Fund for the Republic, 1964.

"Center of the Home: Living in the Kitchen." *NAHB Journal of Homebuilding* 14 (Sept. 1960): 54.

"The Challenge of Right Now: How to Succeed with Today's Serious Buyers." *House & Home* 17 (Jan. 1960): 120–34.

"Characteristics of Single-Family Homes." *PF: The Magazine of Prefabrication* (Apr. 1956): 48, 50–53.

Checkoway, Barry. "Large Builders, Federal Housing Programmes, and Postwar Suburbanization." *International Journal of Urban Regional Research* 4 (Mar. 1980): 21–45.

Clark, Clifford Edward, Jr. *The American Family Home, 1800-1960.* Chapel Hill: University of North Carolina Press, 1986.

———. "Ranch-House Suburbia: Ideals and Realities." In *Recasting America: Culture and Politics in the Age of Cold War,* edited by Lary May, 171-91. Chicago: University of Chicago Press, 1988.

Clark, Thomas A. *Blacks in Suburbs, A National Perspective.* New Brunswick, NJ: Rutgers University, Center for Urban Policy Research, 1979.

"Cliffwood: An Architect-Builder Cooperative Venture." *American Builder* 71 (Mar. 1949): 86-92.

Cobb, Hubbard H. "How to Get Along with Your Builder." *American Home* 54 (July 1955): 37, 82.

———. *Your Dream Home: How to Build It for Less Than $3500.* New York: Wm. H. Wise & Co., 1950.

Coffin, Tristram. "Maryland's Montgomery County: The Changing Suburban Dream." *Holiday* 38 (July 1965): 54–55, 104, 117–18.

Cohen, Lizabeth. *A Consumers' Republic: The Politics of Mass Consumption in Postwar America.* New York: Knopf, 2003.

Colean, Miles L. "After All . . . Should You Own or Rent?" *House Beautiful* 87 (July 1945): 60, 72, 74–75.

———. "Should You Build, Buy or Alter?" *House Beautiful* 87 (Aug. 1945): 62, 87–88.

———. "You Can't Dream Yourself a House." *House Beautiful* 90 (Aug. 1948): 46–47, 88–89.

"Come into the Kitchen." *House & Garden* 104 (Aug. 1953): 39.

"Completely Equipped Kitchen Can Be a Tremendous Stimulant for the Sale of New Houses." *American Builder* 71 (Sept. 1949): 68–69.

"The Consumer Spends His Dollar Differently Than He Used To." *Business Week,* 10 Oct. 1953, 43–44.

Coontz, Stephanie. *The Way We Never Were: American Families and the Nostalgia Trap.* New York: Basic Books, 1992.

Cordtz, Dan. "Taunted by Black Extremists and Balked by White Resistance—The Negro Middle Class Is Right in the Middle." *Fortune* 74 (Nov. 1966): 174–80, 224, 226, 228, 231.

"Cornerstone for a New Magazine." *House & Home* 1 (Jan. 1952): 107.

Cortright, Frank W. "Address." *NAHB Correlator* 1 (Aug. 1947): 2–4.

"Could Houses Cost Less? This Builder Says Yes!" *Better Homes & Gardens* 40 (Jan. 1962): 28–29.

Cowan, Ruth Schwartz. *More Work for Mother: The Ironies of Household Technology from the Open Hearth to the Microwave.* New York: Basic Books, 1983.

Cromley, Elizabeth Collins. *Alone Together: A History of New York's Early Apartments.* Ithaca, NY: Cornell University Press, 1990.

———. *The Food Axis: Cooking, Eating, and the Architecture of American Houses.* Charlottesville: University of Virginia Press, 2010.

———. "A History of American Beds and Bedrooms." In *Perspectives in Vernacular Architecture, V,* edited by Thomas Carter and Bernard L. Herman, 177–86. Columbia: University of Missouri Press, 1991.

Cromley, Elizabeth Collis, and Carter L. Hudgins, eds. *Perspectives in Vernacular Architecture, V, Gender, Class, and Shelter.* Knoxville: University of Tennessee Press, 1995.

Cross, Gary. *An All-Consuming Century: Why Commercialization Won in Modern America.* New York: Columbia University Press, 2000.

Curtis Publishing Company. *Urban Housing Survey.* Philadelphia, PA: Curtis Publishing Company, 1945.

Das, Sonya Ruth. *The American Woman in Modern Marriage.* New York: New York Philosophical Society, 1948.

Davidson, Lisa Pfueller. "Early Twentieth-Century Hotel Architects and the Origins of Standardization." In *The Journal of Decorative and Propaganda Arts 25: The American Hotel,* 72–103. Miami Beach: Wolfsonian-Florida International University; Cambridge, MA, and London: MIT Press, 2005.

Dean, John P. *Home Ownership: Is It Sound?* New York: Harper & Brothers, 1945.

Dean, John P., and Simon Breines. *The Book of Houses.* New York: Crown Publishers, 1946.

"Design: Builders Hear What Architects Think of Their Product." *House & Home* 18 (Nov. 1960): 58.

"Design File: Traffic Flow." *House & Home* 28 (Oct. 1965): 82–86.

"Designing for Today's Reluctant Buyers." *American Builder* 84 (Apr. 1962): 44–45.

di Cicco, Frank. "Our Most-Used Room Is Below Ground." *Better Homes & Gardens* 29 (Nov. 1950): 117–18.

Dietz, Albert G. H. "Housing Industry Research." In Burnham Kelly, *Design and the Production of Houses,* 240–58.

Dietz, Albert G. H., Castle N. Day, and Burnham Kelly. "Current Patterns of Fabrication." In Burnham Kelly, *Design and the Production of Houses,* 137–87.

"The Differences in Tomorrow's Housing Market." *House & Home* 33 (June 1968): 82–89.

"The Dining Room Is the Familiest Room." *McCall's* 87 (June 1960): 110–17.

Doan, Mason C. *American Housing Production 1880–2000, A Concise History.* Lanham, NY: University Press of America, 1997.

Dobriner, William M. *Class in Suburbia.* Englewood Cliffs, NJ: Prentice-Hall, 1963.

———, ed. *The Suburban Community.* New York: G. P. Putnam's Sons, 1958.

"Don't Build Your House on a Handshake." *American Home* 65 (June 1962): 35, 62, 64–65.

"Don't Forget the Children." *House & Home* 4 (Sept. 1953): 148–51.

"Do Split Level Houses Have to Be So Ugly?" *House & Home* 9 (Feb. 1956): 136–42.

Dunn, Samuel O. "Publisher's Page: The Real Promoters of Socialism." *American Builder* 70 (Aug. 1948): 7.

Earnest, Morgan G. "Selling the Minority Buyer." *NAHB Correlator* 10 (Oct. 1956): 100–103.

"Editorial: Here Is the Great New Challenge of Homebuilding." *House & Home* 7 (May 1955): 124–31.

Eichler, Ned. *The Merchant Builders.* Cambridge, MA: MIT Press, 1982.

Endres, Kathleen L. "*Better Homes and Gardens.*" In *Women's Periodicals in the United States: Consumer Magazines,* edited by Kathleen L. Endres and Therese L. Lueck. 22–30. Westport, CT: Greenwood Press, 1995.

Endres, Kathleen L., and Therese L. Lueck, eds. *Women's Periodicals in the United States: Consumer Magazines.* Westport, CT: Greenwood Press, 1995.

"The Engineered Kitchen Is High on Liveability." *American Builder* 100 (Aug. 1967): 45.

England, Kim V. L. "Changing Suburbs, Changing Women: Geographic Perspectives on Suburban Women and Suburbanization." *Frontiers: A Journal of Women Studies* 14:1 (1993): 24–43.

"'Equal Rights' Order Could Ruin Many Builders." *American Builder* 84 (Mar. 1962): 5.

"Everywhere Today More and More People Want Indoor-Outdoor Living." *House & Home* 16 (Aug. 1959): 97–102.

"The Family Room." *House & Home* 11 (Feb. 1957): 138–47.

"Family Rooms." *House & Garden* 109 (Jan. 1956): 40–53.

Faragher, John Mack. "Bungalow and Ranch House: The Architectural Backwash of California." *Western Historical Quarterly* 32 (Summer 2001): 149–73.

"Fast Movers and What Makes Them Go." *American Builder* 100 (June 1967): 46–50.

Faulkner, Ray Nelson, and Sarah Faulkner. *Inside Today's Home.* New York: Henry Holt and Company, 1954.

Federal Housing Administration (FHA). *Technical Bulletin No. 4: Principles of Planning Small Houses.* Washington, DC: U.S. Government Printing Office, 1937.

———. *Technical Bulletin No. 4: Principles of Planning Small Houses.* Washington, DC: U.S. Government Printing Office, 1946.

Ferguson, Gael. *Building the New Zealand Dream.* Palmerston North: Dunmore Press, 1994.

"FHA: Revolution by Accident." *House & Home* 15 (June 1959): 99–103.

Fishman, Robert. *Bourgeois Utopias: The Rise and Fall of Suburbia.* New York: Basic Books, 1987.

Fogelson, Robert M. *Bourgeois Nightmares: Suburbia, 1870–1930.* New Haven, CT: Yale University Press, 2005.

Forester, Leslie R. "Where *IS* the Living Room?" *American Home* 59 (Jan. 1958): 33–43.

Foy, Jessica H., and Thomas J. Schlereth, eds. *American Home Life, 1880–1930: A Social History of Spaces and Services.* Knoxville: University of Tennessee Press, 1992.

Freund, David M. P. *Colored Property: State Policy and White Racial Politics in Suburban America.* Chicago: University of Chicago Press, 2007.

Fuller & Smith & Ross, Inc., for Housing Industry Promotional Operation. "A National Consumer Survey of the Housing Market: A Study of Residential Behavior and Attitudes." Washington, DC: National Association of Home Builders, 1961.

"Functional Planning Assures More Desirable Homes—Today and Tomorrow." *American Builder* 68 (Oct. 1946): 84–85.

Galbraith, John Kenneth. *The Affluent Society.* 3rd ed. Boston: Houghton Mifflin Company, 1976.

"The Garage: Part of the Home Today." *American Builder* 72 (Aug. 1950): 74–85.

"Getting Set for Tomorrow's Bath." *Business Week,* 21 May 1966, 103–4, 106.

Gillies, Mary Davis. "What Is a Modern House?" *Journal of Home Economics* 42 (Nov. 1950): 714–16.

Gillies, Mary Davis, and Douglas Baylis. "Expand Your Living Outdoors." *McCall's* 82 (Aug. 1955): 42–52.

Goldstein, Carolyn M. *Do It Yourself: Home Improvement in 20th-Century America.* Exhibition catalog. New York and Washington, DC: Princeton Architectural Press and National Building Museum, 1998.

Goodman, Charles M. "Do People Want Traditional? NO." *House & Home* 12 (Sept. 1957): 138.

Grief, Lucien R. "Hidden Costs in Building or Buying." *American Home* 54 (July 1955): 37, 78.

Grier, Katherine C. "The Decline of the Memory Palace: The Parlor after 1890." In Foy and Schlereth, *American Home Life, 1880–1930,* 49–74.

Gruen, Gerry. *Modern Home Decorating.* New York: Arco Publishing Company, 1955.

Guglielmo, Thomas A. *White on Arrival: Italians, Race, Color, and Power in Chicago, 1890–1945.* New York: Oxford University Press, 2003.

Haeger, Leonard G. "Facts You Should Know about Building, Buying, Modernizing in 1952." *Parents' Magazine* 27 (Jan. 1952): 47–48, 50, 75–76.

———. "Four Kinds of Builders." *NAHB Correlator* 8 (Mar. 1954): 200–201.

Hahn, Vera D. "Give Your Living Room a Social Life." *American Home* 70 (Nov. 1967): 62–64.

Hanmer, Gladysruth. "Kitchens for Family Living: Family Activities Center in Our Kitchen." *Parents' Magazine* 28 (June 1953): 61.

Harding, T. Swann, and Will Lissner. "The Huge Potential Market for Housing." *American Journal of Economics and Sociology* 5 (July 1946): 533–36.

Hardwick, M. Jeff. "Homesteads and Bungalows: African-American Architecture in Langston, Oklahoma." In *Shaping Communities, Perspectives in Vernacular Architecture, VI,* edited by Carter L. Hudgins and Elizabeth Collins Cromley, 21–32. Knoxville: University of Tennessee Press, 1997.

Harris, Dianne. "'The House I Live In': Architecture, Modernism, and Identity in Levittown." In Harris, *Second Suburb,* 200–242.

———. *Little White Houses: How the Postwar Home Constructed Race in America.* Minneapolis: University of Minnesota Press, 2013.

———. "Making Your Private World: Modern Landscape Architecture and *House Beautiful,* 1945–1965." In *The Architecture of Landscape, 1940–1960,* edited by Marc Treib, 180–205. Philadelphia: University of Pennsylvania Press, 2002.

———, ed. *Second Suburb.* Pittsburgh: University of Pittsburgh Press, 2010.

Harris, Richard. *Creeping Conformity: How Canada Became Suburban, 1900–1960.* Toronto: University of Toronto Press, 2004.

———. *Unplanned Suburbs: Toronto's American Tragedy, 1900 to 1950.* Baltimore, MD: Johns Hopkins University Press, 1996.

Hayden, Dolores. *Building Suburbia: Green Fields and Urban Growth, 1820–2000.* New York: Pantheon Books, 2003.

———. "Building the American Way: Public Subsidy, Private Space." In Nicolaides and Wiese, *Suburb Reader,* 273–81.

Heath, Kingston. *The Patina of Place: The Cultural Weathering of a New England Industrial*

Landscape. Knoxville: University of Tennessee Press, 2001.

Hecht, Fred C. "Should I Trade in My House for a New Model? No!" *American Home* 61 (Apr. 1959): 31, 74.

Henderson, Harry. "The Mass-Produced Suburbs: I. How People Live in America's Newest Towns." *Harper's Magazine* 207 (Nov. 1953): 25–32.

———. "Rugged American Collectivism: The Mass-Produced Suburbs, Part II." *Harper's Magazine* 207 (Dec. 1953): 80–86.

Henderson, Susan R. *Building Culture: Ernst May and the New Frankfurt Initiative, 1926–1931.* New York: Peter Lang Publishing, 2013.

———. "A Revolution in the Woman's Sphere: Grete Lihotzky and the Frankfurt Kitchen." In *Architecture and Feminism,* edited by Debra Coleman, Elizabeth Danze, and Carol Henderson, 221–53. New York: Princeton Architectural Press, 1996.

Henn, Richard, Jr. "A Second Bathroom Boosts Sales." *NAHB Correlator* 6 (Oct. 1952): 144–47.

"Here's How One Custom Builder Operates: An American Builder Interview." *American Builder* 75 (Oct. 1953): 127–28, 131.

Hess, Alan. *The Ranch House.* New York: Harry N. Abrams, 2004.

"Higher Incomes, More Spending: Survey of Consumers' Buying Plans in 1948." *U.S. News & World Report,* 11 June 1948, 16–17.

Hine, Thomas. *Populuxe.* New York: Alfred A. Knopf, 1986.

Hise, Greg. *Magnetic Los Angeles: Planning the Twentieth-Century Metropolis.* Baltimore, MD: Johns Hopkins University Press, 1997.

"The Home Builder—Who Is He? What Does He Build? How Does He Build—Finance—Sell?" *NAHB Journal of Homebuilding* 14 (Mar. 1960): 15–17, 20, 23, 26, 30, 32, 34, 40.

"Home Building under Titles II and III of the National Housing Act." New York: Time and Architectural Forum, 1934.

"Home Ownership—Our Nation's Strength." *American Builder* 69 (Dec. 1947): 68–69.

Hornstein, Jeffrey M. *A Nation of Realtors: A Cultural History of the Twentieth-Century American Middle Class.* Durham, NC: Duke University Press, 2005.

"House & Garden's 1955 House of Ideas." *House & Garden* 108 (Aug. 1955): 66–97.

"House Omnibus." *Architectural Forum* 82 (Apr. 1945): 89–144.

House Report No. 590 from the Committee on Banking and Currency to Accompany H. R. 4009 (National Housing Act of 1949). 81st Cong., 1st sess. 16 May 1948.

"Houses Best Buy for Today's Dollar: Comparison of Values, 1947–1941." *American Builder* 69 (Oct. 1947): 84–85.

Housing and Home Finance Agency (HHFA). *Housing Statistics Handbook.* Washington, DC: U.S. Government Printing Office, 1948.

———. *The Materials Use Survey: A Study of the National and Regional Characteristics of One-Family Dwellings Built in the United States in the First-Half of 1950.* Washington, DC: Housing and Home Finance Agency, Division of Housing Research, 1953.

"Housing: Up from the Potato Fields." *Time,* 3 July 1950, 67–72.

"How Eichler Sells Open Occupancy with No Fuss." *House & Home* 25 (Feb. 1964): 132–36.

"How Much Besides the Down Payment?" *Good Housekeeping* 144 (Mar. 1957): 49–50.

"How Much House You Can Buy." *U.S. News & World Report,* 31 Mar. 1950, 13–14.

"How to Design for the Market." *House & Home* 15 (Jan. 1959): 137–41.

"How to Increase Sales Volume Today: 'Sell in More Places, at More Prices, to More

Prospects.'" *House & Home* 22 (Sept. 1962): 116–21.

"How to Merchandise Your House." *House & Home* 3 (May 1953): 150–55.

"How to Plan for Modern Electrical Living." *American Builder* 71 (Dec. 1949): 106–9.

"How to Plan Your 1956 Bathrooms." *American Builder* 77 (Nov. 1955): 86–91.

"How to Sell." *House & Home* 13 (May 1958): 113–80.

"How to Sell Houses." *House & Home* 15 (Mar. 1959): 146–53.

"How to Sell New Houses to Families Who Already Own Old Houses like These." *House & Home* 18 (Sept. 1960): 136–37.

"How to Tell if You Can Afford to Buy a House." *Good Housekeeping* 134 (May 1952): 108–11.

Hubka, Thomas C. *Houses without Names: Architectural Nomenclature and the Classification of America's Common Houses*. Knoxville: University of Tennessee Press, 2013.

Huntoon, Maxwell C. "'Could Houses Cost Less? This Builder Says Yes!' Max—Let's Find Out How He Did It." *House & Home* 21 (Apr. 1962): 126–31.

———. "The Ryan Story." *House & Home* 19 (May 1961): 126–31.

Huntoon, Max, and Jan White. "The Split-Entry House: A Big Seller and a Big Problem." *House & Home* 20 (Dec. 1961): 138–47.

Hurley, Andrew. *Diners, Bowling Alleys, and Trailer Parks: Chasing the American Dream in Postwar Consumer Culture*. New York: Basic Books, 2001.

Hutchison, Janet. "The Cure for Domestic Neglect: Better Homes in America, 1922-1935." In *Perspectives in Vernacular Architecture, II*, edited by Camille Wells, 168–78. Columbia: University of Missouri Press, 1986.

Hyman, Louis. *Debtor Nation: The History of America in Red Ink*. Princeton, NJ: Princeton University Press, 2011.

"Ideas That Sell Houses." *Business Week*, 23 May 1959, 76–78, 80, 82, 86.

Ierley, Merritt. *The Comforts of Home: The American House and the Evolution of Modern Convenience*. New York: Three Rivers Press, 1999.

"If You're Trying to Build a Home of Your Own." *U.S. News & World Report*, 30 June 1969, 45–46.

Ingersoll, John H. "What to Look For When You Buy Your First Home." *American Home* 68 (June 1965): 52–53.

Irving, Robert, ed. *The History and Design of the Australian House*. Melbourne: Oxford University Press, 1985.

Isenstadt, Sandy. *The Modern American House: Spaciousness and Middle-Class Identity*. New York: Cambridge University Press, 2006.

"Is This a Good Time to Buy a House?" *U.S. News & World Report*, 18 Nov. 1955, 116.

Jackson, Kenneth T. *Crabgrass Frontier: The Suburbanization of the United States*. New York: Oxford University Press, 1985.

Jacobs, James A. "Belair at Bowie, Maryland." Historic American Buildings Survey (HABS) No. MD-1253. U.S. Department of the Interior, National Park Service, 2008.

———. "Beyond Levittown: The Design and Marketing of Belair at Bowie, Maryland." In *Housing Washington: Two Centuries of Residential Development and Planning in the National Capital Area*, edited by Richard Longstreth, 85–109. Chicago: Center for American Places at Columbia College Chicago, 2010.

———. "Master of the House, Master of the Bath." *Ultimate History Project*, Apr. 2012. http://www.ultimatehistoryproject.com.

———. "Social and Spatial Change in the

Postwar Family Room." *Perspectives in Vernacular Architecture* 13:1 (2006): 70–85.

Jacobson, Matthew Frye. *Whiteness of a Different Color: European Immigrants and the Alchemy of Race*. Cambridge, MA: Harvard University Press, 1998.

Jenkins, Douglas Lloyd. *At Home: A Century of New Zealand Design*. Auckland: Godwit/Random House, 2004.

Johnstone, B. Kenneth, and Charles E. Joern, eds. *The Business of Home Building: A Manual for Contractors*. New York: McGraw-Hill Book Company, 1950.

Jones, Bob. "Operative Building—One Way Out." *Better Homes & Gardens* 25 (Oct. 1946): 53, 132–34.

Kammen, Michael. *American Culture, American Tastes: Social Change and the 20th Century*. New York: Basic Books, 1999.

Kaufman, Gerald Lynton. *Homeseekers' Handbook*. New York: George W. Stewart, 1947.

"The Keeping Room Comes Back." *American Home* 48 (Sept. 1952): 49–53.

Kellogg, Cynthia. "Family Rooms Fancified." *New York Times Magazine*, 7 Sept. 1958, 76–77.

Kelly, Barbara M. *Expanding the American Dream: Building and Rebuilding Levittown*. Albany: State University of New York Press, 1993.

Kelly, Burnham, ed. *Design and the Production of Houses*. New York: McGraw-Hill Book Company, 1959.

Kinchin, Juliet, with Aidan O'Connor. *Counter Space: Design and the Modern Kitchen*. New York: Museum of Modern Art, 2011.

King, Charley. "Publicity: Important Aid to Selling." *American Builder* 71 (Apr. 1949): 112–13, 216, 220, 224.

"Kitchen-Family Rooms Are Getting Larger." *American Builder* 85 (Aug. 1963): 90.

"Kitchen Planning: A Science Today." *American Builder* 69 (Oct. 1947): 96–97.

"Kitchens." *American Home* 71 (Nov. 1968): 63–73.

"Kitchens for Family Living." *Parents' Magazine* 28 (June 1953): 59–66.

"A Kitchen to Feel at Home In." *Woman's Home Companion* 81 (Feb. 1954): 62.

Kizzia, Joe. "Profile: The 1967 Home Buyer." *American Builder* 100 (Mar. 1967): 102.

Klaber, Eugene. "Where?" *Consumer Reports* (Jan. 1949): 29–31.

Kruse, Kevin M., and Thomas J. Sugrue, eds. *The New Suburban History*. Chicago: University of Chicago Press, 2006.

Lacy, Karyn R. *Blue-Chip Black: Race, Class, and Status in the New Black Middle Class*. Berkeley: University of California Press, 2007.

"Land-1." *House & Home* 26 (Sep. 1964): 41–45.

"Land: The Squeeze Is On." *American Builder* 81 (Oct. 1959): 143–47.

Lane, Barbara Miller. *Architecture and Politics in Germany, 1918–1945*. Cambridge, MA: Harvard University Press, 1968.

"Large Homes and Big Values Here." *American Builder* 70 (May 1948): 108–9.

Lasner, Matthew Gordon. *High Life: Condo Living in the Suburban Century*. New Haven, CT: Yale University Press, 2012.

"Lesson in Merchandising." *House & Home* 7 (Apr. 1955): 146–47.

Levitt and Sons, Inc. "Belair at Bowie, Maryland." 1962.

Liccese-Torres, Cynthia. National Register of Historic Places registration form for "Arlington Forest Historic District." U.S. Department of the Interior, National Park Service, 2005.

Lippincott, J. Gordon. *Design for Business*. Chicago: Paul Theobald, 1947.

Lipsitz, George. *The Possessive Investment in Whiteness: How White People Profit from Identity Politics*. Philadelphia, PA: Temple University Press, 1998.

Liston, James M. "It's a Good Life, and Your Home Reflects the Way You Live When You Live Without Pretense." *Better Homes & Gardens* 29 (Sept. 1950): 41–45.

Little, M. Ruth. "The Other Side of the Tracks: The Middle-Class Neighborhoods That Jim Crow Built in Early-Twentieth-Century North Carolina." In *Exploring Everyday Landscapes, Perspectives in Vernacular Architecture, VII*, edited by Annemarie Adams and Sally McMurry, 267–80. Knoxville: University of Tennessee Press, 1997.

"Living-Kitchens." *House & Garden* 106 (Aug. 1954): 63.

Lupton, Ellen, and J. Abbot Miller. *The Bathroom, the Kitchen, and the Aesthetics of Waste (A Process of Elimination)*. Exhibition catalog. 2nd ed. New York: Kiosk and Princeton Architectural Press, 1996.

Lynd, Robert S. "Foreword." In *Home Ownership: Is It Sound?* by John P. Dean, vii–xii. New York: Harper & Brothers, 1945.

Lynes, Russell. *The Domesticated Americans*. 1957. New York: Harper & Row, Publishers, 1963.

Lyon, Luther. "Take Your Shopping List with You." *American Home* 38 (June 1947): 31–32.

MacMasters, Dan. "The Housewife Talks Tract Housing." *Los Angeles Times Sunday Home Magazine*, 17 Sept. 1961, 14–27, 29-29, 58.

"Making Sure You Know Their Kitchen Likes." *NAHB Journal of Homebuilding* 14 (Sept. 1960): 53–54.

"Man of the Year: First among Equals." *Time*, 2 Jan. 1956, 46, 48–55.

Mark Clements Research, Inc., for the National Association of Home Builders and *House & Garden*. "Housing Design and the American Family." Washington, DC: NAHB Journal of Homebuilding, 1964.

Marsh, Margaret. "From Separation to Togetherness: The Social Construction of Domestic Space in American Suburbs, 1840–1915." *Journal of American History* 76 (Sept. 1989): 506–27.

Martin, Christopher T. "Tract-House Modern: A Study of Housing, Design, and Consumption in the Washington Suburbs, 1946–1960." PhD diss., George Washington University, 2000.

Matern, Rudolph A. *52 House Plans for 1952: Construction-Tested House Designs of Proven Popularity*. New York: Archway Press, 1952.

———. "Home Buyers Are Voting in a New Type of Architecture." *American Builder* 70 (Dec. 1948): 80–81.

———. "The Trend in Houses—More Height, Less Sprawl." *Practical Builder* 24 (Nov. 1959): 66–71.

Matthaei, Julie A. *An Economic History of Women in America: Women's Work, the Sexual Division of Labor, and the Development of Capitalism*. New York: Schocken Books, 1982.

May, Bridget A. "Progressivism and the Colonial Revival: The Modern Colonial House, 1900–1920." *Winterthur Portfolio* 26 (1991): 107–22.

May, Elaine Tyler. *Homeward Bound: American Families in the Cold War Era*. 1988. New York: Basic Books, 1999.

McAlester, Virginia, and Lee McAlester. *A Field Guide to American Houses*. New York: Alfred A. Knopf, 1992.

McMurry, Sally. *Families and Farmhouses in Nineteenth-Century America: Vernacular Design and Social Change*. New York: Oxford University Press, 1988.

Mehlhorn, Will. "What Makes a Plan Good or Bad?" *House Beautiful* 88 (Oct. 1946): 155–63.

"Memo to Split-Level Builders: You Sure Need a Good Architect!" *House & Home* 5 (Apr. 1954): 120–23.

Mennel, Timothy. "'Miracle House Hoop-La': Corporate Rhetoric and the Construction of the Postwar American House." *Journal of the Society of Architectural Historians* 64 (Sept. 2005): 340–61.

"Merchandising from the Ground Up, 5. The Model House: Make It the Best Salesman on Your Staff." *American Builder* 84 (Jan. 1962): 66–99.

Miner, Curtis. "Pink Kitchens for Little Boxes: The Evolution of 1950s Kitchen Design in Levittown." In D. Harris, *Second Suburb*, 243–80.

Mintz, Steven, and Susan Kellogg. *Domestic Revolutions: A Social History of American Family Life*. New York: Free Press, 1989.

Morgan-Ryan, Kathryn. "This Is Oskaloosa Where Everybody's Trading Up." *House & Home* 13 (Mar. 1958): 90–104.

Mortgage Bankers Association of America. *Jane and Bill Learn How a Mortgage Works*. Washington, DC: Robert M. Gamble Jr., 1957.

"Most of the Land Shortage Talk You Hear Is Nonsense." *House & Home* 18 (Aug. 1960): 106–21.

Mowrer, Ernest R. "Sequential and Class Variables of the Family in the Suburban Area." *Social Forces* 40 (Dec. 1961): 107–12.

"Mr. Average Builder Views the Situation." *NAHB Correlator* 10 (Dec. 1956): 67–69.

Murphy, Kathryn R. "Characteristics of New 1-Family Houses, 1954–56." *Monthly Labor Review* 80 (May 1957): 572–75.

Myers, Daisy D. *Sticks 'n Stones: The Myers Family in Levittown*. York, PA: York County Heritage Trust, 2005.

National Association of Home Builders (NAHB). History of the National Association of Home Builders of the United States (through 1943). Washington, DC: National Association of Home Builders, 1958.

———. *Housing Almanac: A Fact File of the Home Building Industry*. Washington, DC:

National Association of Home Builders, 1957.

"National Home Week." *American Builder* 71 (Apr. 1949): 101–9.

"National Home Week Roundup." *NAHB Correlator* 10 (Nov. 1956): 41–63.

Nelson, George, and Henry Wright. *Tomorrow's House: A Complete Guide for the Home-Builder*. New York: Simon and Schuster, 1945.

"New Concepts in Kitchens." *American Builder* 82 (June 1960): 96–97.

"Newest Marketing Trends: Gimmicks Are on the Way Out . . . and Skillful Staging Is In." *House & Home* 25 (Mar. 1964): 112–17.

Newman, Dorothy K., and Adela L. Stucke. *Structure of the Residential Building Industry in 1949, Bulletin No. 1170*. Washington, DC: Bureau of Labor Statistics, 1954.

Nickles, Shelly. "More Is Better: Mass Consumption, Gender, and Class Identity in Postwar America." *American Quarterly* 54 (Dec. 2002): 581–622.

Nicolaides, Becky M., and Andrew Wiese, eds. *The Suburb Reader*. New York: Routledge, 2006.

"1936–1956: 20 Years in Review." *Consumer Reports* 21 (May 1956): 252–56.

"No Drop in Consumer Buying Plans." *Business Week*, 15 Oct. 1949, 25.

Normile, John. "Open Planning Makes a Small Home Seem Larger." *Better Homes & Gardens* 25 (July 1947): 42–43, 112–13, 116–17.

Nunn, Richard. "50 Money-Stretching Tips for Home Buyers." *Popular Mechanics* 118 (Sept. 1962): 148–49, 216, 218, 220.

O'Callaghan, Judith, and Charles Pickett. *Designer Suburbs: Architects and Affordable Homes in Australia*. Sydney: University of New South Wales Press, 2013.

Ohmann, Richard M. *Selling Culture: Magazines, Markets, and Class at the Turn of the Century*. New York: Verso, 1996.

"One Plan . . . 11 Houses: Getting Real Mileage Out of a Plan with 7 Variables." *American Builder* 77 (Oct. 1955): 106–12.

"On Long Island, Splits Outsell Ranches Four to One." *House & Home* 3 (Apr. 1954): 111–19.

Onslow, Walton. "Impressing the Public." *NAHB Correlator* 2 (Apr. 1948): 39.

"Open Planning: The Answer to Small Houses." *American Builder* 71 (May 1949): 98–101.

Ormston, Harry E. "The Split-Level: Pro and Con." *NAHB Correlator* 10 (Apr. 1956): 75–76.

Packard, Vance. *The Status Seekers*. New York: David McKay, 1959.

———. *The Waste Makers*. 1960. New York: Pocket Books, 1963.

Palmer, Phyllis. *Domesticity and Dirt: Housewives and Domestic Servants in the United States, 1920–1945*. Philadelphia, PA: Temple University Press, 1989.

"Parade of Homes: What Kind Is Best for Your City?" *House & Home* 33 (Jan. 1968): 68–69.

Parker, Jerry. "Need an Extra Shower? Try a Prefab." *Popular Science* 166 (Apr. 1955): 176–78.

Parker, Stanley. *Leisure and Work*. Boston: George Allen & Unwin, 1983.

Pattillo-McCoy, Mary. *Black Picket Fences: Privilege and Peril among the Black Middle Class*. Chicago: University of Chicago Press, 1999.

Paxton, Edward T. *What People Want When They Buy a House*. Washington, DC: U.S. Government Printing Office, 1955.

Pepis, Betty. "Return of the Two-Parlor Plan." *New York Times Magazine*, 30 Sept. 1956, 54–55.

Pickett, Charles. *The Fibro Frontier: A Different History of Australian Architecture*. Sydney: Powerhouse Museum and Doubleday, 1997.

"The Place of Real Estate in Our Expanding Economy." Proceedings of a conference cosponsored by the Committee on Education, National Association of Real Estate Boards and the College of Business Administration. University of Florida, Gainesville. 10 Nov. 1950.

"Plan-itorial . . . Home Buying Motivations." *Urban Land* 19 (July–Aug. 1960): 2, 9–10.

"Planning the Postwar House." *Architectural Forum* 80 (Jan. 1944): 75–80.

Prentice, Perry. "Should I Trade in My House for a New Model? Yes!" *American Home* 61 (Apr. 1959): 30, 72.

"Project Larger Than Levittown Planned." *American Builder* 72 (June 1950): 140, 144.

Radford, Gail. *Modern Housing for America: Policy Struggles in the New Deal Era*. Chicago: University of Chicago Press, 1996.

Rainwater, Lee, Richard P. Coleman, and Gerald Handel. *Workingman's Wife: Her Personality, World and Life Style*. New York: Oceana Publications, 1959.

"Raised Ranch Stimulates Sales." *NAHB Journal of Homebuilding* 15 (Feb. 1961): 62–64.

Ramsay, Edith. "This Kitchen Is a Family Room." *American Home* 54 (Nov. 1955): 110.

Randall, Gregory C. *America's Original GI Town: Park Forest, Illinois*. Baltimore, MD: Johns Hopkins University Press, 2000.

Randl, Chad. "'Live Better Where You Are'— Home Improvement and the Rhetoric of Renewal." PhD diss., Cornell University, 2014.

Rapkin, Chester. "The Heart of the Matter: More Housing for Negroes." *Mortgage Banker* 24 (Feb. 1964): 21–25.

Reese, Carol McMichael. "Separate but Equal? The Case of Pontchartrain Park, New Orleans." Paper delivered at the 62nd Annual Meeting of the Society of Architectural Historians. Pasadena, CA. 2 Apr. 2009.

Reiff, Daniel D. *Houses from Books, Treatises, Pattern Books, and Catalogs in American*

Architecture, 1738–1950: A History and Guide. University Park: Pennsylvania State University Press, 2000.

Reisner, Jedd S. "The Trend to Make At Least Two Uses of Every Room." *House Beautiful* 90 (Mar. 1948): 74–77.

"A Remarkable Split-Entry House." *Better Homes & Gardens* 41 (Sept. 1963): 68-69.

Remsburg, Bonnie, and Charles Remsburg. "What Went Wrong in Dreamland." *Good Housekeeping* 164 (Feb. 1967): 74–75, 136–38, 140.

"Report from Washington." *House & Home* 18 (May 1961): 172–76.

"Report on Interiors: 100 Leading Builders Give You the Inside Story on Their Houses, Checklist for Kitchens." *House & Home* 25 (June 1964): 80–83.

"The Return of the Dining Room." *Good Housekeeping* 146 (Feb. 1958): 56–63.

"The Return of the Large House," *House & Garden* 109 (Mar. 1956): 108 15.

Rice, Andrew. "The Elusive Small-House Utopia." *New York Times Magazine,* 15 Oct. 2010. http://www.nytimes.com/2010/10/17/magazine/17KeySmallHouse-t.html?pagewanted=all.

Riemer, Svend. "Livability: A New Factor in Home Value." *Appraisal Journal* 14 (Apr. 1946): 148–58.

Riesman, David. "The Suburban Sadness." In Dobriner, *Suburban Community,* 375–408.

Robertson, Cheryl. "Male and Female Agendas for Domestic Reform: The Middle Class Bungalow in Gendered Perspective." *Winterthur Portfolio* 26:2 (1991): 123–41.

Roediger, David R. *Working toward Whiteness, How America's Immigrants Became White: The Strange Journey from Ellis Island to the Suburbs.* New York: Basic Books, 2005.

"Rooms Have a New Job Today." *Good Housekeeping* 131 (Oct. 1950): 68–73.

Ryan Homes. "Homes of Distinction." 1960.

S&P/Dow Jones Indices. "S&P Case-Shiller U.S. National Home Price Index," Dec. 2013. http://us.spindices.com/indices/real-estate/sp-case-shiller-us-national-home-price-index.

Scheick, William H. "What's Happened to Housing in the Last 30 Years." *Parents' Magazine* 31 (Oct. 1956): 63–67, 93–97.

Schlereth, Thomas J. "Conduits and Conduct: Home Utilities in Victorian America, 1876–1915." In Foy and Schlereth, *American Home Life, 1880–1930,* 225–41.

Schrader, Ben. *We Call It Home: A History of State Housing in New Zealand.* Auckland: Reed Books, 2005.

Sears, Roebuck & Co. *Sears, Roebuck Catalog of Houses: An Unabridged Reprint.* New York: Dover Publications, 1991. (Originally published as *Honor Bilt Modern Homes.* 1926.)

Seligman, Daniel. "The New Masses." In *The Changing Metropolis,* edited by Frederick J. Tietze and James E. McKeown, 151–61. Boston: Houghton Mifflin, 1964.

Senate Report No. 1131 from the Committee on Banking and Currency to Accompany S. 1592 (General Housing Act of 1946). 79th Cong., 2nd sess. 8 Apr. 1946.

Shanken, Andrew M. *194X: Architecture, Planning, and Consumer Culture on the American Home Front.* Minneapolis: University of Minnesota Press, 2009.

"The Shelter Magazines Know That, More and More . . . People No Longer Build Houses . . . They Buy Them." *House & Home* 10 (Sept. 1956): 155–58.

Sherman, V. L. "Higher Living Standards Encouraged by FHA Financing." *American Builder* 58 (May 1936): 78, 80, 82.

Sies, Mary Corbin. "North American Suburbs, 1880–1950, Cultural and Social Reconsiderations." *Journal of Urban History* 27 (Mar. 2001): 313–46.

Silpher, David. "Progress Report: Homes Get Bigger, Better Throughout the Nation." *NAHB Correlator* 9 (June 1955): 4–40.

"Six 'Building Boners' Customers Talk About—and 24 Ways to Help You Answer Them." *American Builder* 87 (June 1965): 73–79.

Small Homes of Architectural Distinction: A Book of Suggested Plans Designed by the Architects' Small House Service Bureau, Inc. 1929. Reprinted as *Authentic Small Houses of the 1920s,* edited by Robert T. Jones. New York: Dover Publications, 1987.

Soule, Gardner. "How Much House Can You Afford?" *McCall's* 85 (Nov. 1957): 158, 160–61, 164.

Spigel, Lynn. *Make Room for TV: Television and the Family Ideal in Postwar America.* Chicago: University of Chicago Press, 1992.

"Split Levels on Parade." *American Builder* 78 (Oct. 1953): 68–71.

"Split-Levels Set the Sales Pace." *House & Home* 2 (Dec. 1952): 117–21.

"Spotlight on Bathrooms: More and Bigger Bathrooms Desired." *NAHB Journal of Homebuilding* 20 (June 1966): 53–57.

Springer, John L. "Pitfalls to Avoid in Buying a Development House." *Popular Science* 172 (Mar. 1958): 179–82.

———. "What Can You Afford to Pay for a House." *Popular Science* 173 (Feb. 1958): 194–96, 198.

Sternlieb, George, and James W. Hughes. "The Post-Shelter Society." *Public Interest* 57 (Fall 1979): 39–47.

Sternlieb, George, and Robert W. Lake. "Aging Suburbs and Black Homeownership." *Annals of the American Academy of Political and Social Science* 422 (Nov. 1975): 105–17.

Stevenson, Katherine Cole, and H. Ward Jandl. *Houses by Mail: A Guide to Houses from Sears, Roebuck and Company.* Washington, DC: Preservation Press, 1986.

Stilgoe, John R. *Borderland: Origins of the American Suburb, 1820–1939.* New Haven, CT: Yale University Press, 1988.

Strawn, Bernice, and Elizabeth Matthews. "The Companion Plans a House for Family Living." *Woman's Home Companion* 82 (Sept. 1955): 65–67, 70, 72–74, 76, 78.

Stretton, Hugh. *Ideas for Australian Cities.* Melbourne: Georgian House, 1971.

"A Study of Home Planning Preferences." *Residential Appraiser* 26 (Dec. 1960): 15–19.

Sturm, Richard. "Before You Buy a House." *American Home* 46 (June 1951): 108–9.

Sudman, Seymour, Norman M. Bradburn, and Galen Gockel. "The Extent and Characteristics of Racially Integrated Housing in the United States." *Journal of Business* 42 (Jan. 1969): 50–92.

Sugrue, Thomas J. "Jim Crow's Last Stand: The Struggle to Integrate Levittown." In D. Harris, *Second Suburb,* 175–99.

———. *The Origins of the Urban Crisis: Race and Inequality in Postwar Detroit.* Princeton, NJ: Princeton University Press, 1996.

Sutherland, Daniel E. "Modernizing Domestic Service." In Foy and Schlereth, *American Home Life, 1880–1930,* 242–65.

"Ten Plans by a Top Production-House Architect Show How Tastes Have Changed in a Decade." *House & Home* 29 (Feb. 1966): 92–97.

"There's a Lot to Learn from Today's Best Selling Houses." *American Builder* 87 (Dec. 1965): 90–96.

"There's a New Room in the Western House: The Family Room." *Sunset* 116 (Apr. 1956): 74–81.

"39 Ways to Build a Better Bathroom." *House & Home* 3 (Feb. 1953): 93–100.

"31 Best-Sellers Reflect Today's New Emphasis on What Houses Offer." *House & Home* 25 (Mar. 1964): 96–102.

"This Chart Tells You 'The Best-Seller Features' in 25 Cities." *House & Home* 18 (July 1960): 155.

"This House Sells for $7.13 Per Sq Ft of Living Space!" *House & Home* 14 (Aug. 1958): 132–36.

"This Is Our Land—Millions of Miles of It . . . But the Homebuilders Vote 4 to 1 That LAND Is the Most Critical Problem." *House & Home* 18 (Aug. 1960): 98–105.

Tobey, Ronald C. *Technology as Freedom: The New Deal and the Electrical Modernization of the American Home.* Berkeley: University of California Press, 1996.

"Today's Best Marketing and Merchandising: 1." *House & Home* 23 (May 1963): 111–17.

"Tomorrow's Homes Today." *American Builder* 70 (Apr. 1948): 92–95.

"Trends in the Building Field: Residential Building Down 43 Percent." *American Builder* 73 (Oct. 1951): 16.

"Trends in the Building Field: Why People Buy the Houses They Do." *American Builder* 75 (Feb. 1953): 16, 188, 191.

"The Truth about Tubbing vs. Showering." *House Beautiful* 95 (Aug. 1953): 56, 123–24.

Tucker, Lisa Marie. "The Small House Problem in the United States, 1918–1945: The American Institute of Architects and the Architects' Small House Service Bureau." *Journal of Design History* 23 (2010): 43–59.

"20 Outstanding Houses." *House & Home* 27 (Mar. 1965): 76–113.

"22 Ways to Get More Sales from a Model House." *House & Home* 3 (May 1953): 144–49.

"Two Houses by Builder Kinsey Show Trend of Future Building." *American Builder* 67 (Mar. 1945): 104–5.

"The Two-Story House Is Back and Welcome." *Good Housekeeping* 144 (Apr. 1957): 98.

"Two-Story Living Makes Strong Nationwide Comeback." *American Builder* 84 (Aug. 1962): 72–79.

"The Typical White Suburbanite: He's Perfectly Content as a Bystander." *Ebony* 20 (Aug. 1965): 123–26, 128–30.

"The Undaunted Home Buyers: Expense Doesn't Stop Them." *U.S. News & World Report,* 14 Apr. 1969, 50–51.

U.S. Department of Commerce, Bureau of the Census (Census Bureau). "Characteristics of New Single-Family Houses Completed." 2013. https://www.census.gov/construction/chars/completed.html.

———. *Housing Construction Statistics, 1889 to 1964.* Washington, DC: U.S. Government Printing Office, 1966.

———. *Sixteenth Census of the United States, 1940: Housing, Volume II, General Characteristics.* Washington, DC: U.S. Government Printing Office, 1943.

U.S. Department of Commerce, Bureau of the Census (Census Bureau), and U.S. Department of Housing and Urban Development (HUD). *Characteristics of New One-Family Homes: 1974.* Washington, DC: U.S. Department of Commerce, 1975.

———. *New One-Family Homes Sold and for Sale, 1963 to 1967.* Washington, DC: U.S. Government Printing Office, 1969.

"U.S. Life Is Different: Sales Figures Prove It." *U.S. News & World Report,* 13 Feb. 1953, 69–70.

Volz, Candace. "The Modern Look of the Early-Twentieth Century House: A Mirror of Changing Lifestyles." In Foy and Schlereth, *American Home Life, 1880–1930,* 27–36.

Walker, Nancy A. *Shaping Our Mothers' World: American Women's Magazines.* Jackson: University Press of Mississippi, 2000.

Wallace, Edith B., and Paula S. Reed, with Linda Flint McClelland. National Historic

Landmark nomination for "Radburn." U.S. Department of the Interior, National Park Service, 2005.

Watkins, A. M. "How Much House Can You Afford?" *American Home* 72 (Winter 1969): 78.

———. "Keep a Cool Head While Your New House Settles Down." *American Home* 65 (Sept. 1962): 18, 23.

Weiss, Marc A. *The Rise of the Community Builders: The American Real Estate Industry and Urban Land Planning.* New York: Columbia University Press, 1987.

"Western Style Invades the Eastern Area." *American Builder* 69 (Aug. 1947): 103.

"What Can Be Done about It?" *American Builder* 70 (Oct. 1948): 120–21.

"What Do *They* Want in A Home?" *NAHB Correlator* 6 (May 1952): 16–18.

"What Happened to the Saturday Night Bath?" *Cosmopolitan* 140 (June 1956): 57.

"What Home Buyers Want." *House & Home* 7 (May 1955): 78.

"What House Buyers Are Looking For." *U.S. News & World Report*, 15 Oct. 1954, 107–10.

"What Is 'the ECONOMY HOUSE'?" *NAHB Correlator* 2 (Mar. 1948): 20–22.

"What Makes a Floor Plan Good?" *Changing Times* 17 (Dec. 1963): 34–36.

"What Price an Extra Bathroom?" *Good Housekeeping* 145 (Aug. 1957): 58.

"What's So Good about Splits?" *House & Home* 7 (Feb. 1955): 145–55.

"What You Can Expect in a Builder's House Today." *Better Homes & Gardens* 41 (Sept. 1963): 20.

"When Good Housekeeping Builds Kitchens." *Good Housekeeping* 141 (Nov. 1955): 107–24.

"When Your Houses Have Enough Exciting Features, Today's Buyers Will Queue Up for Them." *House & Home* 18 (July 1960): 145–55.

"Where to Keep the Good Things for the Good Life." *House Beautiful* 96 (Aug. 1954): 43.

Whipple, Richard. "Stay Close to Your Buyers." *American Builder* 101 (Dec. 1968): 45–49.

Whitely, Nigel. "Toward a Throw-Away Culture: Consumerism, 'Style Obsolescence' and Cultural Theory in the 1950s and 1960s." *Oxford Art Journal* 10:2 (1987): 3–27.

"WHO Are the Postwar Builders?" *American Builder* 69 (Aug. 1947): 126.

"The Whole House Is Built around a Living Kitchen." *Woman's Home Companion* 82 (Sept. 1955): 68–70.

"Why a Buyer's Market Is Forcing Builders to Customize." *American Builder* 100 (Oct. 1967): 44–47.

"Why and How the Furnished Model Helps Sell Builder's Houses." *House & Home* 1 (Apr. 1952): 134–37.

"Why Buyers Buy: A New Study Examines Motives." *American Builder* 100 (Oct. 1967): 52–54.

Wiese, Andrew. *Places of Their Own: African American Suburbanization in the Twentieth Century.* Chicago: University of Chicago Press, 2004.

"Will It Be a Dream House?" *Ladies' Home Journal* 66 (Oct. 1949): 206–7, 231.

Wilson, William H. *Hamilton Park: A Planned Black Community in Dallas.* Baltimore, MD: Johns Hopkins University Press, 1998.

Winnick, Louis. "Housing: Has There Been a Downward Shift in Consumers' Preferences." *Quarterly Journal of Economics* 69 (Feb. 1955): 85–98.

"The Worst Is Over: Most Non-Defense Building Is Promised NPA Approval for Third-Quarter Starts." *Architectural Record* 111 (Apr. 1952): 11, 26.

Wright, Gwendolyn. *Building the Dream: A*

Social History of Housing in America. New York: Pantheon Books, 1981.

———. *Moralism and the Model Home: Domestic Architecture and Cultural Conflict in Chicago, 1873–1913.* Chicago: University of Chicago Press, 1980.

———. *USA: Modern Architecture in History.* London: Reacktion Books, 2008.

Wright, Mary, and Russel Wright. *Guide to Easier Living.* 1950. Salt Lake City, UT: Gibbs Smith, Publisher, 2003.

Wyatt, Wilson W. "When You Will Get Your Home." *American Magazine* 142 (Aug. 1946): 48–49, 128.

Yarmon, Betty. *Getting the Most for Your Money When You Buy a Home.* New York: Association Press, 1966.

York, Herman H. "The Young Architect's Role in Mass Housing." *AIA Journal: Journal of the American Institute of Architects* 29 (Jan. 1958): 16–17.

Index